Reshaping Education in the 1990s:
Perspectives on Primary Schooling

Edited by

Rita Chawla-Duggan
and
Christopher J. Pole

 The Falmer Press

(A member of the Taylor & Francis Group)
London • Washington, D.C.

UK   Falmer Press, 1 Gunpowder Square, London, EC4A 3DE
USA Falmer Press, Taylor & Francis Inc., 1900 Frost Road, Suite 101, Bristol, PA 19007

First published in 1996

A catalogue record for this book is available from the British Library

Library of Congress Cataloging-in-Publication Data are available on request

ISBN 0 7507 0526 4 cased √
ISBN 0 7507 0527 2 paper

Jacket design by Caroline Archer

Typeset in 10/12 pt Garamond
Graphicraft Typesetters Ltd., Hong Kong.

Printed in Great Britain by Biddles Ltd, Guildford and King's Lynn on paper which has a specified pH value on final paper manufacture of not less than 7.5 and is therefore 'acid free'.

Contents

Contents

Acknowledgments

The papers in this volume derive from the CEDAR 1994 conference at the University of Warwick.

We would like to thank the authors who have contributed to this collection. We would also like to thank CEDAR staff for their help and advice in the planning and delivery of the conference.

Our personal thanks go to Janet Flynn and Sylvia Moore for their efforts towards the administration of the conference and the collection of its papers.

List of Figures and Tables

Introduction: Reshaping Education in the 1990s: Perspectives on Primary Schooling

Rita Chawla-Duggan and Christopher J. Pole

The 1980s saw an unprecedented amount of change in primary schooling. In Britain this included legislation on the content of the curriculum, about mechanisms for its assessment and changes in initial teacher training with implications for teacher development and professionalism.

The Centre for Educational Development, Appraisal and Research (CEDAR) conference in 1994 addressed issues reflecting the impact of change at a variety of different levels of policy and practice in different settings across different countries. In this context, the conference included papers which discussed changes that have taken place in many aspects of primary education. This book, together with a companion volume (Pole and Chawla-Duggan, 1996) which focuses on secondary education, is a collection of eleven of the papers that were presented at the conference, which address some of the key issues in primary education. The papers both look back at legislative changes that have occurred in primary education in recent years and forward to developments in policy and practice as a result of those changes. They provide critical evaluation of many of the key changes in primary education and collectively they provide a view of the general state of primary education as we approach the twenty-first century. The book is divided into three parts. The first of which is concerned with curricula issues.

By 1993, England had experienced three different versions of the National Curriculum over the five year period since its introduction. Initiatives in Britain have created a new framework within which primary education is being delivered and evaluated. The specific aim of these initiatives is to increase the quality of teaching and learning through a mixture of centrally directed policies, in particular, the National Curriculum and standardized assessment. The impact of a centrally directed curriculum has stimulated considerable debate amongst teachers, parents and academics, together with a large number of research projects. Within the areas of investigation covered by the research, questions are raised about what counts as the curriculum — both hidden and formal; what is appropriate educational experience for primary children; what are the implications of a nationally devised curriculum for school staffing and the way teachers work; and what can be learnt by comparative cross-country analysis of curriculum developments.

The second section of the book is concerned with teacher education. Although curriculum changes may have been of principal concern in primary schools since 1988, the changing relationships between schools and universities in the provision of initial teacher training has also been subject to change. In 1992, the Secretary of State for Education in England and Wales announced proposals to alter the nature of all teacher training courses so that 80 per cent of trainees' experience would be spent in schools. The changes in teacher education may also serve to redefine the concept of teacher professionalism (Barton, Barrett, Whitty, Miles and Furlong, 1994). In 1993 the Department for Education (DFE) published their draft circular entitled 'The Initial Training of Primary School Teachers — New Criteria for Course Approval'. Such initiatives raised questions not only about the nature of initial teacher education, but also about processes of policy making. They led researchers to ask who should be involved in delivering teacher training and to question what distinctive contributions different parties make to the process.

The research reported in this book traces through some of the implications for such developments in government policies. In particular, the papers raise questions about a shift in the balance in the training of primary school teachers away from higher education, towards school-based training; and about the perceptions of parents, teacher-training students and tutors in relation to the changes. In addition, the guiding principles and characteristics behind the concept of partnership between schools and universities are examined, in the light of new proposals for initial teacher training. Whilst earlier research (Dart and Drake, 1993) focused on the changing nature of a PGCE school-based teacher training, arguing that this would not adequately prepare teachers for a complex future, another crucial question is whether different training routes do.

Concern with changes at the level of legislation in relation to teaching and learning in the primary school, or initial teacher training, have implications for the developments of teachers' perspectives of their role and their working life. The third section of the volume is concerned, therefore with professionalism.

In England and Wales, the relationship between teachers and the curriculum is embedded, historically, in issues of professionalism, teacher democracy and teacher autonomy (Chitty and Lawn, 1995). How change is managed in the primary school; how teachers become mediators of educational policy change; and what impact that change has had on the subsequent developments on teachers' perspectives of their role and working lives are questions about professionalism. The papers in this section explore perceptions of autonomy, accountability and relationships with colleagues and children in light of recent organizational change. They consider the complexity of interactions between an individual's personal and professional life and the social and cultural frameworks within which she or he works. In short, this final section of the book is concerned with how primary school teachers are accomplishing their job in the light of curricular, structural and organizational changes post-1988.

The papers in this volume highlight concerns of central contemporary importance to primary education which are illustrated by reference to particular curriculum areas such as science or mathematics or to particular sectors such as nursery or teacher education. Each paper raises issues of its own, but also picks up one or more of the general issues of curriculum, teacher education or professionalism which provide the framework for the volume. In more detail, the papers focus on: curriculum issues; teacher training; and, professionalism.

Curriculum Issues

The first two papers in this section are concerned with the immediate impact of the National Curriculum and assessment proposals, in particular the contradictory nature of current curriculum and assessment policy on primary classrooms. The paper by Brown, Black, Simon and Blondel focuses on the assessment framework adopted in England and its relationship to a uniform curriculum content. Acknowledging the differential relationship between intended curricula and implemented or attained curricula, reflected in international studies, the authors question the assumptions and effectiveness behind a uniform curriculum and its relationship to a stage-led uniform assessment system. The authors conceptualize the extent of 'variability of attainment', by referring to the '7 year gap' concept proposed by the Cockcroft Report on the teaching of mathematics (DES, 1982) and also the Assessment and Performance Unit (DES, 1988). With a scarcity of data which addresses comparisons between attainment of curricula subjects of pupils of seven and thirteen, which confirm or refute the '7 year gap' hypothesis, the authors aim to address the omission. This is illustrated with reference to three studies in the ESRC initiative 'Innovation and Change in Education: The Quality of Teaching and Learning'.

In Chapter 2 Penny Munn is concerned with the point of transition between the nursery and primary school stages and its implication for a baseline assessment framework in the National Curriculum. She addresses questions concerned with developmental progress of areas of literacy and numeracy during the year before entering primary school. She argues that the nursery school curriculum emphasizes language and social skills, but the primary curriculum makes extensive use of written symbols. Questions related to the content in the curriculum — particularly, numeric skills and their implication for progression for the diagnostic assessment of literacy and numeric ability at primary school entry — are raised.

Munn explored the symbolic meanings that children gave to aspects of numeracy and literacy. She asserts that children generally learned to recognize and name numerals before they could recognize and name many letters. Moreover, pictorial representations did not function as communicative representations for the children, although conventional numerals did hold a communicative function. She examined the process of progression from concrete to symbolic in reading and literacy; and she argues that the progression in number parallels phases in reading. However, processes are not simply a linear transference. In mathematics and reading, for example, concrete and abstract understandings overlap and interact.

This paper challenges existing primary practice in mathematics. The data are used to illustrate the view that children use conventional symbols to communicate rather than their self-made systems. The self-invented systems function as a stepping stone to the orthodox system, not as a communicative device in themselves.

The third paper in the section on curricular issues, by Gott and Duggan, considers the structure and content of the primary school curriculum. Dimensions of good practice in primary schools, are related to science education. The authors argue for a return to examining the aims of science education as a whole and of its relationship to the values of primary education. Gott and Duggan question assumptions about the guiding principles underpinning primary science. Drawing on a range of literature they take the overall aims of science education to involve: first, generating a lifetime's interest and enthusiasm for science; second, preparing pupils for employment; and, third, empowering people in and by science to become instrumental in everyday life. The authors demonstrate how the science National Curriculum involves some of the ideas identified as being important to employers and to the empowerment of the citizen. They demonstrate that a set of values, based on the requirements of industry and democratic empowerment, leads to a conceptual dimension for science which is reflected in the National Curriculum as a whole.

The paper by Black and Osborn considers the introduction of a subject-based curriculum in England. In particular, they examined its implications for school staffing, and the way teachers planned and worked together. The authors argue that the National Curriculum had replaced a relaxed collaborative relationship amongst teachers with a more formalized structured collegiality. The difficulties of collaboration involved a lack of time to collaborate across the school. Informal collaboration was most successful for sharing ideas of similar age groups; providing support was given by the headteacher. Osborn and Black recognize a tension between the idea of a generalist and specialist primary school teacher. They contend that whilst many teachers welcomed in principle the guidelines of a National Curriculum; heads and teachers were concerned about curriculum overload and about their ability to cover the National Curriculum, particularly the assessment procedures, in the depth and breadth required. They call for more non-contact time so that collaborative activity may develop.

Chapter 4 takes a different perspective as Uwe Hameyer's paper gives an insight into curriculum development processes in primary schools located in other countries. The paper focuses on activity based learning in primary science teaching in the Netherlands, Sweden, United States and Germany and identifies the characteristics of 'productive schools'. Questions about how school-based change began and how innovative efforts were supported over a long period, are explored. The main concern of the research reported in this paper however was to search out properties common to productive schools. The research defined a school as a productive organization if it succeeded in putting a shared innovative idea into lasting practice.

Insights into the culture of each school were identified through an examination of science teaching, observing classroom work and outdoor activities. Hameyer argues that overlapping stages of initiation, implementation and institutionalization existed in all the successful schools that were studied. He identifies four areas which were indicative of successful innovation. These are explained as programme, person, context and process. 'Programme' is defined as involving independent learning experiences — a variety of teaching styles and resources and changing learning environments for effective outcomes. 'Person' relates largely to innovative teachers, and 'context' concerns school structures and their propensity for innovation. Finally, 'process' builds in a temporal aspect which permits the exploration of initiatives.

The paper argues that lasting curriculum change requires meaningful, multiple try-outs and steady rapport, and that lasting change is not a linear process but rather a spiral which may be time consuming.

In the final chapter of this first section, Morrison makes a welcome contribution to the area of the hidden curriculum, in order to shed light upon changing perceptions about what constitutes a curriculum for food and eating. In the hidden curriculum, she argues, the individual consciousness of pupils and teachers will be shaped by the kinds of interpersonal relations that occur within schools. The paper explores the social processes of eating in primary schools and its impact upon the educational experiences of primary school children. A cross-cultural analysis was used where case studies of eating in two primary schools in England and Japan were examined. Morrison argues that in the national context, educational policy has made parental choice a key feature. Childrens' eating practices have become divorced from official interpretations of what counts as schooling or as appropriate educational experience. School-based eating now reflects choices made by parents, governors and decreasingly local educational authorities.

Teacher Training

The second section of the book begins with Hannan's challenging paper which is critical of current government reforms towards initial teacher training. Higher education institutions have been considered the source of problems relating to poorly prepared teachers and the response has been for the Department for Education and Science to impose new criteria on courses approved for initial teacher training. The role of the training institution is seen as one which should provide the subject knowledge necessary for teaching the primary curriculum, whilst schools are considered the best place for student teachers to develop and apply practical skills. By implication, the government has therefore argued for a more influential role to be played by schools in course design and delivery along with shifting funding to help the process.

Hannan argues that whilst there is little support for the reforms there is support for increased partnership between higher education institutions and schools. Moreover, he argues that out of this conflict, parents have become empowered through their increased knowledge of what goes on in schools, and are aware of obstacles which may prevent their children from getting well-trained teachers.

Partnership is also a theme of Whiting's paper which focuses on the organization and experience of an 'Articled Teacher Course', a pilot scheme directed at postgraduate students where 80 per cent of the course was based in schools. Drawing on qualitative data, with a focus on the structures and procedures for partnership, she examined the planning, recruitment, support and assessment for articled teachers through the course.

Whiting challenges the assumptions behind the idea of partnership. She asserts that despite great efforts to make the planning process a joint one, it was in fact the college personnel who were the originators and designers of the course. They, rather than school staff, had the knowledge, experience and time to design and submit schemes for approval and validation. The crucial point the paper makes is that school staff were starting from a different standpoint altogether from those in college and, therefore, perceptions were built from prior experience. In terms of assessment, she explains that the aims and expectations were either unclear to all parties concerned, or there was a reluctance to acknowledge difficulties in the 'assessed practice teaching'. She points out that, as a result, articled teachers were in a weaker position than the traditional PGCE students; finding less support from the college which was not compensated for by support in school.

Professionalism

The final section focuses on professionalism. The chapter by Osborn, Abbot, Broadfoot, Croll and Pollard reports on findings from the first and second phases of the Primary Assessment, Curriculum and Experience study (PACE). The study was concerned with how teachers perceived their role to be changing; the extent to which they felt their professional autonomy and personal fulfilment were threatened by the changes; and how the changes affected their relationships with children in class, their perceptions of classroom practice and their professional relationships with colleagues.

Drawing on concepts of professionalism juxtaposed with concepts of intensification and deskilling, the paper focuses on the extent to which teachers saw themselves as moving from a professional to a technician role; and the extent to which they felt able to mediate the changes imposed on them in order to move towards a new type of professionalism.

In terms of changing perceptions of work and teachers' role, the PACE study presents evidence to illustrate a shift towards perceptions of deskilling amongst teachers, whilst some felt empowered by recent legislative changes despite the pressures of curriculum overload. In general, they argue that teachers felt they had to change their teaching approaches, their classroom practice and their perceptions of their professional role in ways in which they would not have chosen for themselves. Due to pressures from a lack of time, an intensification of workload and a loss in job satisfaction there were, by 1992 and 1993, increasing perceptions of loss of autonomy and fulfilment in teaching. Other research (e.g., Corrie, 1995) in this area has concluded that it is crucial to attend to both the structure and culture of the school if the underlying principles of staff collaboration are to be achieved.

The paper by Jeffrey and Woods reports on a long-term research project into creative teaching in primary schools. Data collected by means of observation of teachers over a two year period, interviews, informal discussion with teachers and pupils, alongside the collection and analysis of documents and photographs are used to highlight issues concerned with creative criteria and to reconstruct the 'atmosphere' of primary classrooms.

Jeffrey and Woods define the concept of 'atmosphere' as involving anticipation and expectation, relevance, achievement and satisfaction: children's personal experiences and interests were used as part of the curriculum; lessening the cultural, racial, gender and social class distinctions helped towards a harmonious ethos; learning was related to their feelings; and there was a constant sense of purpose.

The authors also refer to the 'tone' of the primary classroom. Tone involved sound quality, levels, rhythm, pace and tempo. Different tones produced different purposes depending on what the activity required; for example, seriousness, excitement and enthusiasm. They argue that through the construction of classroom atmosphere and tone, teachers installed in children a desire to learn; feelings of personal involvement and purpose; and a sense of strong intrinsic reward with a mood appropriate to the task in hand.

Whilst the paper by Jeffrey and Woods highlights the processes involved in the art of being a primary school teacher at a micro level, the final chapter in the section on professionalism, considers the professional role of primary school teachers in their capacities as part of a wider social structure.

In 'Gender and School Leadership', Smulyan provides a case study of a woman principal to show how the characteristics of effective leadership and gender interweave with other personal and professional issues. She argues that women and men experience the patriarchal system and bureaucratic structures of school differently. In turn, they respond differently in school situations. In her case study, the individual's life and country, race, ethnicity and class are in play as are organizational structures in school districts and the community. All contribute to the experience of leadership.

Using an ethnographic approach, Smulyan provides a social portrait of the life of an American black principal in an elementary school. She follows the principal's work with an individual African-American student to illustrate her approach to leadership. Smulyan argues that the picture that emerged was one of a principal whose style reflected that of the literature on women managers, administrators and effective school principals, but whose uniqueness was a result of her own personal experience and beliefs about teaching and her role as a black woman in the district and country. The study illustrates the complex interaction of varying influences on a school administrator's goals and actions. Smulyan argues that future research in educational administration needs to examine the lives and work of individuals in schools to lead to an understanding of how the traits, roles and skills of effective administration are shown in response to children, teachers, parents and other administrators.

*

In studies of primary schooling the interpretation provided depends on the perspective adopted by the writers and researchers. A variety of perspectives on primary schooling are evident in this book. Pollard (1992) offered the proposition that whilst primary education was undoubtedly being reshaped by external forces, there was considerable scope for strategic action by teachers and schools. He proposed that any longer term reshaping would reflect the perspectives of parents, governors and teachers, as well as the obvious forms of change emanating from central government. In short, the interplay of agency and constraint would shape change. The contributions to this book support Pollard's contention.

As legislation continues to be developed, implemented and modified, we are left not simply at a pivotal point by the mid 1990s, but at a point where primary schooling is experiencing a total change in circumstances. This raises new questions: first, about the curriculum — its relevance and whose needs it serves; second, about creating different kinds of partnership; and, third, about a concept of professionalism which recognizes the diverse interests within education and which recognizes the very real and different interests and conflicts that converge around the subject of primary schooling. This book attempts to address these questions.

References

BARTON, L., BARRETT, E., WHITTY, G., MILES, S. and FURLONG, J. (1994) 'Teacher education and teacher professionalism in England: Some emerging issues', *British Journal of the Sociology of Education*, **14** (4), pp. 529–43.

CHITTY, C. and LAWN, M. (1995) 'Redefining the teacher and the curriculum', *Educational Review*, **47** (2), pp. 139–42.

CORRIE, L. (1995) 'The structure and culture of staff collaboration: Managing meaning and opening doors', *Educational Review*, **47** (1), pp. 89–99.

DART, L. and DRAKE, P. (1993) 'School based teacher training: A conservative practice?' *Journal for Education and Teaching*, **19** (2), pp. 175–89.

DEPARTMENT OF EDUCATION AND SCIENCE (DES) (1982) *Committee of Inquiry into the*

Teaching of Mathematics in Schools, Mathematics Counts, The Cockcroft Report, London, HMSO.

DEPARTMENT OF EDUCATION AND SCIENCE, TASK GROUP ON ASSESSMENT AND TESTING (1988) *A Report*, London, HMSO.

POLLARD, A. (1992) 'Teachers' responses to the reshaping of primary education', in ARNOT, M. and BARTON, L. (eds) *Voicing Concerns: Sociological Perspectives on Contemporary Education Reforms*, Wallingford, Triangle.

Part One

Curriculum Issues

1 Age or Stage? Research Findings Relating to Assessment Frameworks

Margaret Brown, Paul Black, Shirley Simon and Ezra Blondel

ABSTRACT   It is the practice in most countries to specify a common curriculum for pupils of a particular age, and to grade attainment with respect to this curriculum using a norm-referenced system.

The assessment framework adopted in England and Wales differs in adopting a common structure for all pupils aged 5–14, using a progressive sequence of ten levels, each described in terms of knowledge/skills.

The empirical basis for this stage-led rather than age-led assessment framework is examined, and further results are reported from a study of the attainment and learning of 7–13-year-olds on common tasks drawn from mathematics (measurement) and science (forces).

The Uniform Model

Most countries have a curriculum specified by either central government or by state or regional government. The normal form of specification is to provide a uniform syllabus for each age group; a weaker form involves a syllabus covering a range of age groups. This syllabus may be supported by stronger forms of control, including centrally set examinations at yearly or less frequent intervals, and/or the central specification of a single textbook or an approved list of texts. Centrally organized inservice training of teachers may also feature as part of the system.

The major function of these forms of curricular specification is to define the responsibilities of the teacher by prescribing what is to be taught. Students are generally assessed in a norm-referenced manner, using tests or teacher judgment to rank students within a class or school year group on the basis of their degree of mastery of the syllabus content.

Reasons for a uniform curriculum may be deeply rooted in a political philosophy that demands a common entitlement/provision for all citizens. A uniform system may be underpinned by religious or cultural beliefs that all pupils have similar potential for achievement (e.g., Nebres, 1988), or may merely reflect requirements for bureaucratic simplicity and teacher convenience.

13

It must be admitted that in practice what is taught may be very much more variable than official documents suggest, due to local conditions, teacher knowledge, interpretation and preferences, student backgrounds, attainment and attitudes, and other factors. International studies confirm that whatever the national ideology, implemented curricula not only differ significantly from intended curricula, but also attained curricula vary even more than implemented curricula, with considerable differences within as well as between class groups (Travers and Westbury, 1989; Robitaille and Garden, 1989).

Variability in Attainment

Variability in attainment causes a major problem for the uniform approach to curriculum specification: it opens up questions both of its effectiveness and of its assumptions of a uniform prior attainment level at the start of each year or phase.

The degree of variability in attainment was illustrated clearly in the early 1980s in the UK by publication of the findings of surveys such as those carried out by the Concepts in Secondary Mathematics and Science (CSMS) project (Shayer and Adey, 1981; Hart, 1981) and the Assessment of Performance Unit (APU) (e.g., DES/APU, 1980–82, 1988). These were concerned with assessing pupils' mathematical and scientific understanding across different age groups: in the case of CSMS common items were used with each of the age groups 12–15; while the APU surveys at ages 11 and 15, with age 13 additionally for science, contained some common items. Surveys were carried out also in other subjects (English, modern languages, technology) by the APU. The results demonstrated an unexpectedly wide range of attainment in each year group, especially in comparison to the progress shown by an average pupil in one year.

One way of conceptualizing the extent of this variation, the 'seven year gap', is suggested in the Cockcroft Report on the teaching of mathematics (DES, 1982). Using CSMS and other related data they point out that one aspect of number understanding which is likely to be achieved by some pupils by age 7, is known to be achieved by the average pupil between the ages of 10 and 11, and not by low attaining pupils until age 14 or later. An alternative interpretation suggesting an even wider variation is offered by the APU in their booklet about decimals (DES/APU, 1986); they demonstrate that if a cohort is split into fifths, then the attainment of each fifth by the age of 15 has progressed only to where the fifth who are immediately above them were at the age of 11. For example the lowest fifth at 15 have just caught up with the achievements at 11 of the second lowest fifth but have still not yet achieved what the median fifth could do at the age of 11.

Results of seventeen such cross-age surveys, including attainment in mathematics, science and language and in general tests of cognitive ability, were brought together and discussed by Wiliam (1992). He demonstrated that if all the results were standardized to measure 'attainment age in years', the standard deviation, measured in terms of years, rose with chronological age and was approximately one third of the chronological age. For example, at age 12 attainment in any dimension is likely to be normally distributed about an 'attainment age' of 12, with a standard deviation of four years. Since approximately one third of the population lies outside the interval of plus or minus one standard deviation from the mean, this means that one in six 12-year-olds are likely to perform worse than an average 8-year-old, and one in six are likely to perform better than an average 16-year-old. This result supports an eight year gap enclosing two thirds of the population centred on age 12, quite closely related to the Cockcroft Committee's suggested seven year gap centred on age 11.

Wiliam's results suggested that the more conceptual the style of test the larger the standard deviation and, correspondingly, that a larger knowledge component tended to reduce the variation. Nevertheless, the standard deviation was greater than 1.5 years at age 12 for all tests, indicating that even in the most uniform case one sixth of 12-year-old pupils would be at or below the performance of an average pupil of 10.5 years, with the same proportion at or above the performance of an average pupil at 13.5 years.

National Curriculum assessment results in England provide useful data since they compare pupils of ages 7, 11 and 14 using the same criteria. While no results on the full population are yet available for ages 11 and 14, pilot results seem generally to bear out the predictions. For example, in mathematics, they indicate that the top 5 per cent at age 7 reach the same or a higher level of performance as about the lowest 13 per cent at age 14. However, the actual tests used have so far been different (with the exception of a small and somewhat unreliable sample at age 11 who sat pilot tests for ages 7 and 14). Generally there is a dearth of data making direct comparisons between attainments in curriculum subjects of pupils of age 7 and those of age 13 or more which would directly confirm or refute the hypothesis of the 'seven year gap'.

Three of the projects in the ESRC Initiative, 'Innovation and Change in Education: The Quality of Teaching and Learning', address this omission. One of these is in the field of historical skills (Concepts of History and Teaching Approaches at Key Stages 2 and 3). A paper giving interim results states that 'It is clear that some seven year-olds perform at a higher level than some fourteen year-olds' (Lee, Dickinson and Ashby, 1996). The second project is in Procedural and Conceptual Knowledge in Science, with pupils aged 9–14; 'results so far certainly seem to indicate that the most advanced 9 year-olds out-perform many 14 year-olds' (Duggan, Gott, Lubban and Millar, 1996). The third project (Progression in Mathematics and Science) crosses two subject areas and four age groups from age 6–7 to age 12–13. Again, the results support a similar spread; some detailed findings are described in a later section.

International results in mathematics suggest that the span of attainment is particularly wide in the UK in comparison to other countries; nevertheless, even in Japan, which has unusually uniform attainment levels, there is evidence of at least a 'four year gap' between the ages at which high and low attaining pupils grasp particular ideas (Robitaille and Garden, 1989). However, CSMS mathematics tests have now been replicated in over fourteen different countries and these show remarkably consistent results; considerable international variations in the facilities of single items lose their significance when items are grouped together. The paper referred to earlier, collecting results from different types of tests (Wiliam, 1992), also contained several tests from France — the results covered the same range as those from England.

Alternative Models

In view of this huge spread of achievement, the curricular model in which there is a uniform syllabus for each age group would seem to be seriously deficient, at least for one or both of the extreme groups. Howson (1991) lists the measures taken by different countries in coming to terms with this problem in mathematics teaching.

> So far as actual structures are concerned, four ways of dealing with the problems of differentiation can be identified in the national descriptions supplied below.
>
> (i) No differentiation of students and curricula other than at the teacher's discretion (e.g., Denmark, Japan (in both cases until Grade 9)).
>
> (ii) Differentiation through the provision of 'optional material' within the main course (e.g., Belgium, Germany (where this is provided within differentiated streams)), or through the provision of 'extra' mathematics (e.g., Belgium and (in Grade 9) Japan).
>
> (iii) Differentiation through clearly separate school types, or streams within a single school (e.g., Germany, the Netherlands).
>
> (iv) Differentiation by individual rate of progress through a common curriculum (e.g., England, but note that here in some subjects other than mathematics (ii) appears to be the preferred alternative). (Howson, 1991, p. 9)

The former more uniform model produces different results depending on the level of difficulty at which the common curriculum is pitched (Robitaille and Garden, 1989; Travers and Westbury, 1989). In democratic countries, for example Sweden, the curriculum seems to be targetted at a low level, presumably to minimize failure, with the result that national attainment is low in comparison to other countries and there is concern that more able pupils are not achieving their potential. By contrast, in Japan, where the demands and the resulting standards are high, pupils show anxiety to keep up and generally dislike mathematics, while their parents resort to enlisting them in evening supplementary classes. Other countries, like France, have traditionally coped by making low attaining students repeat years; although this is becoming less usual and is unpopular as a remedy.

Discussions with mathematics teachers from all parts of the world suggested that many deal with a wide attainment range by reducing mathematics to a set of routine procedures with little apparent prerequisite conceptual background. However, as the work of Brown and Van Lehn (1982) shows, this is not likely to be effective in the longer term; students can only 'repair' forgotten steps in procedures by recourse to conceptual underpinnings.

Separate syllabuses clearly have the disadvantage of dividing pupils rather rigidly, a solution which is unacceptable in some societies and increasingly becoming a problem in developed countries where flexible skills are likely to be demanded of most of the employed population. For these and other reasons the government decided to take, for England and Wales, the radical solution in the fourth route described by Howson, which had been proposed in the Report by the Task Group on Assessment and Testing (DES/TGAT, 1988). This involved an assessment framework arranged according to ten levels defined initially according to age norms two years apart, so that Level 2 corresponds to the performance of the median group of 7-year-olds, Level 3 to that of the median group of 9-year-olds, and so on, as judged in the initial years of national assessment.

The organization of the curriculum in England and Wales is more problematic. With the exception of pupils at the extremes, who are expected to be taught the same curriculum as pupils in an adjacent key stage, the curriculum is now presented so as to appear uniform within each of Key Stages 1, 2 and 3 (ages 5–7, 7–11, 11–14 respectively). Nevertheless, the framework of assessment in levels, each with a broad indication of understanding and skills to be achieved in the form of a level description, will lead many teachers to introduce a greater degree of differentiation in the more hierarchical subjects.

Despite fierce argument between opposing factions during 1993, the ten level system has been retained for assessment, although for up to age 14 only (Dearing, 1993). Nevertheless there have been many doubts expressed about whether and in what senses the attainment of a 7-year-old can be equated with that of a 14-year-old. The next section contains some detailed results from the third of the ESRC projects cited earlier, which it is hoped will illuminate the issue.

Results from the Progression in Mathematics and Science Project

The Progression in Learning Mathematics and Science (PLMS) project (funded by the ESRC no. L208252001) has undertaken an investigation of progression in children's learning within linked areas of mathematics and science, aiming to explore some of the issues underlying the ten level sequence of the National Curriculum, in particular:

- whether a progression can be identified and described so that it matches children's observed learning patterns and helps diagnostic assessment;
- the extent of invariance of progression in different children, and in children of different ages progressing at different rates;
- the relation between progression in learning and the teaching experienced.

The notion of progression is clearly complex; in particular, each of the two areas studied — forces and measures — itself draws on several conceptual strands and a conceptual analysis can be used to define a model of progression. However, the relation between the logical/epistemological dependence of concepts as appreciated by the mature scientist/mathematician and the way children themselves begin to construct and link ideas is problematic. The role played by experience of school learning, in relation to any maturational limits, is not well understood. Part of the function of the project has been to try to identify some of the contributory features.

Research Design

In order to explore the notion of progression on the short timescale that the project allowed, we chose to include both cross-sectional studies, using four age groups (years 2, 4, 6 and 8) and longitudinal studies over a limited timescale, observing changes which occurred over a 2 to 4 month period which included some teaching input (whatever was covered by each teacher) related to the topics.

The sample included a set of six children from each of two different schools, at four different age groups (ages 6–7 to 12–13), making forty-eight pupils in all. Each set of six pupils was selected by the teacher to represent the full attainment range in a mixed ability class. The three primary and two secondary schools involved in the study were from London boroughs and were recommended by local advisers as having good science and mathematics teaching and balanced intakes.

The data included pre-test interviews, observations of teaching, and delayed post-test interviews. Each interview was of about twenty minutes in length, and each child was interviewed separately on length, weight and forces. Each interview took the form of a conversation between interviewer and child and the data to be analysed took the form of verbal responses, with additional notes about behaviours. At present the main body of data, from interviews and observations, is in the process of being analysed and written up.

In forces, strands related to observations and predictions, word meanings, the nature of what is offered as explanations, and the identification of the entities acting have been separated. The detailed analysis of progression in science is virtually complete (Simon, Black, Brown and Blondel, 1994). It seems to suggest that there is a steady development in conceptual areas, which broadly follows age but with considerable variation in rate of change. However, the more process-related aspects of prediction, observation and explanation are less age-related and seem to develop more slowly. They also seem to be very much more context-related than the conceptions of forces and equilibrium, which are used more consistently across different contexts. The analysis of overall performance of individual pupils is as yet incomplete; it will be finalized when it can be combined with the mathematics side of the work, on the topic of measurement. Nevertheless it is clear that some of the performances of the 7-year-olds in the work on forces are indistinguishable from those of some of the 13-year-olds. Detailed data given below is drawn from the work on measuring.

Tasks

Although it would have been interesting to explore the differences between measures of several different types in this study, to do so would have introduced too many variables and made the assessment too difficult for the younger pupils. Thus it was decided to focus only on physical properties with ratio scales, taking one property with and one without a visual quality. *Length* was selected as being familiar to young children and having a unique position with regard to the nature of scale, and *weight* because of the contrasting tactile perception, relative familiarity, and link with ideas of force.

Because of the need to assess the range of performance from that of a low attaining 7-year-old to a high attaining 13-year-old, two straightforward practical situations were selected, but a variety of instruments of increasing complexity was offered.

In one, concerned with length measurement, two 'towers' (actually cardboard boxes) were used, of almost the same height of about 25 cm and initially placed just over a metre apart. Pupils were asked which they thought was taller, and then invited to find out, using first a piece of string, then using plastic Duplo blocks (as a non-standard unit). They were finally given a ruler, calibrated in millimetres along one side and inches along the other, and asked to use that both to measure the tower heights and to measure the distance between the towers, which was greater than the length of the ruler. In each case they were first asked to estimate, then to measure and to say how accurate they thought their result was. Pupils were also asked about the units of their result, and about different subdivisions on different ruler scales.

Very similar procedures were used in the weight task which involved a pair of heavy boxes (about 250 gm). Pupils were asked which they thought was the heavier, and to estimate the weight of one of them. They were then asked to find out the weight of one using whatever two-pan balance was used in the school, in terms of ball bearings and, later, in relation to gram weights. Two kitchen scales using imperial and metric units were then introduced, one with conventional scales and one with a digital readout.

Results

Pupils' responses have been analysed, with several refinements of the techniques used. The mathematics results probably show a more consistent picture than those in science because most of the aspects investigated were conceptual in nature. However, there were one or two aspects where there was little noticeable progression. For example, in the ability to estimate the number of concrete units which matched the weight or length of a given object — as in the science aspect of observation — 7-year-olds were not noticeably worse than 13-year-olds at this, and it did not appear to correlate particularly with other results.

The aspects of units, number, continuity and scale have formed the basic framework both for constructing the tasks and for analysing the pupils' responses. Currently the final steps in the individual analyses are still incomplete; however, a tentative structure of seven stages has been identified by examining the changes across age groups.

It should be made clear that while the results are clearly dependent on the preliminary conceptual framework used to design the instruments, the actual developments in the proposed stages and the identification of those steps which appear to be significant arise from the transcribed data. Similarly, where later comparisons are made between pupil performance, this is not on the basis of totals in any predesigned mark scheme but on a detailed qualitative comparison of the relative sophistication of responses.Thus the theory does not claim to be grounded, but rather to represent an iterative development between the understanding of the expert and that of the novice. For example, the fact that the outcome has a structure close to the Piagetian stages — although this was not explicitly intended (Piaget, Inhelder and Szeminska, 1960; Inhelder and Piaget, 1958) — may be interpreted as suggesting either that this structure is implicit in the thinking of the researchers, or that the results act as a validation of Piaget's empirically based work, or, most likely, as a combination of these.

Only one of the 13-year-olds (Year 8) had really achieved most of the ideas in the seventh and hardest stage, but three more were nearly there. The two most advanced 7-year-olds (Year 2), Jason and Kristina, were ahead of the remaining eight (two-thirds of the sample) of the Year 8 pupils, and had achieved some of the ideas in the sixth stage ('Some Year 8s'). However there were variations in sequence. For example, Jason had developed a sound grip on units but regarded mathematics as a game in which there were always right answers, while Kristina was less familiar with all the units but conceptually

Table 1.1: *Relationship between aspects of competency and age*

	Units	Number	Continuity	Scale
Almost all Year 2s	Sensory comparison; uses multiple concrete non-standard units for measurement	Reads whole numbers to 100		Reads off number near end of object
Most Year 2s (age 7)	Physically repeats a single concrete non-standard unit; appreciates less of larger units	Counts consistently; reads numbers to 1000 (e.g., 250)		
Most Year 4s (age 9)	Estimates with non-standard units; sometimes volunteers name of length unit; familiar with names of cm, g, mm, (m?); uses knowledge of size of cm	Uses halves for non-standard units	One or more finite points between wholes e.g., halves	
Most year 6s (age 11)	Sometimes volunteers name of weight unit; usually volunteers cm; familiar with name of kg; uses knowledge of size of mm		Acknowledges inexactness of estimates	Selects the appropriate scale and direction
Most year 8s (age 13)	Volunteers g; familiar with names of imperial units; selects g as correct unit; uses knowledge of size of m	Reads and interprets decimals with 1 place, uses place value to 1000 in adding mentally	Aggregates on long distances and for weights; some sense of inexactness in results; some regard for consistency	Takes account of zero on ruler
Some Year 8s	Uses knowledge of size of mm, in, g, kg, oz, lb; accurate estimation		Recognizes inexactness of instruments	
A few Year 8s	Refers flexibly to several units in single context; converts readily between metric units; understanding of separate metric and imperial unit systems	Uses ratio in conversion and in calculation of subdivisions; uses equivalences of decimals, and fractions	Understanding of infinite density of number line, and therefore the inherent approximation of measurement	Calculates size of subdivision on scale; conversion between different scales

advanced in terms of appreciating the need for consistency and understanding the inexactness of measurement. While Kristina and Jason were from the same school, the next most advanced two Year 2 pupils, Rajesh and Annabel, were both from the second school. Although much less advanced, these two pupils were nevertheless performing at the same level as the two weakest Year 8 pupils, Natalie and Richard, which was around the third stage ('Most Year 4s'). If the Year 2 and the Year 8 pupils are ordered according to their performance in the interviews, the ordering from weakest to most advanced, using the year group number in place of each pupil, would be:

2 2 2 2 2 2 2 2 2 8 8 2 8 8 8 8 8 8 8 2 2 8 8 8 8

In the case of the weakest 13-year-old, Natalie, there were still many aspects in the third stage ('Most Year 4s') which she had not grasped. Interestingly enough the only aspect in which she was ahead of all the 7-year-old pupils concerned familiarity with the approximate size of an ounce, in which her greater period of life experience may have given her an advantage. In fact there were points during each of the length and weight tasks when Natalie demonstrated a classically Piagetian intuitive (pre-operational) response typical of young pupils, in spite of this not being part of the protocol. She volunteered that the ball bearings would weigh more if they were close together in the scale pan than if they were spread out, and she tried putting them in one by one since she thought that would reduce their weight; she also decided to move the tower to the table from her knee, as she thought it might measure more bricks if it were on the table. In each case, the reason for changing the measuring process was because the result was initially not a whole number of units, and she believed it should be.

A further interesting feature of Natalie's method was that having placed the ruler against the tower to find its height, she read the size of the 'air-gap' between the end of the ruler and the end of the tower; a procedure that was also observed to be used by at least three of the 7-year-olds. Again, by doing this, and reading the scale in the wrong direction and in the wrong units, she managed to produce an answer of 45 cm which exactly matched her own inaccurate estimate for the height of the tower (actually about 25 cm)! Natalie was clearly expert at getting by in class, producing in some cases broadly credible answers by using totally illegitimate methods. It is worth repeating that she was included in the sample in one of the two secondary schools chosen to have a balanced intake and a good academic record, not as a pupil with particular special needs but to represent the range of pupils in a typical mixed ability class.

Richard, the other weak 13-year-old, also read the scale of the ruler in the wrong direction and confused centimetres and millimetres, although he held the ruler in the correct place. Thus instead of reading off 263 mm he counted down in millimetres from the 300 mm end to obtain 37, which he gave as centimetres. When aggregating the lengths of 3 rulers (90 cm or 900 mm) and a further 250 mm he again confused the units and added 90 to 250 to obtain (wrongly) 1050. He had originally estimated the distance of about 1.2 metres as 48 metres.

Other Year 8 pupils also had serious problems in measuring. For example, a boy from a different school to Richard could not identify any of the abbreviations for units of weight on the kitchen scales (g, kg, lb or oz). While he knew that g on the weights stood for grams, when he later met a digital scale he seemed perplexed by the abbreviation gm. It was as if he only recognized grams as solid weights, and not as calibrations on any kind of abstract scale.

Conclusion

The ten level scale adopted in Britain as a model for assessment was radical in that it was supported by very little data which crossed the primary/secondary boundary, comparing competences of pupils at very different ages. Nevertheless, the results referred to in the first part of this paper suggest — and data from the Progression in Science and Mathematics project confirms — that there are very many aspects in which the performances of some 7-year-olds and some 13-year-olds are indistinguishable, and that these are mostly conceptual in nature. It is not clear to what extent teachers are aware of these overlaps in performance, or to what extent they will elect to use programmes of study for earlier or later Key Stages for pupils at the extremes.

Where other countries appear to use a uniform syllabus for all pupils, it is uncertain whether this reduces the problem of the wide range of attainment, or whether it merely disguises it. As conceptual knowledge becomes more important in the curriculum than knowledge and routine techniques, attention to differing levels of attainment may become more important.

References

Brown, J.S. and Van Lehn, K. (1982) 'Towards a generative theory of "bugs"', in Carpenter, T.P., Moser, J.M. and Romberg, T.A. (eds) *Addition and Subtraction: A Cognitive Perspective*, New Jersey, Lawrence Erlbaum.

Dearing, R. (1993) *The National Curriculum and its Assessment: Final Report*, London, School Curriculum and Assessment Authority.

Department of Education and Science, Assessment of Performance Unit (1980–82) *Mathematical Development: Primary and Secondary Survey Report nos 1–3*, London, HMSO.

Department of Education and Science, Assessment of Performance Unit (1986) *Decimals*, London, HMSO.

Department of Education and Science, Assessment of Performance Unit (1988) *Science at Age 11/13/15: A Review of APU Summary Findings*, London, HMSO.

Margaret Brown, Paul Black, Shirley Simon and Ezra Blondel

Department of Education and Science, Committee of Inquiry into the Teaching of Mathematics in Schools (1982) *Mathematics Counts* ('The Cockcroft Report'), London, HMSO.

Department of Education and Science, Task Group on Assessment and Testing (1988) *A Report*, London, HMSO.

Duggan, S., Gott, R., Lubben, F. and Millar, R. (1996) 'Evidence in science education', in Hughes, M. (ed.) *Teaching and Learning in Changing Times*, Oxford, Blackwell.

Hart, K. (ed.) (1981) *Children's Understanding of Mathematics 11–16*, London, John Murray.

Howson, G. (1991) *National Curricula in Mathematics*, Leicester, The Mathematical Association.

Inhelder, B. and Piaget, J. (1958) *The Growth of Logical Thinking from Childhood to Adolescence*, London, Routledge and Kegan Paul.

Lee, P., Dickinson, A. and Ashby, R. (1996) '"There were no facts in those days": Children's ideas about historical explanation', in Hughes, M. (ed.) *Teaching and Learning in Changing Times*, Oxford, Blackwell.

Nebres (1988) 'School mathematics in the 1990s: The challenge of change especially for the developing countries', in Hirst, A. and K. (eds) *Proceedings of the Sixth International Congress on Mathematical Education*, Budapest, Janos Bolyai Mathematical Society.

Piaget, J., Inhelder, B. and Szeminska, A. (1960) *The Child's Conception of Geometry*, London, Routledge and Kegan Paul.

Robitaille, D.F. and Garden, R.A. (1989) *The IEA Study of Mathematics II: Contexts and Outcomes of School Mathematics*, Oxford, Pergamon.

Shayer, M. and Adey, P. (1981) *The Science of Science Teaching*, London, Routledge.

Simon, S., Black, P., Brown, M. and Blondel, E. (1994) 'Progression in understanding the equilibrium of forces', *Research Papers in Education: Policy and Practice*, **9** (2), pp. 249–80.

Travers, K. and Westbury, I. (1989) *The IEA Study of Mathematics I: The Analysis of Mathematics Curricula*, Oxford, Pergamon.

Wiliam, D. (1992) 'Special needs and the distribution of attainment in the national curriculum', *British Journal of Educational Psychology*, **62**, pp. 397–403.

2   Assessment of Literacy and Numeracy Acquired Before School

Penny Munn

ABSTRACT   This chapter describes some findings from a study of preschool literacy and numeracy conducted as part of the ESRC's 'Innovation and Change in Education' programme. The patterns of changes in children's responses to written symbols (letter, numerals and story text) and in their use of writing is described. The implications of the findings for ideas about assessment of abilities at school entry are discussed.

Introduction

The introduction of the National Curriculum and of assessment at age 7 has created a need for some sort of baseline (school entry) assessment. Baseline assessments of the curriculum-related skills that have developed before school depend on a clear understanding of progressions in children's abilities. Our understanding of the progression from preschool skills to school literacy and numeracy is problematic. There is an essential discontinuity between the traditional British nursery curriculum and the primary curriculum that makes it difficult to map out a progression that is continuous across the transition. The nursery school curriculum emphasizes language skills and social skills, whereas the primary curriculum makes extensive use of written symbols. We have little idea of the sort of progressions that children make in understanding and using written symbols before they come to school. There is an informal veto on teaching written symbols in the nursery, and the primary curriculum assumes no knowledge of writing on entry to school.

The fundamental issue is that the literacy and numeracy skills acquired before school are presymbolic, and that there is an essential discontinuity in what is taught at the point of transition to school. The preschool skills that are known to be important for learning to read include practical knowledge of stories and books, analytic language skills and a general awareness of print. The processes of becoming literate entail a shift from oral language to written text. These are multiple processes involving 'owning' and recognizing particular words, relating letter patterns to familiar sounds, and relating word patterns to particular stories.

It is only recently that we have understood how crucial children's *writing* is in this shift from oral language to written text. Learning to read cannot rest on a passive process of taking in text because this requires the presence of a hierarchically ordered set of subskills relating to print. The essential difference between skilled reading and learning to read is that in the early development of reading, these subskills are not yet in place. If children are to progress from uncertain text–sound associations to confident interpretations of letter-groupings then they must engage in the active production of meaningful text (Roberts, 1989). At the preschool stage their text creation is more similar to drawing than to writing. There is a continuum reaching from drawings — which are a direct representation of things — to written symbols — which are representations of linguistic symbols.

Ferreiro (1990) has mapped out the transitions that children make in first acquiring literacy. During levels one and two, children's writing is contained in the iconic domain and tends to be constructed on the basis of each written symbol matching a separate idea or a thing. 'Level three' begins to emerge when children develop what Ferreiro called the 'syllabic hypothesis' — the notion that each letter stands for a syllable. It is only at this level (when they have begun instruction in reading and writing) that children develop the more sophisticated alphabetic notions by which letter patterns are related to sounds which then build into words.

Where numeracy is concerned, the nature of the development progression from preschool to school is still poorly understood. We may understand something of how preschoolers' counting and number activity develop (Fuson, 1988; Saxe, Guberman and Gearhart, 1987; Gelman and Gallistel, 1978), but we understand very little of how this essentially verbal activity becomes related to text-based numeracy — a process which often goes astray (Hughes, 1983; Carraher, Carraher-Nunes and Schliemann, 1985). In particular, we lack any detailed descriptions of how children develop an understanding of number symbolization which are sufficient to parallel our understanding of how children come to understand language symbolization.

The study described here aimed to chart developmental progressions in children's literacy and numeracy during the year before they entered school. The aim was to look at both literacy and numeracy in the same children, to see whether there were similarities across these two contexts and to see what relation the general 'shift to text' might have to children's numeracy skills. The description of the progression has some implications for the diagnostic assessment of children's literacy and numeracy at school entry.

Method

Fifty-six children from eight Scottish preschools were seen in their final year of nursery. The children were selected at random and the sample consisted of thirty-one boys and twenty-five girls. The mean age of the children was 46 months at the start of the study and 55 months in the June before school entry.

The children were seen individually each term to investigate changes in their ideas of reading, counting and number symbolization.

Design of the Child Interview

The interview was constructed as an informal assessment of early literacy and numeracy skills and covered three broad areas.

Storybook reading

Each child was invited to read from a beginning reader that contained a clear story in the pictures on the righthand page. The full text of the story was on the lefthand page, and a shortened version of the story ran beneath the picture. Each child was read the story and then asked to read it again. Each child was asked to point to where the story had been read from, and to point to the words. Note was taken of whether children pointed to the picture or to the words in response to these requests. Each child was asked who had taught him/her to read (or whether s/he could read and when s/he would be able to read) and who else s/he knew who could read.

Recognizing symbols

The children were presented, separately, with a set of plastic letters and a set of plastic numerals and asked 'What are these?' 'Do you know the names of any of them?'

Recording quantity (writing numerals)

Each child was asked to write down the quantity of blocks (1, 2, 3, and 4) in a set of four tins. Note was taken of whether the children used hieroglyphics, pictograms, tally marks, or conventional numerals to do this.[1] An extra block was secretly added to the number 2 tin and each child was asked to search for it. The children were also asked to explain their answer. Note was taken of whether the children used their written record in solving the secret addition. It was also noted whether they referred to this record in their explanation of how they knew where the extra block had been put. The children's recording strategies were deemed to be functional (or literate) if they could use their own written record to infer the site of the secret addition.

Results

Recognizing (Naming) Letters and Numerals

Table 2.1 shows the number of children in each category of letter- and numeral-recognition at each timepoint. Whereas there were very few children who could name many letters in preschool, there were increasing numbers of

Table 2.1: Numbers of children naming numerals and letters

	Term 1	Term 2	Term 3	Primary Term 1
Named one letter	3	7	7	4
Named 2–10 letters	7	7	9	15
Named 10–25 letters	0	0	4	9
Named all 26 letters	0	1	1	7
Named one numeral	1	0	2	0
Named 2–8 numerals	11	14	12	12
Named all numerals	7	13	21	31

Table 2.2: Number of children aware of the role of print

	Term 1	Term 2	Term 3	Primary Term 1
Print concept	12	16	27	35

Table 2.3: Number of children using numerals

	Term 1	Term 2	Term 3	Primary Term 1
Numeral users	6	17	24	39

children who could name all nine numerals. This pattern reflects the pattern of progression seen in the majority of the children — they generally learned to recognize and name numerals before they could recognize and name many letters. The ease with which the numerals were learned in comparison to letters was likely due to a combination of their conceptual simplicity, their small number, and the familiarity of the count words with which they were associated.

Understanding the Communicative Function of Print

Table 2.2 shows the steady increase in the numbers of children who showed awareness of the function of print at each time.

Writing Numerals

Table 2.3 shows the number of children who used numerals when they wrote quantity. By the end of the year, around half the sample had begun to use conventional numerals to record quantity. The remaining children used either 'pretend writing' or they used pictograms or tally marks to depict the quantities. These iconic methods (pictograms or tally marks) incorporated the one-to-one correspondence of counting into the written record. Nine of the children carried this correspondence over to their use of numerals in the early stages, recording '4', for instance, as '1234'. The children who drew iconic records of the quantity to be remembered rarely used these records to check quantities during the secret addition task. In other words, these 'iconic' writing systems were not functioning as communicative representations for the children, although the quantity that they represented was immediately visible. Conventional numerals, on the other hand, invariably held (or rapidly developed) a *communicative* function. The development of communicative strategies for recording quantity were linked to the children's attempts to write conventional numerals. These were themselves related to the children's use of a counting strategy on the 'give a number' task (see Munn, 1995, for description). Counting was therefore connected both with numeral use and with children's communicative writing.

There were strong associations between different areas of the children's understanding, particularly between numeral writing and communicative writing. Both these areas of function were in turn related to the development of print concepts. The picture of development in preschool then is one in which first numerals are recognized, then print concepts develop along with communicative writing and representations of quantity using conventional numeric symbols. Very soon after children begin to notice and remember numerals they are able to write and reproduce them (an ability which is dependent, of course, on the possession of the relevant number concepts). Numerals up to nine, being logographs (symbols that represent an entire idea), might be a particularly easy place for some children to begin using their writing abilities.

Assessing Progression

The information presented here makes the point that children's progression from concrete to symbolic is not linear — a point that is of some relevance for early diagnostic assessments of children's literacy and numeracy. There is a widespread assumption that progressions in children's understanding of symbolic activities, such as reading and number, consist of a shift from a 'concrete' function (that is, verbally based) to an 'abstract' function based on written symbols. In both reading and number the assumption is that children first learn a skill or a concept on the concrete level and that they then transfer this to their abstract (symbolic) function. The data presented here suggest that the relation between the concrete and abstract phases of children's progression is far more complex. Not only did the concrete level of function develop alongside the abstract function, and overlap with it, but the two levels also interacted with each other. The children's developing numeric (symbolic) skills both affected, and were affected by, their oral counting skills. This progression in numeracy parallels the phases in reading that mark the transition from a story-based understanding to an understanding of text. Writing may play the same role in understanding numerals as it does in understanding story text.

Conclusions: Implications for Education and Assessment

While children are still in the 'pre-reading' stage, they may be competent at using symbols — providing the symbols have the logographic characteristics of single-digit numerals. It is a different story altogether, of course, when children are asked to use symbols in more complex ways. The idea that letters represent the individual sounds of a word is one which children take a while to grasp since it requires skills in analysing and segmenting spoken language. Equally, the idea that the numerals in double- and triple-digit figures represent very specific parts of a quantity requires understanding of both quantity and of the way in which the digits are related to each other.

Both writing and numeral use begin at the simple logographic stage. The use of logographic symbols indicates that children are actively beginning the construction of symbol systems that have personal meaning. Current primary practice concerning the teaching of mathematical notation can take two forms. The first form follows traditional mathematical thinking, exemplified by the SPMG[2] curriculum, in which conventional numeric notation is 'bolted on' to a carefully assembled structure of concrete number understanding. The second form is developmental in approach and follows the work of Hughes (1986) in granting the importance of children's self-invented notation systems. It is exemplified by the collection of case studies edited by Atkinson (1992). Both of these forms are problematic. The traditional curriculum is restricted and gives too little room to children's personal meaning. The second carries the danger of attaching so much importance to children's personal meaning that the communicative significance of conventional numeric notation may be overlooked.

The data presented in this chapter show that when children's developing symbol systems are studied longitudinally, the use of conventional notation appears strongly related to communicative function. In other words, children use conventional symbols for communicative purposes, but do not tend to use their self-invented symbols for such purposes. The self-invented symbols function as a stepping-stone to the orthodox system rather than as communicative devices in their own right.

The data presented here have implications for assessment of numeracy in the preschool and early primary years. For good reason, teachers are careful not to introduce numerals until children have adequate number concepts. Yet the children in this sample varied tremendously in their competence with signs. Some of the children were quite capable of dealing with written numerals a year before they entered primary school, while others still did not understand numerals or text after having been at school for a term. Writing systems could be introduced to children whenever they are able to use them if the class teacher has sufficient insight into individual children's abilities. This practice could be calibrated to individuals by assessing the way in which children use numerals or other recording strategies, so that the class teacher can acquire a fuller insight into the children's comprehension. The active use that children make of symbols will have an impact on their entry to school mathematics in the same way that their writing helps them in their attempts to read.

Variation in children's symbolic activity is systematically related to variation in many areas of their literate/numerate function. Their symbolic activity is related to their understanding of reading and to their identity as a reader. Assessment of a child's symbolic activity will therefore provide highly individual information about that child's level of function as a reader and as a counter. However, it is important to assess what children do with symbols rather than what they seem to know about them. In the first two years of schooling a diagnostic assessment based on children's use of written symbols could be invaluable for teachers who want to maximize children's progress in literacy and numeracy.

Acknowledgments

The study on preschool literacy and numeracy was supported by ESRC grant no. L208252005 and was part of the ESRC programme 'Innovation and Change in Education'. Thanks are due to the preschool centres who took part in the study and to Strathclyde Region Education Department for help and cooperation.

Notes

1   Illustrations of hieroglyphs, pictograms and tally marks may be found in Munn (1994) and Munn and Schaffer (1995) as well as in Hughes (1986).
2   Scottish Primary Maths Group.

References

ATKINSON, S. (1992) *Mathematics with Reason: The Emergent Approach to Primary Maths*, London, Hodder & Stoughton.

CARRAHER, T., CARRAHER-NUNES, T. and SCHLIEMANN, A. (1985) 'Mathematics in the streets and in schools', *British Journal of Developmental Psychology* (3), pp. 21–9.

FERREIRO, E. (1990) 'Literacy development: Psychogenesis', in GOODMAN, Y. (ed.) *How Children Construct Literacy*, Newark, DE, International Reading Association.

FUSON, K. (1988) *Children's Counting and Concepts of Number*, New York, Springer-Verlag.

GELMAN, R. and GALLISTEL, C. (1978) *The Child's Understanding of Number*, Cambridge, Mass., Harvard University Press.

HUGHES, M. (1986) *Children and Number*, Oxford, Blackwell.

MUNN, P. (1994) 'The early development of literacy and numeracy skills', *European Early Childhood Education Research Journal*, **2** (1).

MUNN, P. (1995) 'The role of organized preschool learning environments in literacy and numeracy development', *Research Papers in Education*, **10**, pp. 217–52.

MUNN, P. and SCHAFFER, H.R. (1995) 'Teaching and learning in the preschool period', in HUGHES, M. (ed.) *Teaching and Learning in Times of Change*, Oxford, Blackwell.

ROBERTS, G. (1989) *Teaching Children to Read and Write* (Chapter 4: 'Conscious efforts to read'), Oxford, Blackwell.

SAXE, G., GUBERMAN, S. and GEARHART, M. (1987) 'Social processes in early number development', SRCD monograph, serial no. 216, **52** (2).

SULZBY, E. (1988) 'A study of children's early reading development', in PELLEGRINI, A.D. (ed.) *Psychological Bases for Early Education*, NY, Wiley.

WYNN, K. (1990) 'Children's understanding of counting', *Cognition*, **36**, pp. 155–93.

3 Primary Science in the Mid-1990s: Grounds for Optimism

Richard Gott and Sandra Duggan

Introduction

One of the main and, to some, the most exciting impacts of the National Curriculum in the UK has been its effect on science teaching in primary schools. Prior to the National Curriculum, introduced in 1989, science education was left for the most part to secondary schools. Provision at the primary level was somewhat haphazard, ranging from little more than nature study in many schools to some inspired science teaching in others. The effect of the National Curriculum is that now, in the mid-1990s, science is a more or less well-established, but certainly accepted, part of the curriculum in every primary school in the UK.

While the place of science in the curriculum now seems secure, the development of its structure and content has been less straightforward, not least because the government inspired documentation has gone through several changes. Moreover the statutory inclusion of science in the curriculum has placed considerable demands on generic primary teachers, few of whom have an in-depth knowledge of science. Consequently, while there is no doubt that curriculum *time* is devoted to science, the *quality* of science teaching in primary schools has been the subject of much controversy (Summers, 1994). Such controversy has focused mainly on primary teachers' lack of subject knowledge (see, for example, OFSTED, 1992–93), a problem which is not confined to the UK (see, for instance, Ginns and Watters, 1995, in Australia). To a lesser extent, the perceived dominance of 'group work' has been criticized. A recent article in the *Times Educational Supplement*, characteristic of the current political agenda in primary education, reflected both these concerns. The article reported that the government's Chief Inspector of Schools criticized the culture in primary schools as one in which

the teaching of knowledge is less important than the development of core skills.

It was also reported that the Chief Inspector

castigates primary classes where children work on different activities in groups, with teachers as facilitators.

Table 3.1: Dimensions of 'good practice' in primary education (based on Alexander, 1995)

Dimensions of good practice	
1. *The value dimension*	beliefs and values shaping views of childhood and the child's needs, of society and its needs, and of knowledge, which inform a coherent view of what it is to be educated.
2. *The conceptual dimension*	a map of the essential elements of teaching, learning and the curriculum and the relationship between them.
3. *The empirical dimension*	evidence about the effectiveness of practice: about the capacity of particular teaching strategies to deliver learning in accordance with a coherent view of what it is to be educated.
4. *The political dimension*	expectations and pressures from within the professional hierarchy, and beyond it from parents, community, employers and politicians.
5. *The pragmatic dimension*	an awareness of the opportunities and constraints of particular school and classroom settings.

Such comments, often political and rhetorical rather than detached and argued in their reporting, are symptomatic of an ongoing debate. Alexander (1995), in attempting to relate these issues to 'good practice' in primary schools, suggests five dimensions within which such rhetoric can be located (Table 3.1). He further suggests that the first three are of more fundamental importance and it is with these dimensions that we shall concern ourselves in this paper. We shall suggest that consideration of the value system of science education must include a greater emphasis on the collection, interpretation and communication of evidence and that such a shift in perception will influence the conceptual dimension that delimits primary science content and practice. We shall then discuss some recent empirical research findings which go some way to legitimating that emphasis and suggest that, in contrast to the press reports of the government's views, there is much that is promising in primary science education.

The Value Dimension: Primary Science as Part of the Totality of Science Education

Science at the primary level should be seen, not in isolation, but rather as the first steps along the road of 'formal' science education ('informal' science education for many children having begun already in the home and in pre-school education). Schools need to lay the foundations for a sound science education, a process which will continue through the compulsory years of school into adult life. In the past, the long-standing debate about the purpose(s)

Table 3.2: The aims of science education

1. generating a lifetime's interest in and enthusiasm for science, engineering and technology

2. preparing pupils for employment in science related work

3. empowering people to question the 'experts' and thereby to contribute to decision making in areas where science is involved, at all levels of society.

of science education has largely been confined to secondary education. If we accept the notion of a continuum, we must look again at the aims of science education as a whole and then ask the question: what do they, and the values of primary education, have to say to each other?

We take the overall aims of science education to include three which are of direct relevance to this paper (Table 3.2). The first of these, giving pupils a thirst for science and a taste of its intrinsic interest and of its value in relation to everyday living, is clearly of prime importance and we shall take it as axiomatic. The second and third do have things to say to us about the content, and by association, the practice of science education.

Science Education and Employment

The second aim is potentially controversial in that some regard education for employment as a politically sensitive issue. We shall not enter into that debate here but we will assume that some sort of preparation for employment, in the sense that it influences the choice of content for the science curriculum, must be part of the equation. A recent report by the Council of Science and Technology Institutes (CSTI) (1993) considered the requirements of employment by mapping a range of occupations where science, technology and maths were used to a greater (e.g., 'pure' scientists) or lesser extent (e.g., farm workers, hairdressers). Over a thousand employers' views were sought. In trying to define what employers in all these occupations, who employ an estimated 3 million, require, the authors of the report identified three 'skills':

1 A central core of skills concerned with the doing of science
2 Communication skills
3 Management skills

The first of these is defined in more detail as the ability to:

- Generate own ideas, hypotheses and theoretical models and/or utilize those postulated by others

- Design investigations, experiments, trials, tests, simulations and operations
- Conduct investigations, experiments, trials, tests and operations
- Evaluate data and results from the processes and outcomes of investigations, experiments, trials, tests and operations

These findings have been confirmed by another study (Coles, 1995) in which some eighteen scientists in three major UK science-based companies, three public service laboratories and three research departments in UK universities were interviewed in depth. This evidence, coupled with a review of the literature on economic development in Europe, employment/recruitment patterns, scientific and technical competence, scientific literacy, education and employment statistics, led Coles to identify characteristics which are seen as being important in potential and current employees. These include the following 'science-specific characteristics':

- The understanding of major science ideas
- Practical capabilities
- Problem solving by experimentation
- Decision making by weighing evidence
- Scientific 'habits of mind' (e.g., scepticism, logical thinking, considering all options) and 'general characteristics' such as communication, interpersonal relationships and teamwork

The results of this work support the CSTI findings: the general characteristics being equivalent to the communication and management skills identified by the CSTI; the science-specific characteristics equivalent to the central core of skills with the addition of the 'understanding of major science ideas'. We might combine the findings of these two reports into the following statement: The essential requirements for employment in science related fields are:

- an understanding of scientific evidence
- an understanding of major scientific concepts
- personal and interpersonal skills

Empowerment In and By Science

Our third aim is arguably the most important: the need to empower people. Too often science is treated as something beyond comprehension and 'best left to the experts'; a dangerous path to tread. There are numerous instances where experts have failed the public. Issues such as the Intelligence Quotient (IQ), or more recently, the debate over the alleged suppression of research findings in the tobacco industry, all demonstrate how particular scientists, or groups of scientists, can wield power with consequences which most would regard as far from benign. We are not arguing that science is a 'bad thing' but rather using these examples to suggest that a greater public understanding of science, which would enable intelligent questioning of such issues, might help to put science in perspective and thereby avoid detrimental consequences. Wolpert (1992) writes in relation to ecological problems:

> ... only if the public have sufficient understanding can they make judgments about major issues. Unless one has some scientific literacy how can one distinguish between ecobabble and hard science in relation to the environment? (p. 9)

It is simplistic, however, to suggest that the possession of scientific knowledge, particularly of the more traditional factual kind, is in itself enough, particularly in complex issues such as those described above. Layton, Jenkins, Macgill and Davey's (1993) analysis of four case studies where members of the public were confronted with real-life problems — e.g., the problems of parenting a Down's Syndrome child or of domestic energy and the elderly — in which science would be expected to be useful in arriving at a solution, sheds some light on the factors involved in using science in everyday life. The case studies showed that what the public used was 'practical knowledge' — that is, knowledge which, while including scientific knowledge, also included other knowledge together with personal judgments. It was this practical knowledge which was then used to underpin action:

> the lay recipients of scientific knowledge were far from passive; they interacted with the science, testing it against personal experience, contextualising it by overlaying it with particular local knowledge and evaluating its social and institutional origins. (Layton *et al.*, 1993, p. 122)

From these findings Layton *et al.* (1993) argue that scientific knowledge needs to be reworked or translated to become instrumental in everyday life. In discussing what sort of science education will enable all citizens to use science in this kind of way, Layton *et al.* (1993) cite work by Wynne (1991) who defines three levels of public understanding of science:

- its intellectual content, which we take here to mean the major concepts of science
- its research methods, which we will regard in the context of this paper as to do with the collection, verification, interpretation and communication of evidence in support of conclusions
- its organizational forms of ownership and control

It is from an understanding of scientific evidence, rather than simply from a knowledge of the facts and concepts of science (substantive knowledge), that questionable practices and conventions can be challenged. The role of major scientific ideas remains important, but to the extent that there is a minimum which is necessary, to permit the penetrating question:

> knowing when one knows enough about a subject to take reasonable action, like deciding on a birth control method or introducing a modification into one's diet. (Atkin and Helms, 1993, p. 16)

The American Association for the Advancement of Science (AAAS) endorses the importance of the understanding of scientific evidence for the empowerment of all:

> People should be able to note when conclusions do not follow logically from an argument, for example. Or when fact and opinion are intermingled. They should be able to detect when graphs distort the appearance of results, or when averages mask important variation, or when sample size is not reported, or when high levels of precision are unwarranted. (AAAS, 1989, p. 139)

Prewitt (1983) widens the debate by introducing the notion of a 'savvy citizen': as one who

> . . . understands fundamental principles that allow him or her to function successfully in the political process, in policy making decisions, and in issues that affect social change, and, although this understanding would be enriched by substantive knowledge of science, it is not co-terminous with it. (p. 53)

The combination of knowledge and fundamental scientific principles related to the quality of the evidence base enables, and hence empowers, the citizen in the face of government organizations, local or national, and 'big business' interests. The issue for the 'savvy citizen' in the case of the debate about mercury amalgam in tooth fillings for instance, is not *how*, in detail, mercury can harm, it is sufficient to know that it does, but rather, what is the quality of the evidence and do the tests that have been carried out encompass the problem.

Requirements for Employment and Empowerment

To summarize our argument so far, Table 3.3 shows that the requirements for employment and empowerment are not dissimilar. They focus on the research

Table 3.3: Summary of the requirements

Requirements for employment in science	Requirements for empowering people
an understanding of scientific evidence	understanding of the research methods of science
an understanding of major scientific concepts	an understanding of the content of science
interpersonal skills	an understanding of its organizational forms of ownership and control

methods of science, its major conceptual ideas and the interpersonal elements associated with teamwork, ownership and control.

Returning now to the dimensions of good practice with which we began, these three requirements, which comprise the *value dimension*, should enable us to define the conceptual dimension — that is, the essential elements of teaching, learning and the curriculum.

The Conceptual Dimension

To what extent does science education meet the needs of the requirements for employment and empowerment which we have arrived at by consideration of 'value'?

Traditionally, science education (which until recently has referred largely to secondary science education) has emphasized the first and second of these requirements, although the balance of these two has been a matter of ongoing debate. While there is no doubt that an understanding of certain fundamental scientific facts and ideas is necessary, there is a feeling that there has been too great an emphasis on teaching the content of science, not only in the class-room but also in the laboratory where illustrative or enquiry work has been targeted at teaching concepts. We believe that the 'major ideas of science' are, of course, a vital constituent of the curriculum but that they may well not be parsimonious enough at any Key Stage.

The second requirement — the need to teach an understanding of scien-tific method *per se* and its associated content concerning the understanding of scientific evidence — has taken root in the revised National Curriculum. The current version consists of four statutory attainment targets: three of which are concerned with facts and concepts and the other with practical work (see Table 3.4). Science 1 cannot, of course, exist in a vacuum of ideas and is intended to be integrated with the teaching of major scientific ideas:

> Contexts derived from Life Processes and Living Things, Materials and their Properties and Physical Processes should be used to teach pupils about experimental and investigative methods. On some occasions,

Table 3.4: The National Curriculum for science (DFE, 1995)

Sc1	Experimental and Investigative Science
Sc2	Life Processes and Living Things
Sc3	Materials and their Properties
Sc4	Physical Processes

Table 3.5: Key Stages in Science 1 (DFE, 1995)

Key Stage 1	Key Stage 2	Key Stage 3	Key Stage 4
Planning experimental work	Planning experimental work	Planning experimental procedures	Planning experimental procedures
Obtaining evidence	Obtaining evidence	Obtaining evidence	Obtaining evidence
Considering evidence	Considering evidence	Analysing evidence and drawing conclusions	Analysing evidence and drawing conclusions
		Considering the strength of the evidence	Evaluating evidence

> the whole process of investigating an idea should be carried out by
> pupils themselves. (DFE, 1995)

Looking in more detail at the programmes of study for each Key Stage (for
Science 1) we see that pupils of all ages are asked to:

> turn ideas suggested to them, and their own ideas, into a form that can
> be investigated. (DFE, 1995)

We should also note the strong emphasis on evidence in all Key Stages (Table
3.5) and the increasing focus on analysis and evaluation from the lower to the
higher Key Stages. The definition of Science 1 is very close to the CSTI definition of the central core of skills required by industry, outlined above. We
have argued elsewhere that there is a 'content' to the skills/research methods
of science which focuses on evidence just as there is a content to Sc2–4. We
have attempted a definition of that content and, for reasons of space, will not
reiterate it here but rather refer the reader to Gott and Duggan (1995) for a full
discussion.

   The third requirement, which concerns personal and interpersonal skills
and the power structures of science, was to some extent explicit in early
versions of the National Curriculum:

> Pupils should develop the ability to work effectively as part of a group in the planning, carrying out, reporting and evaluation of an investigation or task. (Attainment Target 18, DES, 1988)

and:

> They [pupils] should be encouraged to respond to their teacher and to the reports and ideas of other pupils and to take part in group activities. (Key Stage 1, NCC, 1991)

In the current version (DFE, 1995), however, we can find no explicit mention of group work.

In principle then, the National Curriculum for science includes some of the ideas that have been identified as being important to employers and to the empowerment of the citizen, and primary science has been accorded a place in their development. In terms of the defining dimensions of good practice, we see that a set of values, based on the requirements of industry and democratic empowerment, has led us to a conceptual dimension for science which is mirrored to some extent in the National Curriculum.

The Empirical Dimension: Science 1 in Primary Schools

The third dimension, the empirical dimension, concerns the effectiveness of teaching and learning; clearly no amount of high sounding philosophy is of any account if no learning results. This section of the paper will present some research findings about the feasibility of teaching, particularly at the primary level, for an understanding of evidence which we have seen is strongly emphasized in Science 1.

The research involved a detailed look at a small sample of pupils carrying out investigations and was part of the Procedural and Conceptual Knowledge in Science (PACKS) project which was begun in 1991. One of the aims of the PACKS project was to explore how children's performance of investigations changes with age and experience. The sample consisted of approximately sixteen groups (of two to four pupils) of mixed ability pupils at three age points, Year 4 (9-year-olds), Year 6 (11-year-olds) and Year 9 (14-year-olds) for each of seven investigations. Pupils were drawn from more than thirty urban, suburban and rural schools from two regions in the north of England. The tasks were chosen on a number of criteria such as their accessibility to children from the ages of 9 to 14 , ease of completion within the normal science period, use of simple apparatus and the spanning of a range of contexts. Full details of the project aims, methodology, analyses and findings can be found elsewhere (Millar, Lubben, Gott and Duggan, 1994, Duggan and Gott, 1994a, 1994b).

For the purposes of this chapter, we shall consider aspects of children's performance on the following task:

Richard Gott and Sandra Duggan

Figure 3.1: The forces task

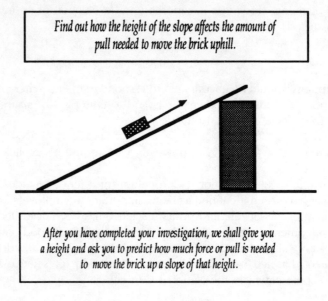

Find out how the height of the slope affects the amount of
pull needed to move the brick uphill.

After you have completed your investigation, we shall give you
a height and ask you to predict how much force or pull is needed
to move the brick up a slope of that height.

A range of equipment was made available:

- half bricks with a hook inserted into one face
- planks approximately 1 metre long
- a variety of forcemeters
- metre rules

If pupils were not familiar with using a forcemeter, its use was demonstrated
before the investigation began. Although the children worked in groups, they
were asked to record their results and conclusions individually.

Both the height of the ramp and the force or pull can be identified quan-
titatively in that both variables can be measured. Alternatively, the height and
pull can be judged or assessed in a qualitative way; for example low, medium,
and high heights or 'little' and 'big' pulls. An additional part of this investigation set a 'competition' which was presented to the participating groups at the
outset. Pupils were told that after they had completed their investigation, they
would be given a height and asked to predict how much pull or force would
be needed to move the brick up a slope of that height. The competition was
intended to encourage pupils to collect quantitative data and to give them a
reason for doing so by requiring interpolation from the data.

When the children's performance on isolated component parts or procedural 'bits' of the investigation were analysed, the results showed a degree of
progression with age in the application of these procedural ideas in the investigation. Two examples will be presented here. The first is an aspect of design
— namely the way pupils define the variables as quantitative or qualitative —

Table 3.6: *Identification of the variables in the Forces II task by age (numbers of groups)*

	Qualitative identification only	Measured independent variable only	Measured dependent variable only	Measured both variables
Y4 (N=16)	4	1	3	8
Y6 (N=17)	0	1	2	14
Y9 (N=14)	0	1	0	13

Table 3.7: *Concepts of measurement selected by pupils in the Forces II task (numbers of groups)*

	2 readings	3 readings	More than 3 readings	Selection of a sensible range	Selection of a sensible interval
Y4 (N=16)	3	3	10	9	4
Y6 (N=17)	1	1	15	13	12
Y9 (N=14)	1	2	11	13	13

which shows a big increase in the number of groups measuring both variables between the two primary age groups as compared to the increase between Year 6 and Year 9 (see Table 3.6). Secondly, if we consider aspects of measurement (see Table 3.7), we see again a marked improvement between Year 4 and Year 6 but little difference in performance between Year 6 and Year 9.

The data were also analysed with the aim of determining children's ability to demonstrate that they could *synthesize* all the parts of the investigation into a whole in working towards an effective solution. An overall judgment or evaluation of each group's performance in the investigation was developed by looking at all the evidence: the written reports of the individuals in the group, the researcher's checklist, and the accompanying case notes (which included the responses to the questions asked by the researcher as the group carried out the investigation). The basis of the judgment was the extent to which all the evidence from the group led to a 'believable' conclusion: was the evidence convincing? The reader is referred to Duggan and Gott (1994a, 1994b) for further details of the categorization. Five categories emerged (see Table 3.8).

The results of imposing these categories on all the data from this investigation are shown in Figure 3.2. The charts in the figure show that, as expected, there is an increasing shift towards the higher categories (2b and 3) with age. More surprisingly, however, when the charts for Year 6 and Year 9 are compared, the relative numbers of groups in category 3 are reversed with more groups falling into the highest category (3) at Year 6 than at Year 9. In other words, the results suggest that pupils' ability to generate believable evidence appears to improve during primary school but then falls during the early years of secondary school.

It should be noted here that the results of imposing the same categorization on children's performance of another task also concerned with forces, namely

Richard Gott and Sandra Duggan

Table 3.8: Group categorization

1a   'Qualitative' groups tested the force or pull by feel, either pulling the brick by hand or using the forcemeter simply as a tool to pull the brick along while ignoring the numerical reading.

1b   Groups of pupils in this category also measured the force by feel but then ordered their data and were able to make some kind of generalization.

2a   These groups took quantitative measurements but in their table or barchart made little or no attempt to order the readings.

2b   These groups also took quantitative measurements and, although they ordered their data, there was evidence to suggest that the data were ordered more by chance than as a result of understanding.

3   These groups ordered the data, drew ordered barcharts or line graphs and showed that they understood the relationship between the independent and the dependent variable in their conclusion.

Figure 3.2: Numbers of groups in each investigation category in Year 4, Year 6, and Year 9

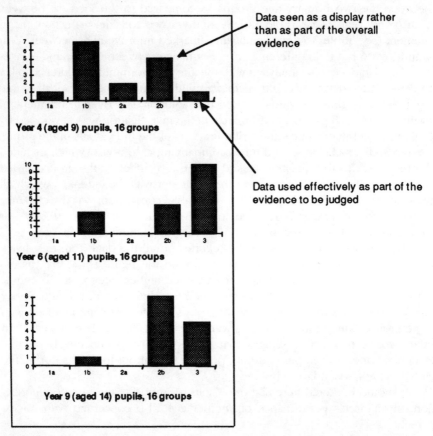

44

Find out how the type of surface effects the amount of pull needed
to drag the brick along

were broadly the same with Year 6 children appearing to be better at making
their understanding of their findings explicit than at Year 9 (Duggan and Gott,
1994a). These results should be interpreted with caution, however, based as
they are on a single task with a relatively small sample of groups of children
at each age point. What other evidence is there to support these findings?

Preliminary analyses of two other PACKS tasks in the context of dissolving
suggest similar but less pronounced trends, a difference which may be attrib-
utable to the relative complexity of the tasks in terms of their implementation
and in terms of the concepts involved. Other tasks in the PACKS project which
were carried out at slightly different sampling points, namely with pupils at
Year 4, Year 7 and Year 9 have not yet been analysed in the same way. The
different sampling points used in these tasks might also be expected to obscure the improvement in performance at the end of primary school (Year 6)
but to illuminate performance in early secondary school (Year 7).

Given the rather small sample involved, we are hesitant to make over-
generalized claims. However, independent evidence from McGrath (1995,
personal communication) supporting our findings suggests that our results do
not appear to be an artefact and indeed convinced us that this is an issue of
some importance and worthy of dissemination. McGrath's work with the Science Challenge scheme was carried out in 1994 with children from different
parts of the country. 'Expert' judges observed children carrying out investigations about a topic called 'Slip and Slide'. They observed, on occasion independently of each other, that overall performance by the primary children was
superior to that of the secondary children. It is coincidental and in some ways
unfortunate that these investigations were, like the data reported above, set in
the context of forces since it is possible that, for some reason, the decline in
performance is restricted to tasks set within this context. Although unlikely,
further work is needed to rule out such a possibility.

The competition described earlier and which was set after the investigation was completed, tested whether pupils were able to apply the idea that a
table or graph represents a picture of the relationship between the two variables, height and force. About half the groups (8/16 Year 4 groups, 7/17 Year
6 groups and 7/14 Year 9 groups) at each age could interpolate correctly from
their investigation in the competition. Did these pupils use their data in tables
or graphs to help them interpolate, or simply predict on the basis of what they
had seen happen? Table 3.9 shows that approximately half the groups of
younger children interpolated correctly from an investigation which included
only a table or list of results. We might expect graphical representation to make
interpolation easier, but it can be seen that although twelve out of the fifteen
groups of Year 9 children drew a graph or barchart, only six groups interpolated from it successfully in the competition. It appears that, in this investigation, successful interpolation does not depend on the method of representation,

Table 3.9: Data handling in the investigation and performance in the competition

	Recorded data in table or list only	Drew barchart or line graph	Interpolated successfully from table in competition	Interpolated successfully from barchart or line graph in competition
Y4 (n=16 groups)	14	2	7	1
Y6 (n=17 groups)	15	2	7	0
Y9 (n=14 groups)	2	12	1	6

but neither does it improve with age despite the increased use of graphs, whose intended purpose is to illustrate the pattern more clearly and hence facilitate interpolation.

To summarize this section, our findings suggest that ideas about scientific evidence are capable of being understood by primary school children. What this research does *not* tell us is which particular teaching strategies helped or hindered that understanding. During the course of collecting the data for this research we observed the effect of the teachers' expectations on pupil performance. For instance, in one Year 9 class, pupils commented that they got extra marks for graphs and this same class were observed preparing graphs before they had even begun the investigation. This kind of ritual performance tends to divert pupils from the purpose of the investigation and leads them to focus on the 'bits' rather than the whole. We tentatively suggest that this might be one possible explanation for the better performance of primary pupils in the investigation described above who were more likely to interpret their results in the 'simpler' tabular form and appeared to keep the purpose of the task in mind throughout. The sample is small, however, so that the results must be interpreted with caution and in the absence of further evidence, explanations must be speculation only.

Implications

If we accept that the aims of science education include employment and empowerment, then these aims require three essential elements to be present in the curriculum. Two of these three elements (the major scientific concepts and research methods focusing on evidence) are now in place in the National Curriculum for science in the UK. This paper has focused on the second of these and has presented research findings concerning pupils' understanding of scientific evidence which suggest that, at Year 6, pupils are capable of demonstrating this understanding.

While the current emphasis on evidence in the science curriculum is a significant step forward which, in our opinion, is to be welcomed, there are aspects of Alexander's (1995) dimensions which are not yet in place. The first of these is the definition of the 'content' of the understanding of evidence. There is a tendency in the government documentation to present evidence as consisting of isolated parts which may lead to teaching which, as we have witnessed, can result in pupils adopting a ritual approach and in a lack of understanding of the purpose of evidence as a whole. While it could be argued that this ritual approach may be the first step on the way to the wider understanding of scientific evidence, in the same way as U-shaped development has been recorded in other areas of learning (Strauss and Stavey, 1982), we have argued elsewhere (Duggan and Gott, 1995) that for those students who do not go on to study science after 16, this seems unlikely to be so. The point we wish to make here is that if the content of this part of the curriculum is not clearly defined, then there is a danger that an emphasis on the 'bits' may divert pupils from the understanding of evidence as a whole which, as our findings suggest, may be a retrogressive step.

The second missing item is an explicit statement of the purpose of teaching for an understanding of ideas about scientific evidence. As in Alexander's (1995) value dimension, the role of an understanding of evidence as a central part of 'education for life' needs to be made clear so that those concerned with science education can locate it within a coherent view of the curriculum. This second item may be more important than the first because if teachers acquire this view, then the content will take on more significance.

What then of the quotes with which we began this article? The first criticized the emphasis on the teaching of core skills as opposed to knowledge. Our application of Alexander's (1995) considerations for good practice to science education would suggest that while the teaching of scientific knowledge, or the major scientific concepts, is an essential part of the curriculum, the development of core skills is equally important, particularly with a view to science education for employment and empowerment.

We would also take issue with the government stance on group work and teacher facilitation (the second quote). At the very least it is difficult to see how children can develop teamwork if they are working alone. This is not to say that there is no room for 'straight teaching'; of course there is. But common sense dictates that we choose teaching styles to suit that which is to be taught; and for investigative work, group activities are a good way of building teamwork and allowing for that ongoing discussion that builds understanding, besides being logistically necessary.

Further, the quality of investigative work where pupils are encouraged to design, collect and interpret their own evidence is dependent on teachers acting as facilitators *and* teachers rather than adopting either a didactic or a 'hands off' role. It seems likely that the autonomy that teachers allow during investigative work in primary schools may be one of the elements which encourages and inspires children and allows them to follow the problem through to the end. A return to individual practical work or to the narrow view of practical work as consisting *only* of guided practicals, is likely to result in a population who are less than scientifically literate, at least in terms of understanding scientific evidence.

To conclude, the introduction of science in primary schools is an important step forward in the history of science education and while there may be legitimate concerns about some aspects of science teaching, our research suggests that there is much that is promising in Sc1 in primary schools. We therefore fully endorse the views of a recent OFSTED report which stated that

> . . . primary science can be counted as major success. (OFSTED, 1994)

Dore (1994) reports the views of a leading physicist, Professor Gago working at the forefront of sub-atomic research. Gago believes that the investigation-based approach science curriculum in the UK places the UK in the lead compared to France and Germany because it

> . . . develops the skills that pupils will need for the job market such as problem solving and teamwork. (Dore, 1994)

To maintain that lead we need to encourage primary teachers to continue what they are doing and at the same time ensure that they have a clear understanding of what constitutes evidence as well as a coherent view of the place and purpose of science education in the modern world.

Acknowledgments

The research reported here was supported by the Economic and Social Research Council Grant No. L208 25 2008 as part of the research programme 'Innovation and Change in Education: the Quality of Teaching and Learning'.

We acknowledge the contributions of Robin Millar and Fred Lubben, University of York, our co-researchers in the PACKS project, to discussions which influenced our thinking about children's investigation performance and its relationship to their understandings of scientific evidence. The use to which these ideas are put in this paper and the interpretations offered are, however, the sole responsibility of the authors.

References

ALEXANDER, R. (1995) 'The problem of good primary practice', in MURPHY, P., SELINGER, M., BOURNE, J. and BRIGGS, M. (eds) *Subject Learning in the Primary Curriculum: Issues in English, Science and Mathematics*, London, Routledge, pp. 50–72.
AMERICAN ASSOCIATION FOR THE ADVANCEMENT OF SCIENCE (AAAS) (1989) *Technology: A Report of the Project 2061 Phase I Technology Panel*, Washington DC, AMERICAN ASSOCIATION FOR THE ADVANCEMENT OF SCIENCE (AAAS).

ATKIN, J.M. and HELMS, J. (1993) 'Getting serious about priorities in science education', *Studies in Science Education*, **21**, pp. 1–20.

COLES, M. (1995) Personal communication.

COUNCIL OF SCIENCE AND TECHNOLOGY INSTITUTES (1993) *Mapping the Science, Technology and Mathematics Domain*, London, The Council of Science and Technology Institutes.

DEPARTMENT FOR EDUCATION AND THE WELSH OFFICE (1991) *Science in the National Curriculum*, London, HMSO.

DEPARTMENT FOR EDUCATION AND THE WELSH OFFICE (1995) *Science in the National Curriculum*, London, HMSO.

DEPARTMENT OF EDUCATION AND SCIENCE AND THE WELSH OFFICE (1988) *Science for Ages 5 to 16, National Curriculum*, London, HMSO.

DORE, A. (1994) 'British science is the real thing', *Times Educational Supplement*, 2 December.

DUGGAN, S. and GOTT, R. (1994a) *Children's Responses to the Forces I Task*, Durham, University of Durham.

DUGGAN, S. and GOTT, R. (1994b) *Children's Responses to the Forces II Task*, Durham, University of Durham.

DUGGAN, S. and GOTT, R. (1996) 'Scientific evidence: The new emphasis in practical science in the UK curriculum', *The Curriculum Journal*, **7** (1), pp. 17–33.

FOULDS, K., GOTT, R. and FEASEY, R. (1992) *Investigative Work in Science*, Durham, University of Durham.

GOTT, R. and DUGGAN, S. (1995) *Investigative Work in the Science Curriculum*, Milton Keynes, Open University Press.

GINNS, I.S. and WATTERS, J.J. (1995) 'An analysis of scientific understandings of preservice elementary teachers education students', *J. Res. Sci. Teaching*, **32** (2), pp. 205–22.

HACKETT, G. (1995) 'Woodhead castigates progressives', *Times Educational Supplement*, 27 January.

LAYTON, D., JENKINS, E., MACGILL, S. and DAVEY, A. (1993) *Inarticulate Science?* East Yorkshire, Studies in Education Ltd.

MILLAR, R., LUBBEN, F., GOTT, R. and DUGGAN, S. (1994) 'Investigating in the school science laboratory: Conceptual and procedural knowledge and their influence on performance', *Research Papers in Education*, **9** (2) pp. 207–49.

NCC (1991) *National Curriculum Council Consultation Report: Science in the National Curriculum*, NCC, York.

OFSTED (Office for Standards in Education) (1994) *Science and Mathematics in Schools: A Review*, London, HMSO.

PREWITT, K. (1983) 'Scientific illiteracy and democratic theory', *Daedalus*, **112** (2), pp. 49–64.

SHARP, R. and GREEN, A. (1975) *Education and Social Control: A Study in Progressive Primary Education*, London, Routledge and Kegan Paul.

STRAUSS, S. and STAVEY, R. (1982) in STRAUSS, S. (ed.) *U-shaped Behavioural Growth*, London, Academic Press.

SUMMERS, M. (1994) 'Science in the primary school: The problem of teachers' curricular expertise', *The Curriculum Journal*, **5** (2) pp. 179–93.

WOLPERT, L. (1992) 'Why it's all Greek', *Guardian*, 29 October.

WYNNE, B. (1991) 'Knowledges in context', *Science Technology and Human Values*, **16** (1), pp. 111–21.

Working Together in Primary Schools: Changing Relationships at Key Stage 2

Marilyn Osborn and Edie Black

Introduction

Teacher collaboration and collegiality are often cited as encouraging teacher development and contributing directly to teaching quality and school effectiveness. Yet we know relatively little about the effect of recent education reforms in England on the extent and nature of such collaboration. This chapter explores the impact of the implementation of a National Curriculum and national assessment on the working patterns of teachers in the upper years of primary schooling. It focuses particularly on the ways in which teachers worked together as colleagues and on teachers' perceptions of the importance of increased collaboration and interdependence.

The findings presented here are drawn from semi-structured interviews carried out in late 1992 and early 1993 with forty-five Year 5 and Year 6 primary teachers and twenty-two headteachers in six local education authorities in England and Wales. The interviews, which contained many open-ended and exploratory questions, were tape-recorded. Extensive notes were also made during the interviews and documentary evidence, such as School Development Plans and whole school curriculum plans, was also collected. A full report of the research methods can be found elsewhere (Osborn and Black, 1994).

Collaboration and Collegiality: Teachers Working Together

There was a general consensus that the National Curriculum at the time the interviews were carried out, and prior to the publication of the Dearing Report (Dearing, 1994), was overloaded and unmanageable. When we asked the teachers in our sample to record their hours of work in a typical week, they reported that they worked an average of 52 hours per week, while 36 per cent reported working over 55 hours per week. Most teachers said that there had been a vast increase in their working day in terms of planning, preparation, and assessment. On average, teachers were in direct contact with children for less than half their working hours. Although the proportion of time spent on planning, preparation, etc., was slightly less than that reported for Key Stage 1 teachers by Campbell (1992), it still represents a considerable investment of time in non-teaching activities. The majority of teachers now took it for granted that they would work regularly both sides of the official school day, some part of most weekends, and some days during half-term and end-of-term breaks. Their responses provided clear evidence of the intensification of teachers' work resulting in a proliferation of paperwork and administrative tasks and the loss of opportunities for more creative work and for developing caring relationships with pupils (Apple, 1986; Densmore, 1987; Webb, 1993).

However, in spite of the vastly increased workload and the associated stress experienced by many teachers, over two-thirds of the teachers welcomed, *albeit* with some reservation, the introduction of the National Curriculum at Key Stage 2, valuing the guidelines and framework it provided, while expressing unhappiness at the overload in terms of subject coverage and paperwork. As a Year 5 teacher in an urban junior school put it:

> The National Curriculum is a useful framework. It's what we needed. It's made us more aware of planning so that we're not repeating work. It's given us a structure to work within. It is, however, too vast; the areas we have to cover at Key Stage 2 are crippling. We just cannot do it all. It's made us more aware that we have to trust each other. We have to realize that things have been taught before, and we don't have to start to teach everything from scratch.

For this teacher, as for most teachers in the study, one of the most positive elements to emerge from the changes was a significant increase in the extent to which teachers planned and worked together as a staff. The theme of trust and a sense of increased interdependency and interrelationship between teachers occurred many times in teachers' responses. Sixty per cent of the sample felt that preparation for Key Stage 2 had made a considerable difference to the way in which they worked collaboratively. The evidence from our sample and from research at Key Stage 1 (Osborn, Broadfoot, Abbot, Croll and Pollard, 1992; Pollard, Broadfoot, Croll, Osborn and Abbot, 1994) suggests that the recent education reforms have brought about a definite diminution in the degree of isolation of primary teachers within their own classroom and an increase in a move to a more 'collaborative' professionalism (Hoyle, 1992).

While as 'autonomous professionals' most teachers argued that they had always shared ideas and consulted with colleagues, 75 per cent now felt that they did much more detailed joint planning and collaboration. Forty per cent mentioned more sharing of curricular expertise and a heightened awareness of the need for continuity and progress. Most had experienced an increased awareness of what was going on in the school as a whole since the implementation of the 1988 Education Reform Act. This was a change welcomed by almost all the teachers we interviewed.

It should be stressed that working together at the initial topic planning stage was the most common form of collaboration, far more common than sharing teaching or working alongside colleagues in the classroom. The most common form of joint planning and working mentioned by 93 per cent of teachers was 'horizontal' rather than 'vertical' in the sense that it took place with other teachers of the same year group or at least with other teachers of Years 5 and 6 rather than throughout the school as a whole. However, 55 per cent also did some planning and working together with subject coordinators and 52 per cent worked sometimes with colleagues in other parts of the school.[1] Much of the latter was done at specific staff meetings or INSET days for planning whole school topics.

Although for many teachers the increase in collaboration was a largely positive outcome of the reforms, there was also evidence from our interviews that for others the National Curriculum had replaced the existing informal, relaxed collaborative relationship with a more formalized, structured 'collegiality'. Hargreaves (1992) has described such a situation, where teachers' collaborative working relationships do not arise spontaneously from the initiative of teachers, but are a result of an administrative imposition that requires teachers to meet and work together, as 'contrived' collegiality. For these teachers, there was a sense of loss as well as gain in their changed working relationship with colleagues. While they met together far more on a formal basis in full staff or year group meetings, they rarely had time for the informal interchanges, the sharing of ideas, discussion about children, and humour which had previously characterized primary staffrooms. For example, one Year 5 teacher in a large junior school argued that she rarely had time to go into the staffroom now. As she put it:

> We used to swap and share before the National Curriculum . . . I love everything about the National Curriculum except that it's taken . . . two things I think it's done which are really bad. One is, it's taken people out of the staffroom. I no longer go in the staffroom because 8.00 am to 9.00 am I'm working, break-time I hardly ever go in. Dinner hour I'm too shattered . . . We used to have schemes whereby someone would say 'Look I'm not very good. I can't get paintings from children like you do. Could you come in and we'll team teach.' But there's just not time for that now.

Acker (1995) in an ethnographic study of an English primary school carried out prior to the implementation of the 1988 Education Reform Act has described the way in which teachers at 'Hillview' had created a workplace culture characterized by collaboration, compassion, and community. However, Acker argues this was in no sense a 'cosy' culture unmarked by tensions. Conflict existed, as in any workplace, but was subdued rather than dominant.

It seemed from our interviews with some of the teachers that they perceived a loss of some elements of this caring, supportive workplace culture. The sense of loss in terms of adult relationships was paralleled by a loss in terms of an informal, relaxed relationship with children, although teachers were concerned to protect this at all costs. The Primary Assessment, Curriculum and Experience (PACE) research at Key Stage 1 documented a similar concern amongst teachers (Osborn *et al.*, 1992, Pollard *et al.*, 1994).

Problems and Difficulties of Collaboration

The pressures under which teachers were working and the problem of curriculum overload had clear implications for the extent to which teachers were able to work collaboratively. A particular limitation on the extent to which teachers felt able to plan together was lack of non-contact time out of the classroom. Because such time away from children was so limited, most teachers gave up some of their own time after school to work with colleagues and had to snatch what time they could at break- or lunch-times, or the occasional assembly-time.

For many teachers, this issue of finding the time to do the necessary work with colleagues as well as their individual planning meant that they extended their work far beyond both ends of the official working day and into weekends. As a Year 6 teacher in a suburban primary school put it:

> We're all in at 8 so I usually spend an hour then planning . . . Not many of us leave before 5, and sometimes later. With colleagues, if we have any planning to do we tend to do that in the evening because there's no after-school time. We have a staff meeting on Wednesday and I have senior staff meeting on Thursday. We run clubs (I run a gym club) so there's no time left. We're doing the English schemes of work at the moment so three of us at the Key Stage 2 level in the upper school are going to get together in the evening. I usually spend about 3 hours at home on Sunday making sure that I'm all prepared for the week ahead.

Lack of time to work with colleagues across the school could easily lead to 'balkanization' where teachers worked not necessarily in isolation, but only in smaller subgroups or year groups within the school, rather than adopting a whole school perspective (Hargreaves, 1994). As one teacher in a small inner city junior school pointed out:

> A major problem that's been identified is that, OK, teachers within a year group work together but there needs to be more liaison between teachers in different year groups. So time needs to be built in to meet those needs.

This issue of the need for time to be built in to the school day to allow for the real increase in collaboration which was already taking place and to facilitate more whole school cooperation was reiterated in many teachers' responses.

Informal Collaboration

For the majority of teachers, collaboration did not extend as far as working together in the classroom. However, it was striking that some of the most successful attempts at swapping and sharing teaching had been set up informally between teachers of the same or adjacent year groups. These arrangements, which occurred in three of the schools in our sample, had the tacit support of the headteacher in each case. However, they were largely the result of serendipity when two teachers recognized that they had complementary skills and acted upon this, using their own professional initiative, while leaving intact the model of the generalist classroom teacher.

For example, in one inner city primary school Janet, a Year 6 teacher who was also the maths and IT coordinator and Elaine, a Year 5 teacher and language coordinator moved frequently between each other's classrooms, each recognizing her own limitations in some areas of the curriculum and welcoming the strengths of the other. Elaine described the way in which they exchanged classes in the following terms:

> I like to build up higher order language and reading skills and she [Janet] is very interested in maths investigation skills. So to support each other, because she's better at doing that than I am, we team teach in that respect.

Janet's perceptions of the arrangement were similar. She said:

> We've developed — and I hope it will develop further — we swap at least once a week. I go and do some of the aspects of maths that I find are most lacking by the time they get to Year 6 . . . Things like problem-solving and investigational maths, algebra and that kind of thing. Elaine is very keen on language development, so she'll pop into my classroom and discuss the development of characters in literature or something like that while I'm doing something else in her class.

Although these teachers had the approval of the headteacher for the exchange of skills in this way, the arrangement was not instigated by the head and did not necessarily reflect the working patterns of other teachers in the same school. Possibly the very success of this method of semi-specialism was that it belonged to the teachers themselves rather than being imposed upon them. However, it would seem that there might be a role for a facilitator within the school, perhaps the head or deputy, who would spot the opportunities for such a dove-tailing of skills where it clearly has benefits for teachers and children.

The Role of Curriculum Coordinators

One of the main ways in which teachers planned and worked together across the school as a whole was as curriculum coordinators with a well-defined distribution of responsibilities for particular areas of the curriculum and/or for cross-curricular themes such as assessment, special needs or equal opportunities. It was through the curriculum coordinators that most schools attempted to plan and work together 'vertically' throughout the school rather than simply 'horizontally' across year groups. In fact, 91 per cent of the teachers in our sample had responsibility for an area of curriculum coordination and 12 per cent of these were also deputy heads — a formidable level of responsibility.

In most schools it seemed that the only teachers excluded from such responsibilities were probationers in their first year of teaching. Moreover, some teachers were coordinators for more than one subject area, or had a cross-curriculum responsibility such as special needs or assessment, in addition. For some, who were asked to take on several areas at once, the curriculum coordinator role could be extremely onerous. For example, a Year 6 teacher who was already responsible for PE throughout the school and for technology, had just been asked to take on maths as well, while gradually relinquishing technology to a new teacher. The PE responsibility involved considerable lunchtime and after-school work. He was also responsible for a range of other things including the school mini-bus, the house system, and timetabling and did not relish taking on a major area such as maths in addition. This type of situation was not uncommon amongst the teachers in our sample.

In general, the title of curriculum coordinator implied very different levels of responsibility in different schools. These ranged from simply making a particular teacher responsible for the ordering, storage, and allocation of resource materials for his/her curricular area, to, at the other end of the spectrum, making a teacher a specialist in a particular curricular area with time spent supporting other teachers in their classrooms, usually teaching alongside them. The former was relatively common, the latter far less so. Between these two ends of the spectrum, a wide range of practices existed. We have summarized these as follows:

(i)   resource gatekeeper
(ii) planning and resource facilitator
(iii) subject consultant
(iv) 'critical friend' — working alongside other teachers in the classroom

The least involved end of the spectrum was the *resource gatekeeper*. This typically involved being in charge of resources and waiting to be approached for help. Approximately 30 per cent of the teachers we interviewed worked in this relatively limited way as curriculum coordinators. Such a role was described by one technology coordinator in a large suburban junior school who said:

> Basically I look after the wood and the hacksaws . . . At the moment I just keep things like sandpaper, wood, hacksaws and so on centrally in my classroom in a big stock cupboard. That tops up individual things which teachers have in their classroom. They all have basic things in their rooms but if they need anything extra then they come to me and chat to me about what they can use.

About 20 per cent of the teachers had a higher level of involvement as curriculum coordinators where the coordinators typically had a role both in making an input into the planning stage for their subject area with colleagues and in playing a more active role in disseminating ideas from courses and suggesting resources. We have called them '*planning and resource facilitators*'. As a maths and IT coordinator in an urban primary school described it:

> I have overall responsibility for seeing that maths equipment is there. I go on courses and feed back, provide ideas for people. I have responsibility for schemes of work and policy documents in maths and IT. Generally you are there as a resource so people come to you. I try to see that planning goes on. I introduced a maths scheme last year and had a workshop evening for parents.

The third type of approach where the curriculum coordinator acted as a '*subject consultant*' but did not actually go into the classroom was used by a further 30 per cent of our sample. They worked very similarly to the teachers who were 'planning and resource facilitators' but a more active role in meeting regularly with groups of teachers to discuss their ongoing teaching as well as their planning. A maths coordinator in an outer suburb of a south-west city had regularly 'had meetings with each year group to discuss their worries, their maths problems, their resources'. She added:

> So I've had four meetings with each of the four year groups which took approximately $2\frac{1}{2}$ hours for each one. That was out of school in twilight time.

A science coordinator in a South Wales school saw herself as:

> . . . making sure that the policies are in order and everyone is working to the same end. Having regular meetings with the year groups and in a way being a consultant, but not because I have particular skills but because I'm the one who is concentrating on that particular subject.

Only 20 per cent of teachers went beyond this level of involvement as curriculum coordinators. In their schools, curriculum coordinators were both resource and planning facilitators, and subject consultants, but in addition they spent some time working alongside colleagues in their own classrooms, acting as a kind of '*critical friend*' (Woods, 1993) who was a catalyst in aiding colleagues to see things from a different viewpoint or to try things in a different way.

For example, in an inner city junior school, the science coordinator, a Year 6 teacher, who was also PE/games coordinator led an INSET day with staff to develop a science policy document, attended science courses and ordered resources after consultation with the other teachers. Not only had she helped colleagues with planning their science teaching, but also she had worked alongside colleagues in their classrooms and had taken their classes with them present to show the approach she had picked up from her INSET courses.

During the whole of the previous term, she had spent most of her non-contact time working alongside Don, a Year 3 teacher, in the classroom. As the following example suggests, her approach varied according to the colleague with whom she was working, but it avoided any pushing of unwanted expertise onto a colleague.

> Initially, I would prefer them to come to me for help because it's better that they come to me rather than I go to them, because they then feel ownership of it. So Don approached me because he felt that he was pushing humanities more than science and he didn't feel he had the expertise there. So we looked at his topic and I brought in a range of resources and showed him which activities I felt would fill the gap and which approach to take. I familiarized him with all these things first before I actually came into the classroom so that he was aware. I tried to get him to participate in it so that it wasn't just me directing it. He was actually doing it with the children so he felt he was the one leading it.

With another teacher she felt it more appropriate to adopt a different approach:

> At the other extreme, I went to Andrea's class because she felt that not enough science was being done. When she had her non-contact time I relieved her and I took the class. On other occasions I asked her to stay in so we'd discuss what was going to happen and she'd raise any concerns that she had. It's no good forcing them otherwise they won't take it on board.

The above example gives some indication of the sensitivity, adaptability and professionalism required of any teacher who works in this way with colleagues. As Wallace (1991) observes, there is a potential tension embedded in the relationship between the role of the curriculum consultant and the degree of autonomy expected by the class teacher and it is therefore not surprising that some curriculum consultants prefer to avoid potential conflict by waiting for staff to seek advice. Above all, the example above indicates the key role played by non-contact time in enabling schools to make the fullest use of their curriculum coordinators. In all the schools we visited where the curriculum coordinators acted as 'critical friends', support from the head in creating non-contact time was a key factor. In fact, heads played a central role in encouraging and supporting interest shown by members of staff and creating an atmosphere in which development could take place.

Some exceptions to the typology described above came with subjects such as music and drama where often the role of the curriculum coordinator came much closer to that of a subject specialist, not so much working alongside other teachers, but taking over some of the music and drama activities for the school as a whole. Thus, a Year 6 teacher in a suburban junior school took the whole of the upper school for music, ran recorder groups and organized upper school concerts.

Another Year 5 teacher who was drama, dance and arts coordinator prepared the whole school policy and planning in that area and more or less organized the performing arts throughout the school, running a drama workshop with sixty children every week as well as a lunch-time (poetry) group. She saw this as an indirect way, through the children, of disseminating new ideas in this area back in their own classrooms and regarded direct work with colleagues as somewhat more problematic. Her main approach to colleagues was through the children and through joint discussions over books for the library. She was aware that her curriculum area was seen as less central than some of the core and foundation National Curriculum subjects and expressed her diffidence as follows:

> If you try to do too much, people start to get submerged. They are submerged really, so you know, with this art competition (school-wide) I was really pushing my luck. You have to work all the time knowing that staff have too much to do and any enthusiastic ideas might be met with stony silence. Adults aren't as enthusiastic as children; you have to be so careful.

Schools tended to use coordination for cross-curricular themes, such as assessment, special needs or equal opportunities, in a rather different way. Typically, such roles might include planning a school policy on the topic in question including contributing to the relevant section of the school development plan, organizing study groups, arranging school-based INSET and liaising with other schools. In some schools, coordinators were appointed for a set time period, such as two terms or a year, to look specifically at how assessment, for example, might be incorporated into teachers' work right through the school.

In all the schools we visited where curriculum coordinators had moved on from simply being resource gatekeepers to a more active involvement in the life of the school, several key factors seemed to be present. The first of these was the existence of at least some non-contact time. The second was support whether from the head, or a deputy or someone else who recognized a potential for more active involvement and took action to facilitate it. In other words, the presence of supportive leadership was essential. In their study of whole school development, Jennifer Nias and colleagues identified a range of factors as important in facilitating successful whole school curriculum development including shared institutional values, organizational structures which facilitated collaborative work, resources of time, commitment, people and materials, and leadership commitment (Nias, Southworth and Campbell, 1992). It would appear that all of these had a part to play where curriculum coordinators were working effectively at all levels of involvement.

A Move Towards Subject Specialism?

In their 1992 discussion paper Alexander, Rose and Woodhead suggested the need to develop subject specialism still further beyond the curriculum coordinator model. They recommended the introduction of specialist and semi-specialist teaching, particularly at the upper end of Key Stage 2 to 'strengthen the existing roles of the class teacher and consultant' (para. 140). They referred to the 'unreasonable and unrealistic' nature of the expectations faced particularly by Key Stage 2 teachers that they should possess the breadth and depth of knowledge needed to teach all the subjects within the National Curriculum successfully (Alexander, Rose and Woodhead, 1992, para. 140). Later, in 1992, the HMI carried out a follow-up survey in a sample of primary schools where they found that over 80 per cent of teachers were generalists who spent virtually all of their teaching time with their own classes (OFSTED, 1993).

Our own data largely confirm this picture. When we asked teachers where they would place themselves along the spectrum of the four teaching roles suggested by Alexander, Rose and Woodhead (1992): the **generalist** who teaches most or all of the curriculum; the **generalist/consultant** who combines a generalist role in part of the curriculum with cross-school coordination, advice and support in one or more subjects; the **semi-specialist** who teaches his/her subject but who also has a generalist or consultancy role; the **specialist** who teaches his/her subject full-time, teachers described themselves as follows:

- generalist   52.5 per cent
- generalist/consultant   40.4 per cent
- semi-specialist   7.1 per cent
- specialist   0.0 per cent

The majority of teachers had a strong identification with their role as class teachers. In the interview they frequently spoke about 'my class' and 'my children', regarding the rewards of primary school teaching as deriving from a close relationship with a particular group of children (Nias, 1989).

A ready recognition of the tension between the generalist and the specialist teacher was shared by both teachers and heads in the sample. A Year 5 teacher in a large, urban junior school said:

> I'd like to have taken away from me the things I don't enjoy doing, the things I don't have any skills in. I'd like things like music, technology and RE taken away from me; things I'm not particularly skilled at or feel I have any expertise in.

Nevertheless, the same teacher said that he would not want to move towards the specialist model of teaching. He argued:

> I certainly wouldn't like to be a specialist who teaches one subject all the time. Being a primary school teacher, I came in to be a generalist. Although I do feel that the way the curriculum is going for the older children, perhaps there is a place for the semi-specialist. When we get to Years 5 and 6, perhaps there is a role for more specialist teaching.

We asked the teachers to rank in order of importance for their work currently, various qualities which might be important for a Year 5 or Year 6 teacher. As Figure 4.1 demonstrates, it was striking that by far the most important quality named by most teachers was 'good relationships with pupils' followed by 'good classroom management skills' while 'specialist subject knowledge' came at the bottom of most teachers' list of priorities.

Figure 4.1: How teachers ranked the qualities of a Year 5 or Year 6 teacher

Good relationships with pupils
Classroom management skills
Understanding of how children develop
Being a good all-rounder
Ability to work closely with colleagues
Skills in assessment
Specialist subject knowledge

Most important

Least important

These findings emphasize the feeling expressed by many heads and teachers in our sample that subject specialism runs contrary to, as one headteacher put it, 'the whole ethos, the whole way primary schools are organized and run.'

Nevertheless, within our sample of teachers, we found that the concept of specialism met with more acceptance in some subjects than in others. In many schools we found some element of shared teaching, usually within year groups, in music and PE/games. Thirty-six per cent of teachers shared games and 21 per cent shared music teaching. In music, particularly, many teachers readily

accepted that the required degree of specialist knowledge and expertise might be beyond their capability. There was no threat to teacher professionalism in admitting this. In other subjects, notably science and technology, teachers expressed anxiety about their level of knowledge. It is particularly in these subject areas that most teachers held ambivalent attitudes towards specialism. On the one hand they were apprehensive about their lack of specialist knowledge, but on the other hand they were uncertain about how this acknowledged deficiency might best be supplemented. We return to this issue in the concluding part of this chapter after a more general summary.

Summary and Conclusions

Although new developments in collaboration and in whole school planning represented a major change in the culture of primary schools, they were on the whole welcomed by heads and teachers in the study. However, despite their willingness to work collaboratively towards implementing the National Curriculum, heads and teachers in all the schools shared a common concern about curriculum overload and about their ability to cover the National Curriculum at Key Stage 2 in the breadth and depth required.

Most teachers reported that there had been a vast increase in their working day in terms of planning, preparation, and assessment. The sheer workload involved in teacher assessment and record-keeping was experienced as overwhelming by many teachers. In spite of these concerns, many teachers welcomed in principle the framework and guidelines provided by the National Curriculum.

One of the most significant changes in teachers' work was an increase in collaboration with colleagues. This mainly took the form of planning initially with colleagues, sharing the distribution of resource materials, and working with others on a consultancy/advisory basis as curriculum coordinators. These elements of the coordinator's role might be described as 'the soft part of the role' (Holly and Southworth, 1989). Relatively few worked alongside colleagues in the classroom even in their role as curriculum coordinators, and a very small minority did some specialist teaching with the children from the classes of colleagues in the same or adjacent year groups.

Most heads and teachers felt very strongly about the importance of the generalist role of the primary teacher and the possibilities it allowed for teaching the 'whole child'. Few teachers would be prepared to give up their classroom-teacher role in favour of becoming subject specialists. Nevertheless many teachers in their role as curriculum coordinators would have liked to develop a little further towards semi-specialism by having some time to teach alongside colleagues in the classroom. Many also felt that the pressures to cover the National Curriculum in the breadth and depth required might mean that some limited degree of subject specialism was necessary, even if the National Curriculum were to be slimmed down.

Of course, it should not automatically be assumed that further development in collaboration are all good and that classroom autonomy is all bad. Isolation and solitude can be important as a strategy for getting work done because it 'protects time and energy required to meet immediate instructional demands' (Flinders, 1988, p. 25 quoted in Fullan, 1991, p. 136). We have referred to the dangers of 'contrived collegiality' (Hargreaves, 1992) replacing a more relaxed informal collaboration. Nevertheless, much research points to the importance of successful teacher collaboration if educational and professional development is to be achieved (for example Fullan, 1991; Nias *et al.*, 1989, 1992). Moreover, it is clear that there may be a particular need for further collaboration and sharing of expertise in some subject areas. Many of the teachers in our sample expressed a lack of confidence in their ability to teach some of the foundation subjects to the depth required and were ready to accept that the required degree of specialist expertise might be beyond their capability. A similar lack of confidence and feeling of insufficient knowledge in many of the foundation subjects, especially technology, was evident amongst the primary teachers studied by Bennett, Wragg, Carré and Carter (1992).

It is possible that recent proposals for the slimming down of the National Curriculum (Dearing, 1994) may reduce the pressures felt by many schools for some specialism or semi-specialism in Years 5 and 6. But, equally, if schools are to avoid the dangers of teaching narrowly to the test and therefore focusing entirely on the basics, they will wish to continue to consider how a broad and balanced curriculum can continue to be delivered at Key Stage 2, while avoiding the excessive overload reported by the teachers in our sample. One way forward would be to encourage greater flexibility in staff roles as suggested by Alexander *et al.* (1992) and to develop further the semi-specialist and curriculum coordinator roles, particularly in Years 5 and 6. Much could also be done through further support and encouragement of the informal arrangements for shared and team teaching which we have described above.

It is clear from our findings that more non-contact time is essential for any further development of collaborative activity. There is a need for such non-contact time to release curriculum coordinators, who are themselves classroom teachers, to work alongside colleagues in their classrooms, as well as for time for coordinators to develop the other aspects of their role. One way to achieve time out of the classroom for teachers would be for attention to be given to the adoption of curriculum-led or activity-led staffing models rather than models based on pupil–teacher ratios. The possibilities for such models are discussed by Simpson (1988) and in a report on *The Staffing of Schools* (NASUWT, 1991). More generally, it is clearly the case that urgent attention needs to be given by policy makers to staffing levels in schools so that teachers can be provided with the non-contact time necessary to do their job well. It should also be recognized that such non-contact time will not always be used for collaborative work with other teachers. Indeed, teachers also need solitary planning and preparation time and time to work with small groups.

A second potential obstacle we identified to developing the role of curriculum coordinators was an understandable reluctance on the part of curriculum coordinators to suggest entering the classroom of a colleague, where they felt that this might threaten another teacher's classroom autonomy. Most curriculum coordinators recognized that a very sensitive approach was needed to work with colleagues in this way. Our findings and those of other research (Burgess, Southworth and Webb, 1993) suggest the need for further inservice training which focuses on the role and on relationships with colleagues and on effective ways of working together inside as well as outside the classroom.

Our findings also suggested that headteachers and deputies had a key role to play in creating the structures and environment which would enable teachers to work together effectively. This implies a need for further inservice training for headteachers and senior staff to enable them to facilitate teacher collaboration and to support curriculum coordinators.

In conclusion, our research suggests that teachers and heads have invested an enormous amount of energy, time and effort in implementing the reforms at Key Stage 2. In spite of the continuous changes imposed upon them over the last few years, their professional commitment remains strong. Indeed, many have been successful in taking active control of the changes and mediating them to professionally acceptable ends. This is particularly apparent in the unprecedented levels of cooperation and collaboration which have emerged within and between schools.

Acknowledgment

The research on which this chapter was based was funded by the NASUWT whose support is gratefully acknowledged.

Note

1   These categories were not mutually exclusive. Many teachers mentioned more than one way in which they worked collaboratively.

References

ACKER, S. (1995) 'Carry on caring: The work of women teachers', *British Journal of Sociology of Education*, **16** (1), pp. 21–36.

ALEXANDER, R., ROSE, J. and WOODHEAD, C. (1992) *Curriculum Organisation and Classroom Practice in Primary Schools: A discussion paper*, London, DES.

APPLE, M. (1986) *Teachers and Texts: A Political Economy of Class and Gender Relations in Education*, London, Routledge and Kegan Paul.

BENNETT, S.N., WRAGG, E.C., CARRÉ, C.G. and CARTER, D.S.G. (1992) 'A longitudinal study of primary teachers' perceived competence, in, and concerns about, National Curriculum implementation', *Research Papers in Education*, **7** (1), pp. 53–78.

BURGESS, H., SOUTHWORTH, G. and WEBB, R. (1993) 'Whole school planning.' Paper given at BERA Task Group on the National Curriculum at Key Stage 2.

CAMPBELL, J. (1992) 'The National Curriculum: A dream at conception, a nightmare at delivery.' Keynote lecture at Annual Conference of the British Association for the Advancement of Science, Southampton University.

DEARING, R. (1994) *The National Curriculum and its Assessment*, London, SCAA.

DENSMORE, K. (1987) 'Professionalism, proletarianization and teachers' work', in POPKEWITZ, T.S. (ed.) *Critical Studies in Teacher Education*, London, Falmer Press.

FLINDERS, D.J. (1988) 'Teachers' isolation and the new reform', *Journal of Curriculum and Supervision*, **4** (1), pp. 17–29.

FULLAN, M. (1991) *The New Meaning of Educational Change* (2nd edn), London, Cassell.

HARGREAVES, A. (1992) 'Contrived collegiality: The micropolitics of teacher collaboration', in BLASE, J. (ed.) *The Politics of Life in School Power, Conflict and Co-operation*, London, Sage.

HARGREAVES, A. (1994) 'The balkanization of teaching', in *Changing Teachers, Changing Times*, London, Cassell.

HOLLY, P. and SOUTHWORTH, G. (1989) *The Developing, School*, London, Falmer Press.

HOYLE, E. (1992) 'An education profession for tomorrow.' Paper given to annual conference of British Educational Management and Administration Society, University of Bristol.

NASUWT (1991) 'The Staffing of Schools.' Report presented to the Annual Conference, Bournemouth.

NIAS, J. (1989) *Primary Teachers Talking*, London, Routledge and Kegan Paul.

NIAS, J., SOUTHWORTH, G. and YEOMANS, R. (1989) *Staff Relationships in the Primary School: A Study of Organisational Cultures*, London, Cassell.

NIAS, J., SOUTHWORTH, G. and CAMPBELL, P. (1992) *Whole School Curriculum Development in the Primary School*, London, Falmer Press.

OFSTED (1993) *Curriculum Organisation and Classroom Practice in Primary Schools: A Follow-up Report*, London, DFE.

OSBORN, M. and BLACK, E. (1994) 'Developing the National Curriculum at Key Stage 2: The Changing Nature of Teachers' Work', Rednal, NASUWT.

OSBORN, M. and BROADFOOT, P. with ABBOT, D., CROLL, P. and POLLARD, A. (1992) 'The impact of current changes in English primary schools on teacher professionalism', *Teachers College Record*, **94** (1), pp. 138–51.

POLLARD, A., BROADFOOT, P., CROLL, P., OSBORN, M. and ABBOT, D. (1994) *Changing English Primary Schools: The Impact of the Education Reform Act at Key Stage One*, London, Cassell.

SIMPSON, E. (1988) *Review of Curriculum-led Staffing*, Windsor, NFER.

WALLACE, M. (1991) 'Flexible planning: A key to the management of multiple innovation', *Educational Management and Administration*, **19** (3), pp. 180–92.

WEBB, R. (1993) 'Eating the elephant bit by bit: The National Curriculum at Key Stage 2.' Final report of research commissioned by the Association of Teachers and Lecturers, University of Manchester.

WOODS, P. (1993) 'Self-determination in the National Curriculum.' Paper presented to the annual conference of BERA at Liverpool University.

5 Profiles of Productive Schools: Processes of Organizational Self-Renewal

Uwe Hameyer

ABSTRACT Productive primary schools in four countries are the focus of this contribution. It draws upon a comparative cross-country analysis of curriculum renewal which was published in 1995. The study is called IMPACT which is the acronym for '*Imp*lementing *Act*ivity-Based Learning in Elementary Science Teaching'. IMPACT was carried out in The Netherlands, Sweden, United States and Germany.

We investigated lasting processes of curriculum renewal in the realm of activity-based learning in primary science teaching of 9- and 10-year-old children. The methods we used are based on qualitative data analysis and the comparison of fifteen indepth case studies. We mapped out what productive schools have in common, for instance sufficient capacity to establish good climates and conditions for putting activity-based curriculum ideas into practice.

This contribution focuses on the methodology of IMPACT, the conceptual model called PROMISE (Process Model of Institutionalization and Self-Renewal), selected preliminary findings, and a checklist guide for school improvement based on basic conditions necessary to facilitate lasting curriculum renewal.

The Angler's Talent

Educational researchers share working styles with detectives or anglers when they unravel secrets in the deep darkness. Success often requires years of exploration. According to the viability of their terrain, they need to invent adequate designs and methods, 'sign posts' and valid theories about where to enter the unknown; some of them may wait for results over a long time while others find the unexpected quite soon.

Educational researchers may be compared to an angler or a fisherman. These cultural artists are highly talented to find what they are searching for without seeing 'it' directly. They are persistent masters of patience and intuition until they reveal the secret. The angler and the researcher have to be confident that their place of activity is well chosen to open darkness. They know that success requires sound information about the terrain to be explored. They need appropriate equipment, methods, and convincing ideas for paths of enquiry.

The talent of the angler is characterized by experiential professionalism in formulating *guiding questions*, be it a hypothesis or an assumption, be it a theory or a complex problem to be clarified. I am not sure if we in our research group behaved in the professional way an angler does. Anyway, we prepared the exploration of our terrain carefully so that systematic knowledge about 'secret spots' could be achieved.

The field of our research is the *school as a unit of analysis*. We wanted to study productive primary schools. How did they start school-based change and how did they support innovative efforts over a longer period? In view of this aim we were sure that *time on task* would be crucial, i.e., sufficient time for extended field studies. Similar to the task of an angler, we had to search for the best places where such schools exist, and we had to develop methods good enough for reconstructing the process of self-renewal.

At the Outset of Discovery

As we do not possess an angler's intuitive talent to use 'local wisdom' about a terrain of discovery, we developed a systematic strategy to unravel the secrets of successful innovations. Searching properties common to productive schools became our main concern. A productive school is conceived of a place where school improvement has been successfully sustained. In particular, we investigated questions such as the following:

- How did primary schools initiate, develop and sustain instructional improvement efforts?
- To what extent do the efforts have an impact on the quality of educational opportunities?
- By which specific activities and decisions were activity-based learning patterns embedded into science teaching practices?
- What does a productive school do to facilitate the adaptation and enculturation of new educational practices?

Our project is called IMPACT which is the acronym for 'Implementing Activity-Based Learning in Elementary Science Teaching'. The findings and cases will be available in 1995 (Hameyer, Akker, Anderson and Ekholm, 1995; Ekholm and Hameyer, 1995). The methods we used are based on qualitative data analysis and cross-case comparison. IMPACT focuses on practices in fifteen primary schools out of four countries each of which is represented by a researcher in the core group (Jan van den Akker, Ronald Anderson, Mats Ekholm, Uwe Hameyer):

- Sweden
- United States
- The Netherlands
- Germany

Inside Productive Primary Schools

The schools we selected are called productive as they show — each of them in its own unique way — to what extent learning can be enriched by an intact culture of educational creativity within the schools which are designed as open learning communities. The development of new ideas to raise instructional quality is expected to be a major task of any reflective practitioner (cp. Schon, 1983).

The term 'productive' alludes to more than intellectual curiosity, creative thoughts, or arguing for an exciting initiative in one's own school. We conceive of a *school as a productive organization* if it succeeds in putting a shared innovative idea into lasting practice. Productive means working effectively to implement *and* institutionalize the idea or 'concrete vision', to reinvent *and* protect something new against traditional routine, to develop implementation requirements *and* to try it out repeatedly, to give chance to 'fuzzy' ideas *and* to support their elaboration, to learn how to master the new *and* to cooperate with others so that experiences can be exchanged in time and mutually supported.

Design of IMPACT

As we focus substantially on qualitative research methods, the type of knowledge we look at is mainly rooted in reconstructed 'biographies' of lasting self-renewal as it occurs within primary schools. Our final report (Hameyer, Akker, Anderson and Ekholm, 1995) specifies how innovations such as activity-based learning are anchored in the culture of a school.

Basic Idea: Enculturation

Shymansky and Kyle (1991) claim that — particularly in science studies — educational research should stress much more vigorously the following research question:

> How are reform initiatives enculturated into the process of schooling? What are the impediments to reform, as well as the constraints upon the implementation of a reformed curriculum? What constitutes reasonable measures of successful curriculum reform? (Shymansky and Kyle, 1991, p. 17)

The process of 'enculturation' or institutionalization, i.e., building the new into the school setting, occurred in all our IMPACT cases stepwise. Our study is about the nature of school-based enculturation and activities to institutionalize new educational practices. Our major concern is to study indepth how these schools created a motivating learning environment and a cooperative culture of mutual development. We were not so much concerned in looking at doubtful short-term success rather than portraying shared innovative practice profiles which lasted over time.

> In the seventies and early eighties, innovators often expected short-term impact from putting a plan into practice. The institutionalization perspective as applied in IMPACT broadens our view of timespans in education necessary for sustained improvement. We know that almost no project is able to succeed effectively in implementation within less than a year. Three or more years seem to be the minimum time requirement for innovative efforts to grow in the field (see Hameyer, 1978). In IMPACT we found that lasting changes demand 5 to 6 years until a minimum level of routine has been reached.

It looks as if we are dealing with a *long-distance running exercise* in education. This metaphor gives a tentative idea of what institutionalized enculturation is about, namely to reach and share a long-term aim successfully. A more precise definition is given by Ekholm and Trier (1987) who conceive institutionalization as a process that appears during and after implementation of a new product, process or capacity in an organization. Implementation involves the refinement of a policy idea or program according to feedback from practice (van Velzen, Miles, Ekholm, Hameyer and Robin, 1985), whereas institutionalization requires stabilized use and enduring efforts to anchor the change in the field. An innovation which is conceived as institutionalized can be defined as follows:

- though it may have taken some negotiation, it is now agreed upon, seen as fully legitimate, valued by the key people involved;
- it is working in a routine, stable way;
- it is a natural, normal part of life, expected without doubt to continue; it may even be 'invisible', taken for granted;
- allocations of time, material and personal resources are made for it. (Miles, Ekholm and Vandenberghe, 1987, p. 244)

These supports are stable. They do not depend on specific persons for continuance any longer. The visibility of the new even diminishes and loses its provocative flavour; it is no longer a matter of controversy. 'It is simply there' (Ekholm and Trier, 1987, p. 17).

We developed a *reconstructive model of analysis* because, particularly in the domain of instructional research and school improvement, investigators still prefer the what-is-missing issue instead of asking why specific new ways of mastering educational demands grow and gain power. Learning from such new ways is, according to our understanding, considered as helpful as the analysis of problems at stake. Reconstructing the conditions under which sustained improvement occurred is the specific perspective we apply.

Focus: Activity-based Learning

To gain insights into the culture of each school (Sarason, 1971), we focused our analysis on science teaching. As activity-based learning methods are proved as a key to increase educational quality, we chose this method, studied its anatomy and its embedding curriculum, we observed classroom work and outdoor activities.

Activity-based learning is associated with inquiry and self-guided exploration. The student investigates nature or other domains of reality, stimulated by her or his own ideas or assumptions, and by efforts to learn from using systematic enquiry methods. Activity-based learning is considered a pattern of learning consisting of the following components:

A

- The pupils develop their own ideas for enquiries, experiments or constructive work.
- They search for explorative methods to clarify and illuminate the questions which they consider meaningful.

B

- Students investigate meaningful questions or problems on the basis of their own ideas.
- They explore their ideas and apply different methods.

C

- Students analyze, discuss and evaluate what they have found or constructed; they display their results in the classroom or at other places.

D

- Students express their understanding of what they have learnt. They exchange findings or constructive results, and they draw conclusions where possible or appropriate.

This framework encompasses various hands-on activities and learning equipment like books, different materials, direct exploration of nature, and uses information resources within and outside the school. Patterns of activity-based learning which are embedding these methods and materials are expected to:

Figure 5.1: *Model of institutionalization overlapping stages of the process*

Implementing
Activity-Based Learning
in Elementary
Science Education

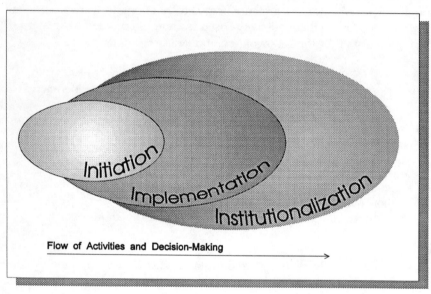

- provide opportunities for students to interact with materials in a multi-sensory way, i.e., observing, constructing, experimenting with equipment, reading, listening carefully, interacting with other students, visualizing and other activities are equivalent;
- relate to educationally meaningful basic issues of science and technology which allow for building on the students' ideas and perception of phenomena;
- facilitate the student's capacity to learn by doing an experiment or other activity;

Figure 5.2: *Promise: Process model of institutionalizing school-based self-renewal*

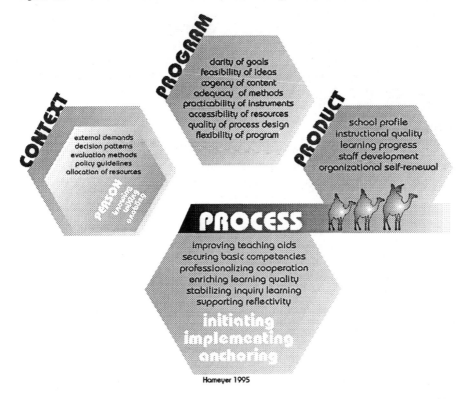

Hameyer 1995

- allow for involvement of students in planning, carrying out an experiment or other activity, and growing self-direction of their learning;
- give room for various hands-on activities (e.g., experimenting with simple equipment, on-site investigation, learning games, field visits, other).

Framework: The PROMISE Model

Figure 5.2 shows that school improvement requires more than ideas. Activity-based learning practices also depend on various conditions inside and outside a classroom. According to improvement research, we learned that any demanding educational approach or method, such as activity-based learning, is complex. Profiles of successful improvement grow over a longer timespan. Overlapping stages such as initiation, implementation and institutionalization occur in all successful cases we studied.

The IMPACT cases were selected according to the criterion whether they covered the final stage at least to some extent. The Process Model of

Institutionalization and Self-Renewal specifies the three I's by five components which serve our data retrieval:

Debut/initiative

Why did the pedagogical pattern of Activity-Based Learning in Science (ABLS) enter the school, and how did it happen?

Explorative try-out

How did the staff, the principal, students, parents, and the administrative authorities become acquainted with the new? What were the first conclusions that they came to? What decision-making criteria emerged from the exploration?

Implementation

Who contributed to ABLS implementation, and in what way? What did the process of implementation look like? What sort of external support helped during implementation efforts conceived as a process of reconstructing current practice?

Beginning routine

What led to activity-based teaching and learning being repeatedly practised in general studies lessons? What were the signs that a routine was gradually being established? Who supported and stabilized the new routine? What made this development easier and what sort of difficulties had to be overcome?

Institutionalization

Why has activity-based teaching become an integral part of normal practice? What indicates this? What were the most important events after the beginning routine?

Profile: Case-study Format

A framework for data collection and case-study description was developed so that systematic comparison across the cases is possible. The framework called *case-study description format* looks as follows:

Case-study description format

A THE CASE STUDY
    Selection of the School
    Study Plan

Methods: Focused Interview Guide

In order to avoid the risk to be confounded by the proudness of schools when they emphasize the good rather than the problems at stake, we developed semi-structured instruments to serve for objectivity. Thus, our cases have a common analytical basis. All are embedded in a *multi-method multi-site approach*. From this we expected a valid understanding of conditions under which innovative efforts are more likely to occur and to survive.

Indicators of Self-Renewal

I will now look at selected results from IMPACT in terms of indicators. They represent clusters of activities carried out in the IMPACT schools. They are grouped into four areas:

Uwe Hameyer

- **Program**
- **Person**
- **Context**
- **Process**

'Program' refers to the aims of the innovation within the school. The 'process' aspect indicates the way the program was implemented and sustained. Was the timetable rearranged and were learning materials jointly developed? What did the decision-making processes look like amongst the staff? Were new encouragement and coordination systems developed? The 'context' is the school and its environment, in which such processes occur — the institutional site of events. Finally, the category 'person' refers to people who 'did it' or who had responsibilities, including their expectations, wishes, attitudes, hesitations and abilities.

Program

Strengthening the child

All IMPACT schools facilitate independent learning in various ways. Teachers provide a bundle of opportunities for students to plan some of their own learning. Appropriate facilities and methods help the children to achieve this aim.

Instruction is much less based on the school book than ten years ago, the classroom environment more attractive, and methods are substantially child-centred. All kinds of hands-on materials are stored in classrooms; many of them are completely restructured.

Experiments and various sorts of explorations are carried out in the class-room. Students are given time and space for explorative studies. They learn by using various information resources and hands-on information materials such as topic card systems and others. Project work is often used.

Increasing the quality of teaching

Independent learning is not necessarily linked to project work or other methods such as weekly plan teaching ('Wochenplan'). We almost always discovered variations of a multi-method sandwich: discovery learning, group work, debates and plenary discussions, more direct teaching methods and individual instruction all build the daily practice profile in the classroom.

Weekly plans are increasingly handled in a routine way. The teachers in successful schools developed many practical ideas to teach in different ways. They intensify cooperation with parents inviting them as experts in schools. They produce all sorts of materials, vary teaching methods professionally, and they foster experimentation in the classroom.

Reorganizing classrooms

What influences those who alter their teaching? We did not look for individual motives. But so much is certain: many want their teaching job to be more fascinating. 'Omväxling' is the key word to note from the Swedish studies — doing work in a different way; changing prevailing roles and routines. It is an important motive for change. There is another motive: the changed learning conditions in schools and a person's environment. In restructured classroom environments children enjoy learning more. A restructured pattern of class-room organization contributes to the well-being of children at school and alleviates direct experiential learning. A teacher from Bremen said that she easily became 'exhausted' but that she could spend the whole day in the changed learning environment where various different activities were on offer.

In the history of progressive education Parkhurst, Dewey and Kilpatrick, Petersen, Gaudig, Lay and Freinet have all stressed the importance of the learning environment for effective meaningful learning outcomes. They stressed the feeling at ease as basic for productive teaching and learning. Much earlier Pestalozzi coined the image of the cosiness of a school living room. Work-shops, school gardens, kitchens, and ateliers — nowadays some people call this a 'learning studio' — played a decisive role for the working school edu-cationalists at the beginning of the twentieth century. Freinet attached a special value to the school printing set.

Person

Acting authentically

The motives of innovative teachers are interesting — hardly concern for their careers, but mostly an intrinsic incentive to undertake new things, occasion-ally, however, spurred on by the principal or by colleagues. Those involved actively look for ways of improving their own teaching, even if the adjustment requires time and brings disappointments with it. The seriousness of purpose is unquestionable.

There is also something else which characterizes their authenticity: the concurrence among knowledge, ability, and the desire to get things done. The development of one's own practice takes place with the increase of personal ability, the desire to progress and the confidence that the goal and the path are the right ones (high degree of consistency).

An interesting second point is pastoral care. Good and bad schools clearly differ in their treatment of pupils and in their perception of common respon-sibility. Wherever a collective loss of responsibility and loss of control are to be found, teachers have clearly already given up pastoral care (cf. Fend, 1987, p. 69).

Uwe Hameyer

Increasing reflectiveness

Teachers from the IMPACT schools are used to being self-critical and to accepting the criticism of others (cf. Sirotnik, 1983). They learn from mistakes and do not feel hurt if others point out the critical aspects of their own behaviour. Schön (1991) attributes three characteristics to 'reflective practitioners':

- they actively educate themselves further
- they recognize where innovations could be started
- mistakes act as correctives in their learning process

The *reflective practitioner* admits that s/he does not know enough and is willing to continue learning and is ready to adapt to new situations. A teacher from one of our schools in Bremen wishes to give her teaching a more individual note and states that there is much to be done in this area. Teachers admit to one another what problems have not been solved yet. Problems are not glossed over, but stated, and serious attempts are made to solve them instead of waiting for initiatives from outside.

Proactive organization of schools

In the German case studies the headteachers are proactive forces in schools; in the American schools this has been reported for some of the schools studied. The principals look for ways of improving things, support teacher initiative wherever possible, contribute to the success of ventures in both a practical and advisory capacity, and create a climate which favours innovation, which encourages involvement and which wards off negative sanctions. The headteachers create protected spheres of action. What can be observed in Nienburg also holds for Kiel schools: the principals consider how schools can be developed further and how the staff could be involved more. The principal is generally at the forefront of things, and almost always regulates them.

The principals promote a school climate which is well disposed to innovation and stand up to those who think differently. I have not found a principal who acted as a damper anywhere in our study of four countries; principals played rather the role of recognized advisors, who offer support but also warn against overloading oneself with bundles of innovations. Such principals argue for divisibility of the new, stepwise procedures, and clearness of the major goals for all staff members. This is how the situation appeared in the Nienburg case study:

> The principal is a rugged example to be followed. He puts emphasis on teaching examples which must be convincing. Feedback which meets his expectations encourages him to continue. The innovatory teaching example must, however, always fulfil the criterion of practicability, if it is to survive in school. Nobody would adapt it in advance,

certainly not somebody who is still not convinced or is by disposition a doubting Thomas. This model behaviour leads to a vortex effect. (cf. Nienburg Case Study)

Looking for new solutions

The schools we examined establish scope for self-renewal, protect it from external attack and develop a spirit of initiative. Teachers pluck up the courage to explore new ground without having to fear negative sanctions if something does not succeed immediately. The expedition is protected by supportive advice on the part of the headteacher. Serious attacks from staff or from outside are few and far between as attempts are made to involve the entire staff in the discussion without putting members of staff under pressure to become involved. The headteacher from Bremen expresses this as follows:

> Hurrying on ahead is never any good. If new approaches are adopted we must avoid making colleagues feel attacked or making them fear extra work. Every innovation requires time. It must be introduced stepwise, primarily because practitioners with years of experience tend to avoid questioning the methods they have used so far. In education we are dealing with stubborn people.

He continued that the implementation of modern mathematics years ago turned out to have negative effects because this reform was imposed on people who suffered from problems which were unnecessary because of its power-coercive approach.

Explorative behaviour is supported by the principals. They are considered tolerant of variety and expect creative solutions from teachers, even if this causes a certain amount of disruption to the administrative structure of the school. Unusual ideas are encouraged provided that they have a stimulating potential for practical work. There is no veto because, perhaps, some conventions are not rigidly adhered to. Support depends on the educational appeal of the new: will it enrich school life and improve teaching?

Network thinking

The principals are characterized by a high degree of prognostic simulation of the results of innovations and possible side-effects. They are concerned with a prognostic weighing up of the pros and cons so as to be able to have an impression of what generally awaits the school and what can be done along the way. This network thinking can also be applied to our four components: seeing the components together is clearly marked in these schools. The introduction of the weekly plan was not only thought through where aims were concerned but was made to concur with the peculiarities of the school concerned. At the same time it was considered what weekly plans would look like

77

in practice so as to be able to estimate what degree of educational turbulence was likely to occur.

Network thinking requires an informed caution where detailed planning is concerned. In both of the Bremen schools the introduction of a weekly teaching plan was accompanied by a partial reorganization of the timetable, flexible cover plans, parallel lessons, mutual observation of lessons and observation groups. In Hamburg special value was attached to the meshing of (a) concrete construction (cf. the annexed learning workshop); (b) the development of motivating learning environments; and (c) the formation of a choice of lessons. The Kiel principal placed much emphasis on the cautious introduction of project lessons; didactic creativity, the search for materials, the development of learning aids, information for parents and so on were carefully carried out.

Context

The context is the school and its environment. I limit my considerations to schools and those characteristics which had a positive effect on the implementation of independence in general studies lessons.

Independence

Innovative schools reward having the courage of one's convictions for professional reasons, i.e., doing something even if the state does not specifically demand or allow it. Legalistic behaviour has no place in 'good' schools. Laws, requirements and curricula are interpreted foremostly according to the criteria of educational quality.

This is also true for control mechanisms. Processes of innovation are mostly guided from within and responsibility is generally assumed for them by the school concerned (see also Corbett, Dawson and Firestone, 1984; Goodlad, 1987). The headteachers and staff are really the inventors or doers. The division between educational planning and administrative control is partly suspended. As schools are responsible for the educational work which goes on within them they lay claim to more control than was once the case, mostly, however, without any recognition.

Innovations which are predominantly implemented from above by senior teachers or state authority are generally critically regarded. Innovations which are produced in schools and which can also be controlled by staff have a considerably greater chance of survival.

School climate

In 'good' schools cooperation is developed to an above average degree (Fend, Gute and Schlechte, 1987; Bessoth, 1985). Teachers observe one another's lessons, coordinate the development of learning materials, arrange classrooms according to joint plans (all Bremen weekly plan classes are arranged in a similar way).

An open interactive structure is common to all schools. This makes it easier to plan lessons differently without having to carry out long debates to justify an innovation. This is supported by an activating school climate, stable forms of cooperation, open and inventive headteachers and a basically reflective approach by staff.

This point is also dealt with in the organization research about successful innovations. In their analysis of addictive organizations Schaef and Fassel (1988, p. 8) state that the following characteristics have a negative influence on work: fear, isolation, dishonesty, suppressed feelings, lack of respect for others, confusion, forgetfulness. Good organizations encourage responsiveness and responsibility for oneself, the concurrence of formal and informal goals and thinking as part of a process.

In his reanalyses, Fend found an excellent characteristic which marked the quality of 'good' schools. In 'bad' schools an above average number of teachers went straight back home after lessons (41 per cent of the good schools and 74 per cent of the bad schools) (1987, p. 65). Mutual visits to lessons took place considerably more often in good schools than in schools where there was less cooperativeness.

Continuity

A low turnover of staff is advantageous up to a point, even if routine then easily gets the upper hand. In Bremen there has been no fluctuation for over ten years. Continuity enables one to hold out: from all of the reports of success which are known to me there is hardly a case in which there was not at least one person who acted as a 'stakeholder', and who made sure that the good points of the innovation were explained to those who were sitting on the fence or who doubted. These 'stakeholders' ensure continuous clarity of purpose and attempt to make the practicability of the innovation clear to all — not just for those who are already convinced anyway.

Serious problems generally occur when key people who get the process of innovation going change schools. These are generally the most able people. This difficulty is also lamented in specialist literature (Timmermans, 1987). This is the moment when it becomes clear whether the innovation can carry on by itself.

Process

The process dimension is the key to understanding school level changes. It alludes to the biography of a self-renewing school and how it works when changes are implemented. I will describe a few selected process indicators and enumerate some more afterwards; the IMPACT book (Hameyer, Akker, Anderson and Ekholm, 1995) gives more details and advice for practitioners.

Uwe Hameyer

Starting from what is familiar

Interventions in social systems assume knowledge of roles in action, conventions and the locus of power control within the system. Innovations such as activity-based learning approaches must be attuned to the culture of the school. What we have found, too, is that productive schools not only protect expeditions into undiscovered terrain, but support also what is tried out on a tentative level before more widespread familiarization in the school is started. According to the Bremen cases, the 'explorers' of new educational practices need respected practitioners as comrades-in-arms: practical educational knowledge and educational imagination — vision-building — are equally necessary. The teachers of the elementary schools that we have examined so far were never outsiders but recognized as good teaching personnel.

Establishing goal clarity

Clarity of aim is one of the most important requirements for constant collaboration of those involved. This criterion was not replaced by comprehensive catalogues of aims or treatment of a different kind; goal clarity was produced again and again by guaranteeing that practical experiments were easy to understand, e.g., within the framework of observation, through reports, the exchange of experience and feedback, and last but not least by the use of materials which provide information about what is really intended by a new way to learn. Opening the classroom allows others who are curious or interested to experience: parents and other children, together with colleagues from next door, can peek over the fence.

Allowing for experimental freedom. IMPACT schools allow for a substantial amount of experimental freedom. They go for variation insofar as they recognize noteworthy impact of the new on educational quality. The important criterion is the potential value of such efforts for the enrichment of school life and the increase of the quality of learning. Principals have made sure that those who were not yet convinced would not be pressured.

In all cases, time for exploration was given so that it was possible to become involved with new ideas, to investigate them thoroughly without the pressure of immediate commitment to the new. Everybody was guaranteed the freedom to withdraw. During the introductory phase the work was carried out by teachers within the schools. The principal as initiator and helper plays a structural role in this process.

Retaining step-by-step progress

Changes in schools do not represent a linear process but require social learning opportunities, e.g., explaining what comes with the new (impact analysis); being able to reflect on one's own practice; discussing what should be retained; not expecting too much from others; getting acquainted with the innovation by learning about earlier attempts of the school to innovate — Fullan speaks of the innovation biography of a school (1991) —; 'getting to grips with it' and trying it out for oneself without having to commit oneself immediately.

Ensuring continued feedback

Principals kept an eye on the lasting receptiveness of the staff to new ideas, and they ensured that good opportunities were given to clarify the current state and to encourage everyone to give and receive feedback. Encouraging feedback is just as important as early criticism. In Bremen, for example, lessons were opened: schools, parents and the general public were often able to convince themselves at first hand of the effects of activity-based teaching on the behaviour of students. The children's fun thus became much more evident, and parents could react to what they had seen. External advice was often solicited, workshops for key innovation tasks were organized, experiences regularly shared with others or all staff, elite circles avoided.

Enhancing cooperation

In IMPACT schools, staff members felt good because they did not have to fight their own corner. There were always at least two or three people who 'sighted new land' together. Principals are always ready to support by advice and help those involved.

In the following boxes some of the above and additional process indicators of self-renewal will be enumerated. Some of them reflect what we know from innovation research.

Interim Lesson[1]

Integrated Curriculum

Common to all cases is the integrated curriculum pattern embodied in the activity-based approach. Three types of integration may be discerned. The most modest is to integrate subjects such as biology, physics, chemistry in 'science education' or 'enquiring nature' (Terebint, De Noor, Pine, Shadow Crest, Jeffco, St. Vrain). In these cases the biology component is usually the most prominent. The second type of integration is to integrate natural and social studies: 'Sachunterricht' in Germany, 'umvärldorientering' in Sweden, 'wereldoriëntatie' in The Netherlands, see Molenwijk, Norrbacka, Bremen-Arsten, Kiel, Bremen-Vahr, Nienburg, Hamburg-Wegenkamp. The third and mostly used type of integration is compared to a general approach of activity-based learning that permeates almost all instructional processes and curricular content in the school (Furulund, Ostansjö, Kiel and Hamburg-Wegenkamp).

Monitoring and clarifying progress

—> Ensuring the students' gain

—> Reconceptualizing 'losses'

—> Documenting exemplary work

—> Posters which the students printed

—> Opening innovative work to externals

   (other students/neighbouring school/parents/

   politicians/)

—> Checking the soundness of clarity before the next

   steps are taken

Stabilizing by infrastructural support

—> Adapting time schedules

—> Putting the new topic on various agendas

—> Using study days for the new

—> Creating principal's commitment

—> Allocating time for consultation/talk/advice

—> Utilizing 'pool hours' for the new

—> Establishing local criteria for teacher recruitment

—> Anchoring the new in the culture of the school

—> Giving assistance by principal (Vertretungsstunden)

—> Creating stimulating school climate

Advocating the new

—> Inviting parents to participate in classroom work

—> Informing the public (newspaper/handouts/ brochures/letters to parents)

—> Sharing experiences with authorities

—> Hiring the best experienced »piloters«

—> Instrumentalizing the snowball effect

—> Writing posters, reports; giving practical advice

—> Showing up at exhibitions/public events

—> Linking to regional centres

Preventing pioneers from proceeding alone

—> At least 2 to 3 people involved

—> Preparing cooperatively through all stages

—> Encouraging each other in case of doubt/conflict

—> Sharing/enjoying success

—> Discussing what is good for sharing with others

—> At least one highly experienced and accepted companion

—> Exercising co-teaching

—> Mutual hospitation and class visits

Securing experimental freedom

—> Redesigning the learning environment

—> Diversifying teaching styles

—> Saving money and time for non-classic tasks

—> Reallocating responsibility to teachers

—> Encouraging risk-taking efforts

—> Enforcing vision-building techniques

Project-oriented Learning

Another common feature in our cases is the large amount of integrating topics and project-oriented activities. These activities are often spread over a longer period, sometimes even months. The original planning for such activities is usually made by the teacher, but there is wide variation in the degree of students' influence on the coverage of the topics, the use of resources, and the character of the discovery and enquiry activities.

Process Skills

In most cases a lot of emphasis is put on process skills for exploration, on 'learning to learn', and on attitudinal goals as curiosity, exactness, and perseverance. That doesn't mean that the content goals are unimportant, but they are probably less in the forefront as in more traditional approaches.

As may be expected from the different kinds of integration offered, the varying scope of content is broad across all cases. We do not present an exhaustive list of all topics, but we can illustrate the variety by selecting some themes of the lessons for the 9 to 10 year old children whom we observed:

> studying heartbeat
> constructing towers
> observing trees around the school

making sounds
analysing the dog's behaviour
exploring the human body
measuring temperature
working with electricity
discovering environmental pollution
experimenting with water
reading the newspaper
working on traffic issues
protecting nature
exploring nature in the city
investigating pace
starting with earth science
protecting the life of whales
investigating rocks and minerals
analysing properties of snow
studying the soil

Various Materials and Resources

Variety is the keyword for describing the materials used in activity-based learning. In contrast with traditional teaching, the *textbook* has lost its prevalent role. Only in two of our cases — Shadow Crest and St. Vrain — textbooks are used as an instructional tool. However, also in those schools the textbooks are not the single source of information and action; they are combined with other instructional materials, kits, and media.

The most frequently used teaching and learning aids are various types of instructional materials, often a combination of teacher guides with worksheets for the students. These materials are developed as much externally as internally. Also common is a documentation centre, a media zone or a recreational area in the classroom which makes background information accessible, which invites for extra-curricular activities, and where many learning resources, games or books are exposed for further reading.

Long-distance Running

Looking at all the cases, we learn that lasting impact can virtually never be ascertained within one or two years. Social organizations such as a school are much too complex and culturally framed to give room for instantaneous renewal. Educational meaningfulness, multiple try-outs and steady support are required which, in turn, presuppose sufficient time for the practitioner to taste the new menu, to make up his mind about its composition and ingredients, to serve in an appealing way, and to remove what he dislikes (Hameyer, Akker, van der Anderson and Ekholm, 1989).

Any school renewal touches upon established patterns of classroom work. It is not so much an addition than a stimulus to reconsider current routine, to unfreeze old components where necessary, and to enrich one's own educational work. Repeated exchange of experience and mutual learning are required to encourage this process which progresses in a spiral rather than going straight from the start to the finish.

A spiral may be time consuming but is more likely to be successful because it gives room for careful feedback and reflection, adjustment and reinvention of the new in close contact with the local environment. Otherwise one would easily miss the chance to explore the daily challenges which consume much of the practitioner's time budget and energy input. A spiral way of renewal involves long distances. This metaphor has been elaborated by Ekholm (in Miles, Ekholm and Vandenberghe, 1987) to clarify pre-conditions for lasting change efforts. Ekholm (1987) argues as follows:

(a) Continued preparation is necessary for 'long-distance runners' such as school innovators to master their task. It does not help very much to be trained only for short-term implementation. Huberman and Miles (1984) show that two, often more years, are necessary to get through well institutionalized patterns of daily practice.
(b) A long-distance runner should neither start too fast nor avoid others who stay at the same speed. It is more bearable to run in company.
(c) A long-distance runner will have severe difficulties continuing if he pauses on his way. Good pacing and a steadily adjusted match between his capacity and the conditions under way are necessary.
(d) A long-distance runner must be tough, aim-oriented, and clear about his speed. If he loses sight of what others do, he might waste too much energy.
(e) An effective long-distance runner will benefit from looking for others at the same speed. This makes his work easier. He will not feel alone nor be too far ahead. Even if he does not see his aim directly, he should be convinced of getting closer to it even if he occasionally becomes weak.

Note

1 Some of the names used here and elsewhere in this section are pseudonyms.

References

AKKER, J. VAN DEN (1988) 'The teacher as learner in curriculum implementation', *Journal of Curriculum Studies*, **20** (1), pp. 47–55.

BERG, R., HAMEYER, U. and STOKKING, K. (1989) *Dissemination Re-considered. The Demands of Implementation*, OECD publication, Leuven (Acco).

BESSOTH, R. (1985) 'Kennzeichen effektiver Schulen', in BESSOTH, R. (hrsg) *Schulleiter-Handbuch. Band 4*. Ergänzung Februar.

BREDDERMAN, T. (1983) 'Effects of activity-based elementary science on student outcomes: A quantitative synthesis', *Review of Educational Research*, **53** (4), pp. 499–518.

CORBETT, H.D., DAWSON, J.A. and FIRESTONE, W.A. (1984) *School Context and School Change*, New York, Teachers College Press.

EKHOLM, M. and TRIER, U.P. (1987) 'The concept of institutionalization: Some remarks', in MILES, M.B., EKHOLM, M. and VANDENBERGHE, R. (eds) *Lasting School Improvement: Exploring the Process of Institutionalization*, Leuven, OECD Publication, Acco, pp. 13–21.

FEND, H. (1987) 'Die einzeline Schule alis padagogische Handlungseinheit', in STEFFENS, U. and BARGEL, T. *Qualität von Schule, Heft 1 der Beiträge aus dem Arbeitskreis*, Qualität von Schule, Wiesbaden, Hessisches Institut fur Bildungsplanung und Schulentwicklung, pp. 55–79.

FREINET, C. (1965) *Die Moderne Französische Schule*, Paderborn, Schöningh.

FREY, K. (1982) *Die Projektmethode*, Weinheim, Beltz.

FULLAN, M. (1985) 'Change processes and strategies at the school level', in *The Elementary School Journal*, **85** (3), pp. 391–421.

FULLAN, M. (1991) *The New Meaning of Educational Change*, Toronto, OISE Press.

GAUDIG, H. (1963) *Die Schule der Selbsttätigkeit. Herausgegeben von L. Müller*, Heilbrunn, Klinkhardt.

GOODLAD, J.I. (ed.) (1987) *The Ecology of School Renewal*, Eighty-sixth Yearbook of the Society for the Study of Education, Part I. Chicago, IL, University of Chicago Press.

GOODLAD, J.I. (1984) *A Place Called School*, New York, McGraw-Hill.

HAENISCH, H. (1987) 'Was ist eine "gute" Schule? Empirische Forschungsergebnisse und Anregungen für die Schulpraxis', in STEFFENS, U. and BARGEL, T. (hrsg) *Qualität von Schule. Heft 1 der Beiträge aus dem Arbeitskreis* 'Qualität von Schule', Wiesbaden (HIBS), pp. 41–54.

HAMEYER, U. (1978) *Innovationsprozesse*, Weinheim, Beltz.

HAMEYER, U. (1978) *Vier Gesichtspunkte zur Förderung von Innovationsprozessen im Bildungssektor*, Kiel, IPN.

HAMEYER, U., AKKER, J. VAN DEN, ANDERSON, R. and EKHOLM, M. (1989) *Implementing activity-based learning in elementary science education. A plan for a comparative study in four OECD countries*, IMPACT booklet, Kiel, Institute for Science Education.

HAMEYER, U., AKKER, J. VAN DEN, ANDERSON, R. and EKHOLM, M. (1995) *Portraits of Productive Schools: An International Study of Institutionalizing Activity-based Practices in Elementary Science*, New York, SUNY Press.

HAMEYER, U., AKKER, J. VAN DEN, ANDERSON, R. and EKHOLM, M. (eds) (1996) Implementation of activity-based learning in elementary schools (IMPACT) — 15 case studies in four countries (Germany, Sweden, The Netherlands, USA). Kiel — Karlstad 1996 (Institute for Science Education — University of Göteborg/Karlstad).

HAMEYER, U., LAUTERBACH, R. and WIECHMANN, J. (eds) (1992) *Innovationsprozesse in der Grundschule. Fallstudien, Analysen und Vorschläge zum Sachunterricht*, Bad Heilbrunn, Klinkhardt.

HUBERMAN, M. and MILES, M.B. (1984) *Innovation Up Close*, New York, Plenum.

KYLE, W.C. JR. and SHYMANSKY, J.A. (1988) 'What research says ... about teachers as researchers', *Science and Children*, **26** (3), pp. 29–31.

MILES, M.B., EKHOLM, M. and VANDENBERGHE, R. (1987) *Lasting School Improvement. Exploring the Process of Institutionalization*, Leuven, Acco.

MILES, M.B., VELZEN, W. VAN, EKHOLM, M., HAMEYER, U. and ROBIN, D. (1985) *Making School Improvement Work. A Conceptual Guide to Practice*, OECD publication, Leuven, Acco.

MORTIMER, P., SAMMONS, P., STOLL, L., LEWIS, D. and ECOB, R. (1988) *School Matters. The Junior Years*, Somerset, Open Books.

NIENBURG CASE STUDY (unpublished document) *An IMPACT Case About Activity-based Learning*, Kiel.

PETERSEN, P. (1927) *Der Kleine Jena-Plan*, Weinheim, Beltz.

PURKEY, S.C. and SMITH, N.S. (1983) 'Effective schools: A review', *Elementary School Journal*, **83**, pp. 426–52.

ROLFF, H.-G. and ZIMMERMANN, P. (1985) *Kindheit im Wandel*, Weinheim, Beltz.

SARASON, S.B. (1971) *The Culture of the School and the Problem of Change*, Boston, Allyn and Bacon.

SCHAEF, A.W. and FASSEL, D. (1988) *The Addictive Organization*, San Francisco, Harper and Row.

SCHÖN, D. (1983) *Educating the Reflective Practitioner*, New York, Jossey-Bass.

SHYMANSKI, S., KYLE, W.C. and ALPORT, J.M. (1983) 'The effects of new science curricula on student performance', *Journal of Research on Science Teaching*, **20**, pp. 387–404.

SHYMANSKY, S. and KYLE, W.C. (1991) *Establishing a Research Agenda: The Critical Issues of Science Curriculum Reform*, Washington, National Science Foundation.

SIROTNIK, K. (1983) 'What you see is what you get — consistency, persistency and mediocrity in classrooms', *Harvard Educational Review*, **53**, pp. 16–31.

TIMMERMANS, R. (1987) 'Institutionalization of the MAVO-project — A Durch case study', in MILES, M.B., EKHOLM, M. and VANDENBERGHE, R. (eds) *Lasting School Improvement: Exploring the Process of Institutionalization*, OECD publication, Leuven, Acco, pp. 125–142.

VAN DEN BERG, R., HAMEYER, U. and STOKKING, K. (1989) *Dissemination Reconsidered. Demands from Implementation*, Leuven, Acco.

VAN VELZEN, W.G., MILES, M.B., EKHOLM, M., HAMEYER, U. and ROBIN, D. (1985) *Making School Improvement Work. A Conceptual Guide to Practice*, Leuven, Acco.

WALBERG, H.J. (1988) *Productive Teaching and Instruction: Assessing the Knowledge Base*, Chicago, University of Illinois, Chicago.

6   Cross-cultural Perspectives on Eating: A Hidden Curriculum for Food

Marlene Morrison

Introduction

> The diets of U.K. school children are too high in fat, especially saturated fat, and in sugar. They are too low in iron, calcium, dietary fibre, and probably in anti-oxidant vitamins such as vitamin E. Obesity is becoming more prevalent, and where it occurs, should be tackled as early in childhood as possible . . . a poor diet clearly creates short-term health problems in relation to growth, and long-term health problems in relation to anaemia, low bone mass, hypertension, coronary heart disease and some cancers. Poorer children may be more vulnerable. A very poor diet is likely to affect children's activity levels and academic performance. (Nelson, 1994, p. 19)

Alongside increased nutritional and social concerns about the quality of British schoolchildren's diets there has developed a commensurate belief in the ability of education to affect changes in *both* attitudes and behaviour towards more 'healthy' eating linked to individuals' lifestyles. Such a belief, it has been argued, has often been both ill-founded (Rodmell and Watts, 1986) and, where beneficial, likely to impact most upon the well-being of those least threatened by the association between health and lifestyles (Blaxter, 1990). For the last decade, health educators have devoted a good deal of energy in the search for 'objective' strategies to determine how best to impart health messages through food-focused education. For school pupils, most of that attention has focused upon the formal curriculum, namely the formal corpus of school knowledge that is imparted through legislation and texts and then filtered and acted upon by teachers. Where the knowledge content of the curriculum is itself a selection of the stock of knowledge retained within the culture of a society, such 'objectivity' is, of course, more apparent than real. Yet, in its most recent manifestation, food-focused education has been ranked the number one priority for all age groups — but, in particular, for those of school age — by the Nutrition Task Force (Department of Health, 1994) established in the wake of *The Health of The Nation* White Paper (Department of Health, 1992).

Since 1988, links between food use and the role of schooling have been heavily reliant both upon the formal curriculum *and* a political ideology

of individualism to underpin strategies 'encouraging individual responsibility, awareness, and informed decision-making' (NCC, 1990, p. 7). 'Self-
empowerment' is the mechanism advocated for enabling individual pupils to
make healthy food choices and, it is argued, such advocacy needs to begin as
early as possible in the primary school. From such perspectives, the child is
encouraged to develop the potential to act rationally upon his/her health. This
is based upon the food-focused education received as knowledge,
understandings, and skills made available through the formal curriculum. Yet
we know that the curriculum comprises much more than its formal components and includes not only the perspectives that primary school teachers
bring to their curriculum work but also the many day-to-day interactions of the
hidden curriculum that tacitly teach the norms and values of schooling. The
focus of this chapter is upon eating arrangements in primary schools that are
investigated as aspects of 'all the other things that are learned during schooling
in addition to the official curriculum' (Meighan, 1986, p. 66). (This recognizes
that there are important messages in the formal curriculum which are also
hidden but, for the purposes of this chapter, are beyond my major concerns.)

As an area of interest for sociologists of education, eating in school has
received little attention. Yet food, and what we do to it and with it, lies at the
core of our sociality (Van der Berghe, 1984). Schools are important settings for
studying food consumption in a variety of forms, including its institutional
arrangements. For young primary school entrants, eating provides initial en-
counters with food beyond the home and in the presence of outsiders. Daily
eating rituals are continuing, if occasionally poignant and tearful reminders
of irrevocable shifts in the locus of their lives. Such experiences straddle an
intriguing halfway position between 'eating in' and 'eating out' (Mennell, Murcott
and van Otterloo, 1992). On the one hand they stand in contrast to the public
commercialized world of fast food outlets and restaurants, and on the other
hand diverge from, or substitute for, familial and domestic routines. If sharing
food signifies togetherness and inclusion (Douglas, 1975; Goody, 1982), by
implication similarities and differences in eating patterns within and between
schools also involve exclusion. Eating is thus linked to issues of social access,
control, divisions, and power. In this sense, schools are micro-political arenas
in which government policies and cultural practices are filtered, negotiated,
and mediated as school practice (Ball, 1987). Moreover, at the micro-level, the
construction of links between eating at home and at school both distort and
mirror the relations between parents and the state which are thought to underpin any educational system (David, 1992). This chapter explores the sociality
of eating and its impact upon educational experience in order to shed further
light on changing perceptions about what constitutes a curriculum for food
and eating. An important dimension to this discussion of the hidden curriculum is the proposition that the individual consciousness of pupils (and teachers) will be shaped by the kinds of interpersonal relations that occur within
schools. Schools create specific contexts for formal and informal learning about
food use. It will be argued that eating arrangements pose both sensitive and

powerful images in children's and teachers' constructions of reality and provide complementary and contradictory messages about food use.

Though institutionally based, the evidence presented in this chapter will be seen also in terms of the wider structures, in particular home–school relations, to which the curriculum is linked. The analysis is cross-cultural and includes case studies of eating in two primary schools, one in England (for children aged five to eleven years) and one in Japan (known as an elementary school, for children aged six to twelve years). Here, the potential pitfalls of 'massive cultural difference' attendant upon comparative analysis (Howarth, 1991) are balanced alongside opportunities to move beyond an ethnocentric focus of eating in school. Such interest is timely. A conflation of recent nutritional concerns about the quality of British schoolchildren's diets (National Forum for Coronary Heart Disease Prevention, 1994) and a decline in families taking meals together (Fischler, 1979; Herpin, 1988) find echoes in Japanese commentaries (Holdenson, Thomson, Bullis and Davis, 1988). Here, the decline of the extended family, growing numbers of 'Kagibbo' — literally latch-key kids — coupled with the large scale internationalization of cuisine and food choice have raised fears not only about the nutritional value of food eaten by Japanese schoolchildren (Monbusho, 1992) but also about the marginalization of Japanese food and eating patterns. In both countries it looks as if 'worries about "the decline of the family meal" are also signalling worries about "the decline of the family"' (Mennell *et al.*, 1992, p. 116), a familiar phrase in recent political debates about 'basic values' in the UK. (Such concerns have a Scandinavian equivalent: in a Swedish study, Ekström, 1991, found similar concerns about a loss of shared meals but little evidence to support it, or for trends towards solo eating.)

The National Context

In the UK there is a need to reassess emerging political, nutritional, and educational interests. Convergent and divergent trends in food use are visible in and beyond schools. Among important connections are those linked to terms like freedom, choice, efficiency and responsibility when applied to education in general and school meals' provision in particular. Murcott (1987) rehearses the arguments well. Freeing local education authorities (LEAs) from the 1944 Act to provide meals of a specified nutritional standard, legislation of the early 1980s reflected an underlying political philosophy that has gathered momentum. Adults are now urged to take responsibility for their own welfare and 'families ought to be accepting the responsibility to know what is and what is not a healthy, nutritious diet and eat accordingly, but at the same time be free to do so and make choices as they fancy' (Murcott, 1987, p. 247).

Making educational choices as parents 'fancy' has become the hallmark of educational policy since the Education Reform Act (1988) for England and Wales. Market forces and parental choice have come to define most aspects of the English educational system *albeit* within the framework of a curriculum which is centrally driven. Paradox, then, is a feature of educational links between food and eating as it is elsewhere. As legislation has defined the scope for food in the National Curriculum, as aspects of subject choice and cross-curriculum themes, children's eating practices have become increasingly divorced from official interpretations of what counts as schooling or as appropriate educational experience. Instead, school-based eating now reflects the 'responsible' and 'efficient' choices made by parents and governors, and, decreasingly, by LEAs. Within school, eating practices are largely controlled by 'non-educational' supervisors — dinner ladies — acting in lower statused (and increasingly insecure) positions as 'stand in' parents or teachers (see also Morrison and Burgess, 1993; Burgess and Morrison, 1993). All this seems a far cry from Mortimore's findings (1989) based on a major junior schools project (1988) that effective schools were those with

> . . . evidence of a positive climate [which] included: the organisation of lunch-time and after-school clubs for children; . . . [and] teachers eating their lunch at the same tables as children. (pp. 171–2)

Current emphasis upon parents' rights rather than collective duties to consume education eschews ambiguities about the role of parents in school, whether as voluntary or paid helpers, for example, in classrooms or in dining halls. Parents, it has been argued, frequently present 'a symbolic challenge' for teachers (Stierer, 1988, p. 189). Even in schools committed to 'community education', Burgess (1992) comments how the time parents spend with teachers in the classroom is thought 'to create inner conflict on one level and harmony on the other' (pp. 48–9). Evidence from recent research (Burgess and Morrison, 1995) suggests that employing parents as supervisors at lunchtime and as volunteer helpers in class-based cooking activities, for example, may signify as much about the low educational status of cooking and/or eating as it does about parental partnership in education and the availability and use of human resources in primary schools.

An International Context

In Japan, parents also consume education and do so voraciously. 'In the old days, Japanese parents might forego food so that their sons [*sic*] could attend school . . . now, as then, this concern for learning and dedication to knowledge have made education Japan's most important social priority' (Holdenson, Thomson, Bullis and Davis, 1988, p. 18). Elementary schools play a pivotal role, operating with mixed ability classes, an 'explicit mastery [*sic*] framework', and with a high proportion of 'time on task' (Rohlen, 1983). What Rohlen describes as the central paradox of Japanese education is an educational egalitarianism which co-exists with the rigorous application of individual assessment, the significance of which accelerates as a sorting mechanism through junior and senior high school. In a 'frankly' competitive system, the order of merit produced stratifies individuals to many grades of work in society whilst, at the same time, schooling serves to sustain collective notions of what it means to be Japanese, and what it means to contribute to the collective life of school.

In Japan, external parental influence outweighs internal influence, and has important economic links. Parents and teachers preserve distinct and separate roles for home and school. Competition for places in non-compulsory kindergartens, for example, is oversubscribed and expensive. So important are the age-graded transfers between schools that parents financially support an extensive range of 'juku', which offer remedial and enrichment opportunities after school. (Such trends are also discernible in an increasingly differentiated English school system, *albeit* in different historical and cultural contexts.) At its extreme (Tobin, 1992) the Japanese school system has been observed as 'a Godzilla like monster with Monbusho [the Ministry of Education] for a brain and pre-schools for a mouth, each spring swallowing alive cohorts of happy, spoiled kids, chewing them up, and then spitting out armies of robot-like businessmen, bureaucrats, housewives, and office ladies' (p. 21).

In considering the balance between home/school influences, the reality is one in which Japanese teachers and parents take implicit and explicit account of separate roles. Thus Tobin (1992) argues that Japanese (pre)schools do not seek a renunciation of individuality or self-hood as much as they offer children the chance to develop dimensions of self difficult to cultivate at home (p. 22). An interesting illustration of distinctions preserved between home and school is to be found in the use of space in Japanese schools. In contrast to many English primary schools which have sought to reduce visible and spatial distinctions between home and school, it is at the entrance — the 'genkan' — that school principals greet parents, children, and visitors. 'Custom and architecture facilitate separation' (Tobin, 1992, p. 33) and formalize the differences between family and school life. This is accentuated by the physical absence of parents who rarely accompany primary age children to or into school.

Eating and Welfare: Recent Constructions

In both Japan and in the UK, eating in school dates back to its welfare functions. Legislation for school meals has been a feature of post-war policy in both countries, introduced to the UK and Japan in 1944 and 1947 respectively. From early perspectives, then, eating in school was a question of practicality and diet, and meals programmes were introduced to regulate the minimum conditions under which children might be encouraged or expected to learn.

From the early 1980s, eating policies have taken divergent paths. In the Japanese system there is continuing recognition of the symbolic as well as nutritional significance of food not only as a means of ensuring children's physical survival and well-being, but also as a means of children expressing themselves socially and educationally. Thus:

> . . . the school lunch program is operated *as part of educational activities.* (Ministry of Education, Science and Culture, Government of Japan, 1989, p. 94, my emphasis)

By 1986 a national programme for school meals had been established, with costs borne by the state, by local authorities, and by parents. In 1992, 99 per cent of elementary school children received a school meal. In England and Wales, the 1980 Education Act abolished a national fixed price for the school meal, scrapped minimum nutritional standards, and removed the statutory duty upon LEAs to provide a hot school meal. In 1990, 44 per cent of school-aged children in England had school meals (Leather, 1994, p. 32).

Japanese programmes are aimed at 'contributing to the sound mental and physical development of children, as well as to an improvement in the eating habits of the Japanese' (Monbusho, 1992, p. 27). Japanese nutritionists have identified a number of concerns linked to 'rich' 'unbalanced' diets which lead to 'overweight' children. More importantly for our purpose are the links made between the nutritional and the social; in Japan, social concerns centre upon a decline in breakfasting, increases in solo eating, and an increasing popularity in occidental food and eating. The educational response has been to inject moral questions about whether children *ought* to share food with peers, *ought* to ignore Japanese food and *ought* to share food in specific settings. Such questions have been addressed in schools.

Paradoxically, in the UK an overriding emphasis on nutritional aspects has sidelined and fragmented the social and educational dimensions of school eating. By focusing on the neediest and the poorest it has been hard to argue against the importance of children having access to a 'free' school meal (Leather, 1994; Mortimore and Blackstone, 1982). Yet focusing on this aspect of eating alone it is, as Murcott (1987) points out, difficult enough to untangle 'the conundrum' of whether school meals contribute significantly to children's eating. However, the process of disconnecting the nutritional issue of eating from its educational significance, including links to teaching and learning about food, has made it peculiarly vulnerable to the vagaries of political philosophy. In 1995, LEAs in England and Wales are not only freed from most of their statutory responsibilities, but at the same time teachers are freed from the duty to make school eating part of their daily responsibilities, even though, of course, school managers continue to face the overall organizational issue (some might say headache) of containing large numbers of children in school over the lunch break, under the supervision of non-teachers.

In such ways children's eating is becoming essentially a private and parental matter, yet subject to discipline, containment, and control on educational premises. At the same time, the what, where and how children ought to eat is expected to be the subject of cross-curriculum guidance (NCC, 1990). Advocacy of this kind has placed 'moral entrepreneurs' in the paradoxical position of asking schools and teachers to take a moral lead on issues like food and nutrition which are 'simultaneously held to be properly none of their concern' (Dale, 1989, p. 86). In the following case studies, such issues are explored at the micro-level in two schools, to be called Fieldgate (in England) and Sakuda (in Japan). Pseudonyms are used throughout.

Sakuda Elementary School

Sakuda School is a co-educational school with two hundred and fifty-seven pupils, and is situated in one of the most densely populated urban areas of Japan. Not large by Japanese standards, it shares with other post-war elementary and high schools, standardized features like multi-storeys, wide passage ways, and basic classroom configurations which comprise rows of desks and chairs. These, in turn, contrast markedly with the science laboratory, equipped music, craft, and home economics areas, a large gymnasium and a swimming pool. The school's socio-economic catchment is one of high, regular employment, with head of household described by the headteacher as 'the salaried man' engaged mainly in administrative and commercial employment.

At Sakuda, lunchtime marks a boundary between most of the subject-based lessons of the morning and the extra-curricular activities of the afternoon like sport or cooking. As in the UK, morning activities include an interval for morning break. However, the highly visible in *loco parentis* model of the UK primary school teacher, stereotypically on patrol with cup of coffee in hand, has no Japanese equivalent. Children remain in classrooms if they wish, socialize in corridors, or go out to the playground. Where teachers remain in classrooms this is an overspill of class-based activities.

If lunchtime demarcates morning and afternoon activities, it is also part of the daily continuum of teacher–pupil relations. Eating and drinking is confined to the lunchbreak, which consists of a school meal provided as part of the region's school lunch programme, and is taken by all children as an assumed and routinized event in the school day. In lunchtime eating there are combined and rotating roles for children and class teachers, augmented by two ancillary staff whose function it is to prepare the food as it is delivered to the school, and whose visibility remains low. Unlike many activities carried out in the UK by non-teaching staff, for example, caretaking and cleaning, arrangements for food consumption are among the daily responsibilities of children and teaching staff at Sakuda School. Lunchtime eating occurs within classrooms where children have their main base. Except for a termly event when children share eating with those in other classes, Sakuda children eat alongside those with whom they engage in learning activities; this takes place at their desks which are re-arranged for communal eating purposes. Children assist in the delivery of food to the classroom, in preparation for serving, in apportioning food to classmates, and in clearing up. These roles are shared with the class teacher. Whilst retaining an overall supervisory role, the class teacher also eats with the children.

Eating arrangements were observed on my second visit to Sakuda. Here, as the fieldnotes record, I join a class of first graders a few minutes before lunch commences:

> This week's servers have already collected today's food, and tables have been re-arranged at the back of the class to form a serving counter. For the servers, uniforms of white coats and hats not only symbolise their responsibilities and roles but also attaches a significance to the links between preparations for eating and matters of hygiene. Teacher wears a similar outfit. Children take turns to receive food and drink from their classmates and return to their desks with their meals on trays.

> Except for the most disadvantaged children in the class, most parents will have paid a modest monthly sum for a set menu displayed weekly, and comprising a traditional Japanese style meal of cooked vegetables, a thick meat or fish soup, with bread or rice, a piece of fruit, and a bottle of milk. The only visible reminders of home or of individual preference are the embroidered traycloths which children bring to school and the chopstick bags from which they take their eating implements. There is a quiet hum of conversation as the children and I begin eating. Next to me Tomomi senses my insecurity about the order in which I am to eat. Amidst a few giggles, she slows down her pace of eating and through sympathetic eye contact and slow motion activity instructs me appropriately. Once assured of my new found dexterity she accelerates her own pace of eating.

In eating groups of six, food consumption is confirmed as an integral part of the school day and of teacher–child relations. The spatial constraints of the classroom make it imperative that this is a carefully orchestrated activity. At the end of the meal children take turns to clear away their companions' dishes and return them to the counter in preparation for removal. The latter is re-arranged in preparation for the afternoon's class and a brief period of social activity and movement along corridors and between classes takes place before the afternoon bell and a timetable which extends to 2.25 pm, after which some children remain for extra activities.

For children at Sakuda, the social mores of school eating will pertain for most of their school careers. Whilst differences emerge in some (but not all) high schools in terms of regional arrangements, specified dining areas and cafeteria systems, most Japanese schoolchildren will experience daily eating events which confirm occidental patterns of consumption as integrated educational features of the school day, and the only legitimate event to include eating. This is, of course, not to argue that food-focused education as distinct from eating-focused education does not take place in other school settings as curricular or extra-curricular activities. In both arenas, food and eating are confirmed as learning activities which are mediated by teachers. Parents provide ingredients for food-focused curriculum activities, but their main involvement will be via parent associations, through external interest and influence, and by opportunities to visit children in situ on periodic 'observation days'.

Fieldgate Primary School

Fieldgate School is a co-educational primary school with three hundred and fifty pupils on roll and is situated in a village on the outskirts of an English town. Its catchment draws widely from surrounding villages, and increasingly from the neighbouring town. With a declining 'rural' population, a growth in owner-occupied housing, and a nearby motorway network, Fieldgate parents are predominantly mobile parents who have elected to live in an area which they consider to be economically, socially, and educationally conducive to their families' well-being. Pressures upon school accommodation create continuing demands for teaching and learning space.

Fieldgate School is sited within a local education authority which, two years previously, had decided to end its school meals' provision in response to educational priorities deemed more pressing. The LEA meets its legal obligation to provide free school meals for the economically disadvantaged by providing packed lunches. These consist of: sandwiches/roll, biscuit, fruit and drink items delivered to school in distinctive brown paper bags. The demise of the school meals service has brought one major advantage to Fieldgate School, namely the conversion of its canteen into a large well-equipped classroom currently occupied by a Year 2 class. Changes in local policy have reinforced a view among some teachers of 'school dinners' as mixed administrative and educational 'blessings', a view reinforced by the removal of lunchtime duties from teachers' responsibilities since 1986. For teachers and parents interviewed, responsibilities for food and eating are part of a parent–school partnership, and yet also subject to compartmentalization; 'eating' is here seen as a parental responsibility, as distinct from teaching and learning about 'food' as a teaching responsibility. A vociferous minority among parents and teachers regret the passing of school meals provision mainly for 'other' families' children but also for families with working, professional parents who need to engage in multiple strategies for the timing and content of what they describe as the 'main meal' event in the evening.

At this school, lunchtime eating resembles a large indoor picnic which takes place in two sittings in the school hall. Children have the choice to go home for lunch, but 85 per cent of children remain at school, bringing an array of lunchboxes which are stacked each morning in classrooms. Each lunchtime, individualized eating takes an institutionalized form. This comprises mainly sandwiches, crisps, a chocolate biscuit and a drink, with fruit and yoghurts not uncommon. What is labelled 'a packed lunch' or 'school dinners' by parents and children is, in effect, a collection of snacks. When children open their lunchboxes they are, in effect, displaying some of the opportunities and constraints of familial consumption choices. In interviews, parents explain that their influence over food choice for the box is mediated not only through their children's preferences, but also what is affordable and practically stored in a lunchbox. It is also acknowledged that children's preferences are mediated through the peer group. Parents and lunchtime supervisors note peaks and dips in the popularity of certain items, with lunchtime supervisors more willing to acknowledge the influence of current advertising than parents. Changes in popularity of some items are underpinned by consistency in, for example, the provision of crisps, and parents' inclination (not always shared by children) to perceive the sandwich as an essential constituent of the packed lunch. What is most notable about individualized eating at Fieldgate is not its variety (there are isolated pockets of difference like raw vegetables and hot soups in flasks) but its standardized format. Care is taken not to make the free packed lunches distinct from those of their classmates. Eleven children deliver their lunchboxes to the school secretary who repackages the free school meals into the lunchboxes and places them in the classroom lunchbox stands during first break. Free school meals are dull and unimaginative. An unintended consequence is that even when a family's needs remain unchanged, few children take them consistently.

If lunchtime eating is the main eating event of the school day the first break constitutes an important supplementary eating encounter. At Fieldgate, children experience institutionalized snacking as part of the daily activity known as schooling. A few minutes before break children are allowed to take one item from their lunchboxes to eat in the playground. Crisps proliferate although some children have alternative choices; sandwiches 'must' remain a feature of lunchtime eating. Sweets are not permitted in school but both parents and teachers are ambivalent about what constitutes a sweet and what constitutes a chocolate snack. Generally parental choice is paramount, although parents are contacted if snacks predominate over more 'acceptable' 'healthy' foods like bread. Parents are also informed if children become persistent non-eaters; the deputy head readily acknowledges a 'sandwich graveyard' at one corner of the school site. Overall the provision of food as one aspect of home–school relations is recognized as a potentially sensitive issue with parental rights to choose prioritized except in very exceptional circumstances, as in the case where a parent only provided chocolate bars.

A recent commentator (Young, 1993) has argued that opportunities within education to learn about nutrition and health need to coordinate classroom-based learning about food and eating with the food and eating which children experience at school at break times and other eating events. At first sight, then, prospects for coordinating formal and informal teaching and learning about food at Fieldgate School do not look promising. Here, as elsewhere in increasingly differentiated kinds of schooling — as LEAs abrogate their responsibilities — parents are exercising rights to control what children eat in school (*albeit* subject to the usual familial and economic opportunities and constraints) whilst schools focus on the social context for eating and its implications for containment and control.

Freed from the ties of lunchtime supervision, the head and staff have used what resources they *do* have to maximize food-focused educational opportunities for children in the classroom. Most opportunities are interpreted in the National Curriculum context of subject-led teaching and learning where a judicious blend of expertise available in food is used to complement the science, technology, language, history, geography, and physical education curriculum. Fieldgate exploits its advantages; these include guidance from an enthusiastic Year 2 ex-home economics teacher, a local employer, and a pool of parents in the locality, including former primary teachers who enter the school as parent helpers to engage in food-focused activities like cooking, food handling, food festivals and educational trips. Moreover, in a locality where teachers and parents are often neighbours, parents' use of language and learning frameworks is not dissimilar to that espoused by teachers in classrooms and staffrooms. Their 'cultural capital' is applied to food use.

Whilst there is minimal influence on *what* is eaten at lunchtime, some opportunities are taken to maximize the social and educational impact of eating arrangements. This is promoted via close liaison between lunchtime supervisors (also local parents) and school managers. Children picnic at tables of eight. At the start of each academic year discussion takes place to decide upon an eating partner. Table groups are mixed across four classes; this is a deliberate attempt to foster interrelations between age groups and classes. Where children wish to change partners 'this has to be an exercise in democracy' (the head) and cleared by partners before changes are made. Whilst teachers accompany children to the dining hall, there are deliberate strategies to signify supervisors 'taking over'. The latter take a firm but friendly stance, clearing spillages, opening difficult packages, encouraging children to sample and finish all items in the box. Swapping is discouraged as it is thought to thwart parental choice, although there is a tension here between the positive social aspects of sharing and the more problematic features of swapping. There are many social and educational opportunities lost, not the least of which is the possibility for children to sample a variety of hot, nutritionally balanced foods as meals. As importantly, children are unable to share, apportion, or assess foods in different ways, nor do they experience the use of knives, forks, or plates. Teachers are absent from this eating experience. Children do not observe teachers sharing or eating food or vice versa.

What is the cumulative effect of children's daily eating upon their day-to-day consumption patterns? Most parents interviewed at Fieldgate School argue that the existence or non-existence of a hot school meal service is not reflected in their propensity to offer a hot meal in the evening, and children's diary returns illustrate the continuing importance of an evening meal. This may be partly a reflection of the school's prosperous catchment (for a contrast, see Morrison and Burgess, 1993). Of equal significance, however, are diary records and interviews that suggest important modifications to familial evening eating on school days. This is linked both to adult working arrangements and a variety of after-school pursuits by children. For children eating in 'shifts', or alone and/or with and without a knife-and-fork evening eating event, the practice of day-long institutionalized snacking reinforced by grazing at home, further inhibits opportunities for communal eating.

Summary and Conclusions

In both the UK and Japan, schools aim to be caring communities which look after the social and educational well-being of those who work and study within them. Previous research (Young, 1994; 1993) confirms health promotion as part of that well-being, often expressed in terms of food and nutrition. This is seen as 'a combination of health education within the curriculum and *all other actions a school takes to protect and improve the health of those within it*' (Young, 1994, p. 38, my emphasis). A key feature of such combinations is the connection between the formal and informal, the overt and hidden curriculum. The focus of this paper has been upon the formal and informal processes of school-based eating, though the influence of the food curriculum in the classroom is readily acknowledged (Burgess and Morrison, 1993) and is discussed elsewhere (Morrison, 1995). The curriculum includes relations between home and school, between parents, dinner ladies, children and teachers, as well as the exemplar role of the latter, each influenced and mediated through the institution and through wider local and national policies.

At Sakuda School the formal and informal curriculum for food and for eating are merged as part of a school day in which eating is a routinized aspect of daily educational experience. Where teacher–pupil interrelations are dominant, and the Monbusho a guiding force, parental influence upon eating is externalized. In contrast, what has been described at Fieldgate School is, in part, a reflection of the belief that adults and children given advice and information about healthy eating are 'rational actors who are able to choose and enact rational choices' (Leather, 1994, p. 30), and that those choices are possible through a separation rather than integration of food- and eating-focused education. Where schools have enacted whole school eating policies, previous research indicates that this does not necessarily affect children's overall consumption of different kinds of food (Young, 1993). Rather, that school provides an environment in which specific approaches to eating might be safeguarded, even formalized for limited timespans.

We continue to learn most about food through our daily experience of it; much of that experience is influenced by what is available inside as well as beyond school. In the UK, the governmental approach to children's eating is underpinned by an ideology that individual choice is in everyone's interest. Yet there is incompatibility between the freedom to choose and the what, when, and how to eat. It is also conceivable — but increasingly unlikely given the current fragmented and marginalized status of the food-focused curriculum

(Morrison, 1995) — that among children who acquire the understanding, knowledge, and skills to 'choose' at school will be those who continue to opt for food which others view as 'unhealthy'. Whilst the key variables of social class, age, and gender provide a baseline for explanations of the social and cultural bases for the distribution of food choice, differential accessibility to food choice and food knowledge is also inexorably linked to relations of power and control, and to notions of inclusion and exclusion. This exploration of the significance of eating in school has used a case-study approach which, in the English context, explores a school caught in a pincer movement in which legislation has increasingly segregated formal 'knowledge' about food from the everyday experience of eating. At Sakuda School in Japan, partial cohesion is retained by enclosing eating within, rather than outside, its educational operations.

As long as we do not eat everything we could or should, school-based eating will continue to be a complex mix of choice and necessity as children receive and act upon a variety of daily messages from schooling. Information-only led messages about 'healthy food' which pay little attention to the social, educational, and economic contexts in which eating is operationalized, seem likely to continue to demoralize those children with least power to change their eating habits:

> If you keep telling people they ought to do something they cannot you sever that connection — a connection which is essential to moral discourse and a sense of self. (Leather, 1994, p. 37)

For children in the UK, as in Japan, that sense of self is subject to a complex and sometimes contradictory blend of curricular and familial interests. As we continue to examine curriculum issues and the changing role of home and school, school eating emerges as an essential rather than peripheral arena for assessing the social, symbolic and educational significance of food and eating, and for re-evaluating individualistic as well as collectivist interpretations of primary school curricula in the 1990s.

Acknowledgments

Part of this paper is based on research conducted on the project entitled 'Teaching and Learning about Food and Nutrition in Schools' (Grant no. X209 25 2006), directed by Professor Robert Burgess, and funded by the ESRC as part of the Nation's Diet programme, which is coordinated by Professor Anne Murcott. The paper also draws on research, funded by the Daiwa Anglo-Japanese Foundation, and conducted jointly by CEDAR and the Osaka Kyoiku University, on the effects of recent educational reforms in both countries. Whilst they remain anonymous, I gratefully acknowledge the contribution of headteachers, staff, voluntary helpers, parents and children at Fieldgate and Sakuda schools who made the work possible. Thanks also to Barbara Muldowney who typed the script.

References

BALL, S.J. (1987) *The Micro-Politics of the School*, London, Routledge.

BLAXTER, M. (1990) *Health and Lifestyles*, London, Routledge.

BURGESS, H. (1992), 'A time for community in the primary curriculum', in MORRISON, M. (ed.) *Managing Time For Education*, CEDAR Papers 3, Warwick, University of Warwick.

BURGESS, R.G. and MORRISON, M. (1993), 'Ethnographies of eating in an urban primary school'. Paper presented at the AGEV Conference on Eating Habits, 14 October, Potsdam, Germany.

BURGESS, R.G. and MORRISON, M. (1995) *Teaching and Learning about Food and Nutrition in Schools*, a Report to the ESRC as part of the Nation's Diet Programme: The Social Science of Food Choice.

DALE, R. (1989) *The State and Educational Policy*, Milton Keynes, Open University Press.

DAVID, M. (1992), 'Parents and the state: How has social research informed education reforms?' in ARNOT, M. and BARTON, L. (eds) *Voicing Concerns: Sociological Perspectives on Contemporary Education Reforms*, London, Triangle Books Ltd.

DEPARTMENT OF HEALTH (1992) *The Health of the Nation White Paper*, London, Department of Health.

DEPARTMENT OF HEALTH (1994) *Eating Well: An Action Plan from the Nutrition Task Force to Achieve the Health of the Nation Targets on Diet and Nutrition*, London, Department of Health.

DOUGLAS, M. (1975) *Implicit Meanings*, London, Routledge.

EKSTRÖM, M. (1991) 'Class and gender in the kitchen', in FÜRST, E.L., PRÄTTÄLÄ, R., EKSTRÖM, M., HOLM, L. and KJAERNES, U. (eds) *Palatable Worlds: Sociocultural Food Studies*, Oslo, Solum Forlag.

FISCHLER, C. (1979) 'Gastro-nomie et gastro-anomie: Sagesse due corps et crize bioculturelle de l'alimentation moderne', *Communications*, **31**, pp. 189–210.

GOODY, J. (1982) *Cooking, Cuisine and Class: A Study in Comparative Sociology*, Cambridge, Cambridge University Press.

HERPIN, N. (1988) 'Panier et budget: l'alimentation des ouvriers urbains', *Review francaise de sociologie*, **25**, pp. 503–21.

HOLDENSON, W., THOMSON, E., BULLIS, L. and DAVIS, S. (1988) *Exploring Japan: An Anthology of Photo Essays*, Canon Chronicle, Tokyo, Canon Inc.

HOWARTH, M. (1991) *Britain's Educational Reforms: A Comparison with Japan*, London, Nissan Institute/Routledge, Japanese Studies Series.

LEATHER, S. (1994) 'What changes in national policy could improve children's eating patterns?' in National Forum for Coronary Heart Disease Prevention, *Food for Children: Influencing Choice and Investing in Health*, London, National Forum for Coronary Heart Disease Prevention.

MEIGHAN, R. (1986) *A Sociology of Education*, London, Reinhart and Winston.

MENNELL, S., MURCOTT, A. and VAN OTTERLOO, A.H. (1992) *The Sociology of Food: Eating, Diet, and Culture*, London, Sage, for the International Sociological Association.

MINISTRY OF EDUCATION, SCIENCE AND CULTURE, GOVERNMENT OF JAPAN (1989) *Education in Japan 1989: A Graphic Presentation*, Japan, Gyosei Publications.

MONBUSHO (1992) *The Current Main Activities of the Monbusho*, Japan, Monbusho.

MORRISON, M. (1995) 'Teaching and learning about food and nutrition in schools: Choices at the curriculum table'. Paper presented at the 4th International Food Choice Conference, April, University of Birmingham.

MORRISON, M. and BURGESS, R.G. (1993) 'Chapatis and chips: Encountering food use in primary school settings'. Paper presented at an International Conference on Children's Food and Drink: Today's Market, Tomorrow's Opportunities, Chipping Campden Food and Drink Association, Chipping Campden, Gloucestershire.

MORTIMORE, P. (1989) 'School matters', in MOON, B., MURPHY, P. and RAYNOR, J. (eds) *Policies for the Curriculum,* London, Hodder Stoughton for the Open University Press.

MORTIMORE, J. and BLACKSTONE, T. (1982) *Disadvantage and Education,* London, Heinemann.

MURCOTT, A. (1987) '"Feeding the Children", A Review of the Diets of British School Children', *Journal of Educational Policy,* **2** (3), pp. 245–52.

NATIONAL CURRICULUM COUNCIL (1990) *Curriculum Guidance 5, Health Education,* York, NCC.

NATIONAL FORUM FOR CORONARY HEART DISEASE PREVENTION (1994) *Food for Children: Influencing Choice and Investing in Health,* London, National Forum for Coronary Heart Disease Prevention.

NELSON, M. (1994) 'Nutritional content of children's diets and the health implications' in *Food for Children: Influencing Choice and Investing in Health,* London, National Forum for Coronary Health Disease Prevention.

RODMELL, S. and WATTS, A. (eds) (1986) *The Politics of Health Education: Raising the Issues,* London, Routledge and Kegan Paul.

ROHLEN, T. (1983) *Japan's High Schools,* Berkeley, CA, University of California Press.

STIERER, B. (1988) 'A symbolic challenge: Reading helpers in school', in MEEK, M. and WILLS, C. (eds) *Language and Literacy in the Primary School,* London, Falmer Press.

TOBIN, J. (1992) 'Japanese pre-schools and the pedagogy of self-hood', in ROSENBERGER, N. (ed.) *The Japanese Sense of Self,* Cambridge, Cambridge University Press.

VAN DER BERGHE, P.L. (1984) 'Ethnic cuisine, culture in nature' *Ethnic and Racial Studies,* **7** (3), pp. 387–97.

YOUNG, I. (1993) 'How much can a school do about healthy eating?' *Research in Education S.C.R.E. Newsletter,* Issue 53, Autumn, pp. 4–5.

YOUNG, I. (1994) 'The Health Promoting School', in *Food for Children: Influencing Choice and Investing in Health,* London, National Forum for Coronary Heart Disease Prevention.

Part Two

Teacher Training

7 The Reform of Primary Teacher Training: The Views of Parents

Andrew Hannan

Introduction

In the demonology of the Conservative Party, 'loony left' local education authorities and 'child-centred progressives' in schools and Higher Education Institutions (HEIs), both teachers and teacher trainers, are held responsible for much of what is wrong with our education system. On the other hand, parents are seen as the repositories of good sense, who must simply be given the power to choose in order to refashion that system in a way which will reflect their priorities (Hillgate Group, 1986). Since children, particularly those of primary school age, are considered too young to exercise their full role as consumers of education services, that task is allocated to their parents. These surrogate consumers are then invited to exert their influence in a quasi-marketplace by choosing to send their offspring to schools which meet their definition of children's education needs (as well as making their views felt through annual parents' meetings and by representation on school governing bodies). The assumption here is that there is considerable overlap between the agenda of the Conservative Party (and in particular the 'new right' thinkers who have contributed so much to current government policy) and the views of parents. Although parents may want a degree of diversity of provision (DFE, 1992), however limited by the constraints of a National Curriculum, what they really value is high levels of pupil attainment and good discipline, or so we are led to believe. There is some evidence of schools struggling to meet such perceived requirements, with a shift to school uniforms and an emphasis on the public presentation of orderly behaviour and academic success, particularly in secondary schools (Gerwitz, Ball and Bowe, 1993).

For teacher education, the direct consumers are, presumably, the student teachers, although it is the schools who 'consume' the output from the training process by employing newly qualified teachers. However, it is the children who are the intended consumers of the teaching actually undertaken and it is their parents who are frequently portrayed as sceptical about the sort of primary education that is provided. One contradiction which is often pointed out about current government reforms of teacher education is that the intention is to give schools more control over the training process whereas these same schools are seen as the defenders of outdated ideologies detrimental to true progress (see the first annual lecture by Her Majesty's Chief Inspector, Chris

Woodhead, as reported in Hackett, 1995). However, this assumes the schools concerned remain the same, whereas the intention of the wider process of reform is to transform their character through the three-fold pressures of national regulation, inspection and parental influence, the last exercised through both governing bodies and the quasi-market. The 'new' primary school, shorn of child-centred ideology, invigorated by a strong commitment to moral and spiritual education and accountable to parents whose main wish is to maximize the academic attainments of their offspring, is then seen as the ideal place for new teachers to acquire their skills.

In contrast, the HEIs are much less susceptible to market pressures and are themselves seen as the very source of the problem, if that is defined as Plowdenesque approaches to primary education. This is why the government are to apply what the draft circular (DFE, 1993a) called 'tough' (p. 1) and the final version (DFE, 1993b) called 'strict' (p. 3) new criteria which the HEIs have to meet and why schools are seen as 'best placed to help student teachers develop and apply practical teaching skills' whereas the role of the HEI is to provide 'the subject knowledge necessary for sound teaching of the primary curriculum' (DFE, 1993b, p. 3). This is why 'schools should play a much larger and more influential role in course design and delivery, in partnership as appropriate with HEIs' (DFE, 1993b, p. 5) and why there should be a shift of funding to schools to make this possible, backed by the Secretary of State's intention 'that the transfer of funds from individual institutions to schools will be monitored and made public' and his commitment to 'look carefully at any evidence that individual schools have been treated arbitrarily or unreasonably and take action as necessary' (DFE, 1993b, p. 12). Ultimately, then, the ivory tower world of HEIs is itself to be rendered accountable through the twin forces of market mechanisms directly driven by funding considerations and inspection by the Department For Education (DFE) intent on applying their 'strict' criteria.

This project is based on a number of assumptions and has already been challenged through, in particular, the resistance of teachers to the testing regime which is at the heart of the market mechanisms (Hatcher, 1994) and more recent campaigns by Parent Teacher Associations and school governing bodies against cuts to school budgets. The HEIs, however, despite the best efforts of UCET (Universities Council for the Education of Teachers) and the CVCP (Committee of Vice-Chancellors and Principals) have been able to exert little influence on the government, with the newly established TTA (Teacher Training Agency), containing a membership largely sympathetic to the government's agenda, about to begin its task of transformation.

For those who wish to understand what is going on here, and still more for those who wish to influence, resist or re-direct the process of change, it is important to take account of the views of those the reformers see as their natural allies, the parents. This chapter does so by means of a comparison with the views of primary school headteachers, tutors involved in initial teacher education and student teachers, as revealed by means of a recent survey.

The Survey

The research reported here was launched immediately after the DFE published their consultation document/draft circular with the title *The Initial Training of Primary School Teachers: New Criteria for Course Approval*, dated 9 June 1993 (DFE, 1993a). Questionnaires were sent to the headteachers of all the county and voluntary-aided primary sector schools in Devon (one of the largest counties in England), to parents of pupils at seven of those schools, and to students and tutors at the Rolle Faculty of Education of the University of Plymouth.

Of the 433 headteachers who were sent copies of the questionnaire, 264 replied, giving a response rate of 61 per cent. The nature of the sample in terms of size of school was as follows: seventy-seven schools with less than 100 pupils (29.1 per cent); 128 with 100 to 299 pupils (48.5 per cent); 41 with 300 or over pupils (15.5 per cent); and 18 schools (6.8 per cent) which did not provide this information. 1,040 copies of the questionnaire were distributed to parents at seven primary sector schools, 267 were returned, a response rate of 26 per cent. These seven were an 'opportunity sample' with a reasonable degree of representativeness for Devon county schools, i.e., in terms of pupil age ranges, location (rural, small town, large town) and pupil numbers.

The attempt to reach students in teacher training was hampered by the timing of the survey, as it took place at the very end of term when many students were without lecture commitments, so it was not possible to contact them all. None of the fourth year Bachelor of Education (BEd) students were available as they had finished their exams and had dispersed. All students who took part in the survey were undertaking courses of initial teacher education in order to work in primary schools. Those taking the BEd were engaged in a four-year honours degree. Those graduates (with BA or BSc or equivalent) taking the primary Postgraduate Certificate of Education (PGCE) could take either a one-year course or spend two years as Articled Teachers (a school-based course involving partnership between school and the university). Overall, whereas 769 students (not counting those who had just finished the fourth year of their BEd) were eligible to take part, it was only possible to distribute 593 copies of the questionnaire. Of these, 242 were returned, a response rate of 41 per cent. Tutors were easier to reach making it possible to send the questionnaire to 53 full-time tutors and 18 part-time tutors of Rolle Faculty of Education, a total of 71. Of these, 50 were returned, 41 from full-timers and 9 from part-timers, giving response rates of 77 per cent and 50 per cent respectively and 70 per cent overall.

The questionnaire instrument was designed in close consultation with the Devon Association of Primary Headteachers (DAPH) who sponsored its distribution amongst headteachers and parents. The project was intended to serve a dual purpose in that it aimed to provide immediate feedback to the DFE (by 31 July 1993) from all these groups as part of the consultation exercise (on behalf of the University of Plymouth and of DAPH) and to provide valuable research evidence about the perspectives of those who would be directly affected by the reform of primary initial teacher education. The questionnaire explained the government's proposals to the respondents in terms which were an attempt to paraphrase the language used in the DFE circular (DFE, 1993a) and to avoid any accusations of leading them towards a negative reaction. The version of the questionnaire sent to parents contained three general items of most direct relevance to their concerns whereas that for the other sets of respondents contained an additional four questions of a more specific kind.

General results of the survey are published elsewhere (Hannan, 1993; 1994) as is an analysis of the responses of headteachers who favoured the proposal for School Centred Initial Teacher Training (SCITT) which was to enable primary schools to offer teacher training without necessarily involving an HEI (Hannan, 1995). Here the focus will be on the responses of parents to the proposals, with some comparison to the views of the other groups.

The seven schools involved in the survey of parents provided a reasonable cross-section of Devon primary schools. They and their contribution to the overall sample, may briefly be described (by reference to their pseudonyms) as follows:

- Shannon Primary School — 356 pupils on roll, 83 (23.3 per cent) of whom have free school meals. Situated on the outskirts of a large seaside town, with a mix of owner-occupied, privately rented and council house accommodation. Wide range of social class. (90 parents replied, making up 33.7 per cent of respondents at a response rate of 34 per cent.)

- Cotton Primary School — 85 pupils on roll, 15 (17.6 per cent) of whom have free school meals. Situated in a small village with a dispersed rural catchment area. (8 parents replied, making up 3 per cent of respondents at a response rate of 13 per cent.)

- Wade First School — 213 pupils (aged 3–8) including 35 at the nursery, with 64 (30 per cent) receiving free school meals. Located in a large town, approximately half the families living in council housing. (48 parents replied, making up 18 per cent of respondents at a response rate of 28 per cent.)

- Salter Primary School — 123 pupils, 7 (5.7 per cent) of whom receive free school meals. Located in a small village populated by families with a wide range of social backgrounds, including farm labourers and a relatively high proportion of people earning high incomes. (33 parents replied, making up 12.4 per cent of respondents at a response rate of 39 per cent.)

- Whiver Primary School — 85 pupils, 12 (15.6 per cent) of whom take free school meals. Located in a village and catering for children from the families of professionals who commute to a nearby large town as well as locals of a range of social backgrounds, including manual working class. (21 parents replied, making up 7.9 per cent of respondents at a response rate of 36 per cent.)

- Maxton Primary School — 309 pupils, 86 (27.8 per cent) of whom take free school meals. Located in a large seaside town, with approximately one-third of families living in council housing but with the full range of social backgrounds, including a significant proportion of those in the professions. (45 parents replied, making up 16.9 per cent of respondents at a response rate of 21 per cent.)

- Linstead Primary School — 295 pupils, 20 (6.8 per cent) on free school meals. Located in a small market town. Mainly private housing. (21 parents replied, making up 7.9 per cent of respondents at a response rate of 11 per cent.)

An overall response rate for parents of 26 per cent is by no means impressive, although the fact that as many as 267 of them were able to respond within the relatively short time limit imposed by the consultation process (of just two weeks) should be taken into account. Nonetheless, we cannot take the results as representative of this population (defined as the parents of children at these seven schools) as a whole. It seems safest to assume that those who did respond were those most likely to be interested in the issues raised by the questionnaire, but we have no grounds for assuming that they were more likely to represent a particular point of view, either for or against the government's proposals for primary teacher training. It remains true, however, that we have before us the views of 267 parents, on issues which were of some concern to them and that no other survey has provided us with similar information.

Findings

The first proposal put to all four categories of respondent was that:

> **One-year courses of training should be established for parents and other mature students with considerable previous experience of working with young children who have the necessary academic qualifications** (such as two 'A' levels and English and Maths at GCSE grade C or above), **to train them to teach nursery and infant pupils only.**

This idea (often known as the 'Mums' Army' proposal) was overwhelmingly opposed by headteachers (96 per cent), students (89 per cent) and tutors (96 per cent). Although more parents were against (48 per cent) than were in favour (42.4 per cent, with 9.4 per cent neutral), the extent of opposition was significantly less than for the other groups. However, the 'in favour' category can be subdivided to separate those who indicated 'support' (96, or 36 per cent) from those who indicated 'strong support' (17, or 6.4 per cent) and the 'against' can be separated in terms of those who indicated 'oppose' (48, or 18 per cent) or 'strongly oppose' (80, or 30 per cent). It would seem from this that the extremes of response were not in balance, that far more parents were strongly opposed to the proposal than were strongly in support.

Only 17 of the parents who favoured the proposal took up the option to provide 'further comments' and of those just the following gave their reasons:

I think that mature students and parents often have a lot of useful experience that they can bring to the job. (Parent 41)

I would only support this proposal if it meant increased teaching staff in individual schools, thus reducing numbers of pupils in the class-room or to enhance teaching for pupils with learning difficulties. (Parent 54)

Real Time 'experience' with young children and an understanding of their needs and expectations is more than a substitute for over quali-fied people with little practical experience. (Parent 119)

Mature students will already have good communication skills with young children, which will create a relaxed but confident approach to the learning environment from which the child will benefit. (Parent 129)

In contrast, 76 parents who were against the proposal added 'further com-ments'. They gave their reasons for opposition in terms of a range of factors. Thirty-one mentioned the need for nursery and infant teachers to be highly trained, 27 placed particular emphasis on the importance of the early years as a foundation for future learning and 22 stated that they thought that one year was an inadequate period for the preparation which was necessary. Thus:

Is school at this level meant to be child-minding or educating? These early years are the foundation on which later education is based so thorough training is necessary not just to introduce trainees to the breadth and complexity of the National Curriculum but also to ensure that they have a working knowledge of how children learn. One year would not be long enough for reflection, adjustment and learning. (Parent 35)

One year does not seem long enough to equip someone with enough information and firsthand experience to be a teacher. I heard about this proposal on the radio and was horrified to hear a government official refer to the 4–7 age range as the 'easy' stage, which would suit these less qualified teachers having the one-year course. It is, of course, the most important foundation stage. (Parent 138)

I strongly feel that young children need and are entitled to just as highly qualified and properly trained teachers as older children. The formative years are known to be the most important of a person's life and with the emphasis on upping the standards in schools I consider this to be very short sighted and detrimental to the children's education. (Parent 199)

I feel that infant teachers have a huge responsibility and require at least as much training as other teachers. A child's introduction to basic literacy and numeracy is absolutely vital for their subsequent education, as is a smooth transition from 'home' to 'school'. I would be very unhappy for my children to have (had) minimally trained and qualified infant teachers. (Parent 250)

I believe the early years of education are of paramount importance. I believe that children require the type of teachers whose experience in education extends beyond that of an able, enthusiastic parent. A knowledge and experience of requirements further along the academic road are important. Both my children have had the benefit of excellent nursery education, and my older child the benefit of an infant education that has been provided by exceptional people. We should oppose any 'soft' route to teaching these children. If someone seriously wants to teach small children, I think an excellent test of the required commitment would be the completion of the current course. (Parent 266)

Nine parents attributed the proposal to an ill-considered attempt to cut costs, 6 stated that they saw it as an insult to current nursery and infant teachers, 6 remarked on the dangers of creating a two-tier teaching force, 5 made particular mention of the likely fall in the standards of teaching and learning which they saw as a consequence and 5 pointed out that the experience of looking after children was not necessarily relevant.

The next proposition put to all four categories of respondent concerned the amount of time student teachers should be in schools:

The minimum time to be spent in schools by student teachers should increase (from 20 to 32 weeks in 4-year, and from 15 to 24 weeks in 3-year BEd and equivalent courses; and from 15 to 18 weeks in one-year primary PGCE and 2-year BEd and equivalent courses).

Here, all four categories of respondent had sizeable majorities (71 per cent of headteachers, 77 per cent of parents, 71 per cent of students and 60 per cent of tutors) in favour of increasing the period of time student teachers spend in schools (by the amounts proposed by the DFE). Sixty parents (22.5 per cent) indicated 'strongly support' (144 or 54 per cent indicating 'support') and just eight (3 per cent) gave 'strongly oppose' (with fifteen or 5.6 per cent giving 'oppose'). Fifty-five of the parents in favour offered 'further comments' almost all of which explained their reasons in terms of the advantages of practical experience over theoretical learning. For example:

> The longer the better — more hands-on experience. (Parent 2)

> I am sure students benefit immensely from classroom experience. Surely being with children and putting into practice what is learnt at college is a lot of help, especially with the help of an experienced teacher. (Parent 4)

> The only way to learn the job is in the classroom — only that way will you find out if you are suited to it. (Parent 6)

> I support this proposal because, as with all occupations, experience can be far more valuable than theoretical knowledge, and surely nothing can be better than being able to cope with normal classroom situations after having experienced them firsthand rather than from a textbook. (Parent 209)

Given the widespread support for this proposal it is no surprise to find its provisions incorporated in the new regulations (DFE, 1993b).

The final proposition put to respondents referred to what became known as the SCITT scheme:

> **Groups of schools wishing to take the lead in designing and running their own course of training for primary school teachers should be able to obtain direct government funding for this purpose** (without necessarily having to involve HEIs).

Opposition was strongest amongst the tutors (94 per cent) but was also high amongst both headteachers (69 per cent) and students (76 per cent). Although more parents were against the proposal (48.3 per cent) than were in favour of it (32.8 per cent, with 18.9 per cent neutral) the extent of opposition was again significantly less strong than for the other groups. However, over twice as many parents were strongly opposed (fifty-nine or 22.1 per cent) than were strongly in support of the idea (twenty-eight or 10.5 per cent), with fifty-nine (22.1 per cent) indicating 'support' and sixty-nine (25.8 per cent) 'oppose'.

Of the ten parents in favour of the idea who offered 'further comments', only two were unreservedly in favour:

I feel primary schools should take an active part in running their own training courses for primary school teachers. They are the places where these teachers will later work and know what they should be learning to equip them for the job. (Parent 81)

Yes, I think this is important because each area has different needs, which may only be identified by the schools in that area. (Parent 238)

Otherwise, even those in support expressed concerns in terms of the financing of the scheme, the narrowness of the training offered or the need for careful external vetting. Fifty-nine of those against offered 'further comments', of which twenty-two explained their opposition in terms of the dangers of varying standards and the loss of national comparability, for example:

Who will standardize training levels? Who will train the students? Teachers don't have time to teach their children never mind students because of National Curriculum recording and assessing pressures. Some educational theory is necessary — who will provide this? Can the government cope with large numbers of redundant college tutors? (Parent 97)

While I think Maxton would make an excellent job of teaching students, would the teachers have time (they already work flat out)? There is the problem of a common nationwide standard to be achieved with different approaches. Would the government be tempted to reward certain schools financially, which they approve of? (Parent 218)

Seventeen expressed reservations in terms of the extra burden on schools and teachers whose prime purpose was to educate children, for example:

This would surely detract from their *raison d'être*. Partnership between training institutes and schools can result in freshness. Schools running their own training courses would tend to be more inward-looking and increasingly stale. The burden of administration would be heavy. Who would do the lectures and the training? Surely not the teachers with their workload? (Parent 35)

This sounds like off-loading the responsibilities from the HEIs to the primary schools. We should in fact be looking at greater liaisons between schools and colleges, enabling students to enhance the school whilst training. (Parent 176)

The purpose of schools is to teach children, not to train teachers. (Parent 213)

Thirteen argued that HEIs had an important role to play which should be retained, for example:

> Do we need to re-invent the wheel? These HEIs have a wealth of experience which should be utilized and not ignored. Any group of schools wishing to set up their own course would presumably need to be recognized by some body — what body? How? Isn't this merely adding another collection of officials? (Parent 69)

> Any teacher training should include a balance of academic and practical experience, with a variety of tutors and different schools to visit in order to get a balanced view of the role of a teacher, and to give them a well-rounded education before they start educating others. This proposal could be very dangerous in my view. (Parent 138)

> This is simply a government ploy to remove initial teacher preparation from higher education by offering financial inducements to schools which are suffering from under-funding. The assumption being that parents and governors wishing to obtain the best deal for their children will support this in order to obtain the money needed to run the school. The preparation of teachers to teach primary and junior pupils should not be separated from the preparation of teachers in other parts of the school sector. It is important that the education system be an integrated system in which all children can be helped to develop to the best of their ability. (Parent 221)

Five parents actually championed the role of HEIs in terms of providing guidance on education theory. For example:

> This would mean that teachers would get only a narrow spectrum of teaching methods and probably not enough theory of the process of learning. (Parent 214)

> This is likely to lead to biased training in terms of educational philosophy. It is important for students to find their personal niche. (Parent 229)

> Student teachers need to be taught in a largely academic environment where there is a wealth of ideas and opinions. Training courses such as suggested would be too narrow. (Parent 265)

Conclusion

Looking at the pattern of responses from parents, it seems true that, although they appear somewhat more sympathetic to the government proposals on teacher training than do headteachers, students or tutors (who might be expected to be stronger in their resistance because of vested interests in the status quo), there is little evidence of a wholesale adoption of the agenda for educational reform set out by the 'new right'. Where a majority of parents are in favour of one of the government proposals (on increasing the amount of time to be spent by trainee teachers in schools) headteachers, students and tutors take a similar stance, although the highest percentage support comes from parents (77 per cent compared to 71 per cent of headteachers and students and 60 per cent of tutors). The call for more 'on the job' training seems difficult to resist, with many respondents from each category favouring school-based learning over that taking place in HEIs, at least in terms of changing the relative proportions in favour of the former, although not in overall support of a total shift as in the SCITT scheme. It seems that HEIs are still vulnerable to attack from those who doubt the value of their contribution, at least in terms of the proportion of training which is their responsibility (with even the HEI tutors favouring a shift to schools, which must be somewhat like turkeys voting for Christmas). The parents were not asked to give their views on a survey item setting out the government's proposals for obliging HEIs to enter into partnerships with schools in which the latter would play a more influential role than previously in course design and delivery, but 64 per cent of headteachers, 48 per cent of students and 56 per cent of tutors were in favour of such an arrangement. However, several parents suggested in their responses to other items that they favoured partnerships with HEIs rather than the takeover of teacher training by the schools.

Although there are indeed higher percentages of parents than headteachers, students or tutors in favour of the other proposals they are nonetheless in a minority in each case, with higher percentages in opposition. In the case of the 'Mums' Army' idea (eventually dropped in the face of overwhelming opposition) and the SCITT scheme (still very much alive although not yet popular amongst primary schools), those strongly opposed greatly outnumber those strongly in support (being over four times as many in the first case and over twice as many in the second). All the parents surveyed had children at primary schools in Devon. This county has not previously been known as a hot-bed of anti-government feeling, although at the time of the survey the local authority shifted from Conservative to Liberal-Democrat Party control. Nonetheless, most of the parliamentary constituencies in the region remain bastions of Conservative support, with just one Liberal-Democrat seat and no Labour Party seats outside of one in Plymouth (none of the seven schools involved in the survey of parents were within or close to that city). If anything, then, we would expect the sample of parents to be biased in favour of the proposals on the basis of the political characteristics of the wider population. Yet, the weight of opposition to the 'Mums' Army' and SCITT schemes was considerable, with far more parents in both cases strongly against than strongly in favour. Certainly, those opposed to these reforms were much more likely to provide 'further comments' explaining their views than those in favour.

Andrew Hannan

There appear to be a significant number of parents who are articulate, keen to express their opinions and well informed. It seems that the government's ploy of delegating power to parents has helped to make them aware of what is going on in schools. Any threat to the quality of education offered to their children is quickly identified, with much reference to the dangers of cost-cutting and a defence of teachers, and even HEIs, where the reforms are interpreted as endangering standards. Parents are, it seems, demanding consumers, keen to get the best for their children and impatient of ideologically based critiques of what is currently on offer.

References

DEPARTMENT FOR EDUCATION (1992) *Choice and Diversity: A New Framework for Schools*, London, HMSO.

DEPARTMENT FOR EDUCATION (1993a) *The Initial Training of Primary School Teachers: New Criteria for Course Approval*, Draft Circular, 9 June, London, HMSO.

DEPARTMENT FOR EDUCATION (1993b) *The Initial Training of Primary School Teachers: New Criteria for Courses*, Circular 14/93, London, HMSO.

GERWITZ, S., BALL, S.J. and BOWE, R. (1993) 'Values and ethics in the education market place: The case of Northwark Park', *International Studies in Sociology of Education*, **3** (2), pp. 233–54.

HACKETT, G. (1995) 'Woodhead castigates progressives', *Times Educational Supplement*, 27 January, p. 3.

HANNAN, A. (1993) *The Initial Training of Primary School Teachers: Response to the DFE (an Interim Report)*, Exmouth, University of Plymouth.

HANNAN, A. (1994) 'Headteachers', parents', students' and tutors' responses to the reform of primary Initial Teacher Education', in REID, I., CONSTABLE, H. and GRIFFITHS, R. (eds) *Teacher Education Reform: Current Research*, London, Paul Chapman, pp. 199–208.

HANNAN, A. (1995) 'The case for school-led primary teacher training', *Journal of Education for Teaching*, **21** (1), pp. 25–35.

HATCHER, R. (1994) 'Market relationships and the management of teachers', *British Journal of Sociology of Education*, **15** (1), pp. 41–61.

HILLGATE GROUP (1986) *Whose Schools? A Radical Manifesto*, London, Hillgate Group.

8 The Realization of Partnership in a Primary Articled Teacher Course

Caroline Whiting

The Articled Teacher (AT) course was a pilot scheme delivering a postgraduate training based in schools (DES, 1989). It represented a developing trend towards more school-based training for teachers which culminated in legislative changes first in the secondary sector and then in primary (DFE, 1992; 1993). These changes mean developing the partnership between schools and Higher Education Institutions (HEIs), and giving the schools a more leading role. Data from the AT course can inform those new courses. In my research, I collected detailed qualitative data from a cohort of eleven courses throughout the two-year course beginning in September 1991. Awarding a Post Graduate Certificate in Education (PGCE), 80 per cent of course time was to be in schools, based in one school (but with opportunities for visits and a practice in another school) and under the supervision of a mentor. Mentor training was available at the college (as the HEI was invariably referred to), with a format of day or half-day sessions; one session before the course and several more during the course. The training was supported by supply cover in the schools and amounted to four days over two years. The cohort I was studying was the second to start at the college.

Structures and Procedures for Partnership

Throughout the setting up of the course there was evidence of a will that there should be an ethos of partnership between the college and schools; the main way that this was to be brought about was for there to be representation from both in the *planning* process, in *recruitment* and for the *support* and *assessment* of ATs through the course.

Planning Together

Although the college was responsible for designing the course, putting together a submission document and getting validation, it was recognized that schools must play a part. After a planning seminar in March 1990 the PGCE course director, in distributed notes, stressed that shared perceptions were of utmost importance and could be reached 'by full involvement of all partners in the planning process'. (The local education authority (LEA) was also involved because proposals for Articled Teacher schemes had to be put to the Department of Education and Science (DES) jointly). So, an eye to school involvement was evident at the outset. The DES itself claimed that they had 'explored informally with interested LEA officers, teacher trainers and teachers the idea of setting up some experimental courses for school based schemes — to be called articled teacher schemes' (DES, 1989). As far as this consortium, which included three HEIs and the LEA, was concerned, meetings began in earnest by the end of 1989, but involving as it did large numbers of people, only small representations from each of the three groups were initially involved. As the college developed its own plans, after the consortium proposal was accepted local headteachers and teachers became involved in planning, validation and submission. A member of the college staff accepted the role of convenor of the planning group which was to include a number of teachers agreed by the LEA. A *'validation event'* was held at the college. The panel consisted of thirteen college staff, three external advisors of which two were from other HEIs and one a headteacher, five other school representatives and one LEA representative. The documentation for the 'event' stressed the proposed links between the college and school parts of the course, and the Council for the Accreditation of Teacher Education (CATE) submission set out the following as ways to illustrate and achieve co-operation between the partners:

1 A feature of the course design was regular discussion with senior LEA officers and chief advisor.
2 'Early involvement of head teachers and mentors has also characterised the planning process.'
3 All the partners were to be involved in delivery, monitoring and assessment.
4 In curriculum studies — 'all components are professionally focused. The course is led by students' experience in schools. This provides the focus for professional analysis and extension in college based sessions'.
5 The professional tutor was to have a 'key role': continuity, co-ordination, illustrating general principles from the students' concrete experience. 'In addition they will ensure that proper attention is given to the appropriate cross curricular themes.'

By July 1990 the course had validation. By August approval came from the DES after requesting more detail and receiving *inter alia* the following:

> The intention is that the mentors, the professional tutors and the student teachers will monitor carefully the work done in each of the core curriculum subjects and across the breadth of the National Curriculum

foundation subjects . . . to monitor progress through the professional log, to ensure . . . they have covered at least that amount of content. The relative responsibilities . . . are still being explored . . . seen as a full partnership where all parties are involved in the monitoring of progress . . . ensuring all aspects of the primary curriculum and its assessment are covered.

This is evidence that the partnership was acknowledged as being responsible for the provision for a minimum course content in terms of school curriculum, but how that was going to be monitored in practice was only explained by the proposed professional log and a system of 'relative responsibilities' which were still being explored. It also reveals a possible contradiction: an 'amount of content' was to be ensured by a course that 'was to be led by students' experience in schools' (point 4 above).

The planning team was a small group and included several local heads and deputy heads, including a deputy head who was already on the college site as a temporary associate tutor so it was easier to meet often. The drafts were shown to the PGCE course committee and participating heads and mentors for comment.

The first cohort began their course in September 1990 and at that time an AT course committee was set up. The first meeting was in September 1990 when they considered the programme of the course, including mentor training. A planning day for the teaching team was held the following month, October 1990, to consider more closely the role of the mentor, expectations of the AT in school and the nature of the ATs work in faculty. One of the proposed outcomes of this meeting was 'a statement of principles/guidelines to inform teaching teams'. Despite great efforts to make the planning process a joint one it would be true to say that the college was the originator and designer of the course. It was in a unique position of knowledge in respect of a task like this. Designing and submitting courses for approval and validation was part of its established function. The fact that a new course had just been written for the PGCE meant that the nature of the new CATE requirements was already in close focus for the individuals in college, but not in schools where heads and teachers had quite enough pressing concerns of their own. Only members of staff at the college had time to carry out such a task. In fact the task fell upon two people in particular, the PGCE course director and the AT course director who was going to be the professional tutor for the first cohort. Others were only brought in to the process as approvers, rather than instigators. These others were members of staff at the college as well as the LEA but most particularly schools. It was said by those who were setting up the course that at this point the intention was to involve participating schools and mentors. However, those individuals who were actually going to participate in the course had still largely to be decided at this time. Those who were actually going to be working with the ATs in their schools were in the main not involved in this planning process. When we come to the second cohort of ATs

— the group that I was studying — we had moved even further away from the initial planning process and therefore from the initial planners. The new professional tutor was not involved in the original process; the PGCE course director and the AT course director were not regularly involved in delivery of the course for the second cohort.

Recruitment

ATs

Interviews were initially to take place at the college, just as for those applying for the traditional PGCE course. A further interview took place at a school and at this point the school was free to accept or reject the prospective AT and in theory the AT was free to accept or reject the school. The procedures at the schools varied in terms of time and of personnel involved to do the 'vetting'. The most schools did was to have the prospective AT in school for the whole of one day; a formal interview was given by the head, opportunities were given for the mentor to spend some time with the AT and the AT was able to learn quite a lot about the school and the mentor and the class she would be working with at the outset.

However there were cases where the AT was in school for much less time and in some cases did not meet the mentor at all, or only briefly. At a meeting for new mentors for ATs beginning in 1993 there was evidence that schools were still able and willing to take on new ATs in this way, and that college members did not feel in a position to prevent it. The feeling of partnership did not extend to individuals being prepared to comment too closely on their perceptions of the way the role of other partners was carried out, even when they were uneasy. Internal school arrangements were the schools' concern as college's were college's.

Schools

Schools were to be identified by the LEA phase adviser, the college or the AT herself but approval was to be a joint decision. Three very local schools already had a strong tradition of being involved with the college through the acceptance of students on TP. Finding further schools was not an easy task and arrangements were still being made in the summer term prior to the start of the course. There were not so many schools available that ATs had any real choice about where they were to go; in practice all the ATs reported that they felt in a weak position in this respect. They knew that the ultimate success of their application to join the course was dependent on them finding a school placement. To accept the school was to accept the mentor too. Headteachers were in fact in a very strong position here; they had no compulsion to accept these (or any other) students and the motives for them doing so were not always altruistic. Although several heads mentioned a feeling of responsibility to be part of preparing new teachers, all of them agreed the benefits the school felt from the presence of students. But it was the heads who took decisions about accepting students, not class teachers, or the college.

Mentors

The choice of mentor, too, was entirely up to the headteacher. Although teachers could have said no to the 'request' for them to take on a mentoring role, in general, they didn't. ATs usually worked within the mentor's class, alongside the mentor, in the first instance. The mentors themselves had been chosen by the head to various criteria. They were chosen for reasons of seniority and experience in teaching, for career advancement, because they were teaching a class within the age range the AT preferred, because they volunteered or because simply because they were available. The fact that ATs would, at least by the second year of their course when they could be given more responsibility, become a useful extra pair of hands also influenced choices. At one school it was admitted that the AT was accepted to relieve staffing problems so this influenced the decision as to where to place her, and therefore who her mentor would be. Mentors were often chosen in haste and sometimes not until after the initial mentor training session.

Supporting and Assessing the ATs through the Course

The course was delivered by a number of people, most of whom were not involved in planning it and who never were able to get together as a whole group. Although mentors and sometimes heads would attend mentor training days at the college, class teachers in base schools and practice schools would have no contact with college except possible meetings with the visiting tutor. The team of people who would be directly and formally involved would consist of the professional tutor and curriculum staff at the college and mentors and heads in schools in which the ATs worked. All these were part of a team providing the ATs with opportunities for learning which constituted their initial preparation for their working lives as teachers. Because of this diverse and disparate team it was acknowledged by the planners that there was the need for partnership between those delivering the course at several levels:

- a sharing of aims and procedures;
- a necessity for participants to see their contribution as a component within a whole;
- some sort of quality assurance for the ATs.

The next section describes how this was to happen through the delivery of the course.

Delivery through Partnership

Course Structure

The course was designed around a framework of four 'stages'. Intentions and principles of work in schools within the stages were described in general rather than specific terms, but at the end of each stage a corresponding set of clear outcomes, a written assignment and assessment of practical work were anticipated. This format, with its emphasis on outcomes rather than content, was to allow for individual arrangements as best fitted the AT, the mentor and the school to produce a comparable result for all the ATs. The intention of the course is given as 'enabling the articled teachers, as successful graduates, to focus on the complex and challenging task of teaching young children.'

Documentation and Mentor Training

Documentation had a major role to play. Mentors and ATs each had a course handbook which was intended to provide the basis of the information they needed for the course. It set out the framework which I have described above and was a document which was to give a shared overview of the course for mentor and AT. In addition to the handbook, mentor training was to provide opportunities for college and school staff to work together on a variety of issues and to provide support and sharing opportunities for mentors. The mentors had mentor training sessions which began in the summer before the ATs started. (Mentors also had opportunities to speak with the college tutor on his visits and to gain information from the ATs themselves about what was happening at college.)

Mentor training was a source of some complaint, at least at the outset. All the mentors I interviewed were critical both of timing and content. Attendance at sessions was patchy. Several mentors out of the eleven did not attend the first training session in the summer before the course began which set the scene and emphasized roles and agendas. The course tutor was aware of something less than satisfaction with the sessions and an uneasiness amongst the mentors about the precise nature of their role. He was quick to point out that many of their questions could in fact be answered by reference to the mentor handbook. Unfortunately, many of the mentors did not have the same perception of the handbook as he seemed to; it was criticized as being 'vague' or too long and complex for them to assimilate. It was used as a guide through the course for some, and it seemed to be understood better as the course progressed, becoming increasingly valuable. But this sometimes caused more anxiety; there was still worry if they felt they were not complying exactly with its description of what should happen and were further concerned if, at mentor training sessions, they discovered that others were doing something completely different.

Although they tended to see the problem as being with the document itself, one could query the expectation that such a document could function as a core focus for groups of people whose starting point and experience was so different from those who had designed it. The mentors and ATs had difficulty in 'connecting' with the document. It was not written within their frame of reference. Not just ATs but mentors, too, were learners in this instance.

There was a marked difference in perception, certainly through the first of the two years, between the college and the school. Those who had written the handbook considered the framework described was sufficiently rigid to provide quality control, but flexible enough for individual circumstances to dictate and pace the style of things. ATs were never going to have the same *experience* as each other, but they must have the same *entitlement*. Somehow quality control had to be provided. Mentors and ATs, however, seemed to have insufficient confidence to take control until some way on in the course. When they did decide to take the onus on themselves to decide what to do, it was with a feeling of defiance, only gradually coming to the realization that this was in fact what was intended. Thus there was continued complaint, at least at the outset, but in many cases even at the end, from mentors that they didn't know what they were supposed to be doing. (The only mentor I heard say he was confident about what he should be doing right from the very start was one who was effectively abandoned by his AT after quite a short time, in favour of support from other members of school staff.)

Typical remarks by mentors about their role and mentor training reveal a number of concerns which highlight a lack of true understanding between the partners and the inadequacy of the documentation and training sessions to deliver this. Documentation and talk about the course did not start from where the teachers were:

> This was college jargon. We were pretending to be people we weren't.
> You need more before you start.

Mentors felt at least at the outset in a subordinate role, their professionalism in doubt and with an unclear brief:

> It was a reactive role. I didn't know what I was supposed to be doing. What is it they wanted?

> It [*mentor training*] was grossly inappropriate. They were struggling to find what to do with us. It was almost an insult to our professionalism ... I kept expecting something to improve; I was made very welcome but it was a waste of my time. Perhaps they couldn't do anything else. What could they do?

A consequence was that decisions by mentors and schools were not based on an understanding of a joint perspective but only with an eye to their own context:

> We were able to think what was best for here. We constructed it as we liked. I haven't a clue about what [college] wants. They seem too distracted to think about things like that. They're busy implementing courses, worrying about timetabling.

Yet they still felt the gathering together of mentors was important and valuable. This last comment represents what most of them said was best about mentor training:

> I went three times. The first one I wished was earlier. J [her AT] had been here 6 weeks already . . . the main reason the training was good — it gave me confidence in what I was doing.

So the main plus point was that the sessions gave them opportunities to talk to other mentors and find out what they were doing. They identified similar problems and grievances, had then less of a feeling of isolation and gradually recognized and began to accept that they were all doing it differently and that this was all right. The problem was that this took time and meanwhile the course was passing by. It was only a few individuals in college who had initiated the course structure and fully understood the ways in which they believed partnership to be realized. They were, in the perception of the mentors, in the lead and could only share ideas through documentation, visits and mentor sessions. Those from schools who had been involved in the development of the course were not the ones on the whole who were actually working with the ATs. But the crucial point is that school staff were starting from a different standpoint altogether from those in college and perceptions are built from prior experience. Teachers in schools generally only have knowledge of teacher training based on their own experiences. These teachers had trained to earlier models. As they pointed out:

> I trained 20 years ago and things have changed.

> I only know what I did at college 21 years ago.

Their previous knowledge of current training was through students on a few weeks' teaching practice with a tutor visiting once a week and curriculum and professional studies taking place outside school. Now they wanted to make connections with the other parts of the course and expected to be told what to do within a framework of *content*. They wanted to know what was happening in curriculum studies so they could tie in their curriculum content in school. This would be, however, a reverse of the intention for the course to be *led* by the school experience. Alternative ways of understanding the training only began to grow out of the mentors' experience of the AT course itself. But as one of them said:

I felt I hadn't had the initial guidance. I needed more structure. Was I doing the right thing?

The feeling of the mentors — that they were working within a framework they did not fully understand — was sharpened by the way in which they failed to see the training as an integrated whole:

The two parts weren't really integrated. There was progression in school, not in college. I don't think I felt part of a team, I was too far away.

They felt they were working in isolation, not as a part of an overall team. Even the mentors' group, with members looking to their school context for promotion, was apt to change:

We met other mentors in isolation from anyone else. I never felt a part of anything except the mentors' group and they changed. Generally mentors were up and coming so they up and went.

Mentors relied largely on the ATs themselves to keep them in touch with what else was happening for them in the course:

T [the AT] did her best to keep me informed.

I used to ask J [the AT] a lot what was going on . . . we were not told what they were covering.

I didn't know what she was doing at [college] in advance; only what M [her AT] told me.

So, there was apparently no true realization of the partnership envisaged at the planning stage of the course and this feeling of separateness was unrelieved by documentation or mentor training sessions. They were anxious to make their contribution integrate with the whole, yet with lack of information and no vision of a whole, they were finding this very difficult:

I needed to know what [college] was going to do. We need things in black and white.
We plan ahead so we need to know *when*. We could have chatted about what was going on at [college] if I knew in advance. In the end you work on feedback.

I think the parts were separate. I didn't know enough of what was going on. It was too difficult to link in with. There were no school tasks to go back with.

127

> She [her AT] regards days in [college] as separate. I never met any tutors. It was never suggested that we should. I don't know how tutors evolved what they did. I suspect none of the tutors met each other. We were not aware of them and their problems.

Assessment

School representatives, as well as college and external members, made up the assessment board which oversaw both written and practical work, but the actual marking of assignments was done by college staff. Written reports of practical teaching was done by school staff, with input from the visiting tutor. Assessment was through the four written assignments and two prolonged periods of overall responsibility for a class: 'teaching practices' (TPs) as they were invariably referred to. Mentors were not involved in planning or marking assignments. The two TPs were organized by the schools usually in conjunction with the ATs themselves and approved by the college tutor. The first TP, of three weeks, was usually organized in another school. These schools were often schools with experience of ATs; sometimes a straightforward swap was organized. On occasion they were schools which did not have ATs. The mentors generally worked quite closely with the class teacher in setting up the practice, but there was a large variation in how much the mentor was involved during the practice. It was much harder during a TP where the AT was in another school for the mentor to keep such close contact. But even where the TP took place in the same school as they usually did for the six-week second practice, mentors worried about the resulting loss of contact time with their ATs. It meant that ATs were sometimes working with teachers who had an even less clear idea about the nature of the course; this certainly was true of other staff in schools who weren't familiar with ATs; and that the mentor's function of monitoring the AT's experience was weakened.

The college tutor came in no more often during this time so the ATs could be said to be less supported by college than the usual style PGCE one-year students who were likely to get a visit about once a week, but also removed from their other possible support, the mentor. This did not prove a problem where things were going smoothly, where ATs or class teachers or mentors or all of these felt confident, but it became clear that it was not a set up which satisfactorily dealt with problems if they did occur. For example, the TP of one AT which apparently was going smoothly was not identified as needing help until very late on in the practice, by which time it was necessary to extend the practice in order to make a fair assessment. Aims and expectations were either not clear to all the school staff involved or there was a reluctance to acknowledge difficulties in this assessed practical teaching.

Although the course handbook suggested that it was not appropriate to talk of TP as a separate issue from their teaching performance over the two years, the focus for assessment was on the final TP: a less than satisfactory performance on this meant the possible failure of the student. How could it be that an AT who had been progressing apparently satisfactorily through the course could find themselves in danger of failing at the last ditch and with the prospect of an extended teaching practice? The fact was, that the work they did in schools apart from TPs could not be regarded as for the purpose of assessment. If that had been so, the mentors would be in a far more difficult situation with regard to the conflict between their role as supporter and assessor. But it meant that at the point of assessment, ATs could be in a weaker position than the traditional PGCE student finding less support from college which was not compensated for by support in school.

The Professional Tutor

The function of the overall coordinator, the professional tutor, was seen as crucial. He was the one person who would maintain contact with all involved in the course and the person who provided a central focus for both ATs and teaching team, including mentors. He would have particularly regular contact with the ATs themselves at college sessions and tutorials and was to keep a record of the school experience of each AT. This was to ensure the structure of the experience was wide and satisfying each individual AT's needs while at the same time operating a form of quality control. However, the ATs' main problems centred round a confusion of status; where they felt their loyalty lay, the source of control and the holders of responsibility for them (Whiting and Hannan, 1993).

What is clear from what they said was that they felt the lack of integration in their course. It largely failed to produce for them a complete experience and ultimately they felt their loyalty to be with their schools. Initially the school, and the mentor in particular, may have been unclear about their role. However, except in the one case where there was a complete breakdown in the relationship between AT and school, the effect of a joint working through the AT's needs meant that the school experience was the central one, with the possibility of an understood purpose and structure. This was usually achieved almost solely through the mentor, but where relationships between AT and mentor was less than ideal, or where mentors were changed during the course, other members of staff and in particular head teachers performed this function. It meant that ATs too, were in control of their learning. This was fine where ATs were confident and able or where they felt they had a good support structure. It was commented on by the professional tutor that those strong ATs who had been unlucky with their mentors had succeeded in spite of them, but where weaker ATs were unlucky, there was a danger of them foundering. They would not have the same confidence to take control and take help and support from where it was available.

The ATs generally said they had enjoyed the course and that it had prepared them well for working in schools. They were full of praise for many of the people who had worked with them. But they were all too aware of weaknesses. They valued the basic structure of the course which enabled them to be working in schools for a large percentage of their time and to become a real part of those schools, not a visitor. But it seemed they felt that the onus was on them, ultimately, to be responsible to make the best of the course. They felt that the professional tutor was the one person they should have been able to look to for complete support but they came to recognize that he was also expected to give support to those who may sometimes have conflicting interests with their's: school and college staff. Some examples of their comments illustrate this:

> Occasionally I felt the need for more support from college. I didn't feel college felt responsible.

> He soft soaps so doesn't tread on people's toes — why come in?

> Still not getting enough support [towards end of course] . . . in the first year you feel you're drowning.

re TP:

> I got no help from [the college tutor]. I had to sort it out. I needed an arbitrator.

The roles of the professional tutor were then to an extent at odds with each other. He couldn't be seen to 'take sides', but who then would be the AT's ultimate support within a course delivered from so many different directions?

The Professional Journal

This was to be 'an ongoing record of professional activity and reflection' (as described in the course handbook for mentors) and was partly intended to help ATs monitor their own development. But in its use as a document on which discussions with mentor and professional tutor could focus, it was also intended to function as a source of shared knowledge for the three of them, thus making it a potentially invaluable tool for partnership. But the journal was never mentioned to me by ATs or mentors as a central pivot to mentor sessions. There was a lack of clarity about the ownership of the journal, and it was therefore used in a more superficial way than it might have been, owing to a worry about who might read it. My impression was that it did not always function in as full a way as the planning team hoped it would, and that both ATs and mentors were either aware of this, or failed to see the importance of the journal. Time seems to be a factor and also a failure on the part of ATs to see the importance of evaluation, the possible sharing of reflection and monitoring of progression through the journal. For instance:

I didn't do loads of evaluations. I'm not a student. I do brief individual lesson plans, no detailed reflection. I've no time. I'm more involved in the school as a whole.

One AT went so far as to say: 'The file was a farce.' Similar comments may no doubt be found about files of students on traditional teaching practice, but the professional journal was to have been far more central to the monitoring of a school-based training which was student led.

It seems, then, that the structures set up for partnership did not function in such a way as to provide for wholly effective integration of the courses as far as the mentors and ATs were concerned. Furthermore, it is difficult to see how they could have performed this function for college staff either given the large number of personnel involved in covering the whole of the primary curriculum. Documentation specifically for college staff in line with the hand-books for ATs and mentors did not exist. Only core staff were involved in planning meetings (and a large part of those were concerned with timetabling). Curriculum tutors revealed that they were at a bit of a loss knowing what to do in such a short time and often gave a slightly diluted version of their PGCE course. The ATs commented that the best sessions were given by tutors who really thought about their particular needs and responded to their concerns. But some tutors admitted that they did not really know what the AT course was about and they had no knowledge of the ATs' situations in school. They only knew the number of hours they had to deliver. In the passing on of the concept of the course as a whole it became the victim of a sort of 'Chinese whispers' effect emanating from the original course planners and then out through the course director through planning meetings, mentor training sessions and the professional studies tutor to school and college staff. Every time the message was passed on it became less clear and prone to misunderstanding and alteration.

Away from mentors and core subject staff even the use of documentation to establish the nature of the course and therefore the function of particular components within it began to diminish. Mentors found difficulty with grasping the nature of the course but there were many others who relied on word of mouth, both in college and school. Those in school, apart from the mentors, did not even have the opportunity of attending any sort of meetings. College staff had opportunities which were not always taken up, mainly on account of time. One of the subject staff I interviewed had only been told that he was to deliver these sessions two weeks previously.

I asked college staff and mentors about the agendas to which they worked and their model of the teacher. In fact, the mentors I asked were quite broadly in agreement about what they hoped for in a class teacher; they talked of enthusiastic teachers who liked children and could manage the class and curriculum. However, they often referred back to their own training and were adamant about the importance of a theoretical base on which to build. They recognized that things may have changed since they qualified, and that it was important for newly trained teachers to bring in an understanding of new ideas which were borne out of the study of research and critical reading and they didn't see themselves as being in a position to provide that. It was this model which provided the agenda for their work with the ATs. On being asked to articulate it, they were sometimes quite surprised to find that they did have a clear model and that it could be articulated with some feeling. It was for them maybe a realization or confirmation that the sheer practical slog of teaching had not rid them of their passion for the job and an acknowledgment that it was an intellectual as well as practical one. In fact, many of the mentors said that this was a real plus point; having an AT meant that they were continually questioning their practice. But this was not something which was shared with the other members of the course team; particularly the college tutors. And the mentors were not knowledgable of any college model:

> I probably don't know. I hope the same. Aims were not made explicit. College didn't interview me!

> In an ideal world I would know more about college.

> I've no idea.

> . . . not articulated . . . I'm not sure what their perception is . . . there is a gulf in understanding . . . (*between school and college*).

There was no articulated college model. In fact, I was aware of the college identifying a disparity of aims, focus and certainly of style between members of staff. It was difficult for staff in the faculty to attend all meetings so there would be a lack of scope for planning 'teams', teaching 'teams', certainly the college as a whole, to discuss models of the teacher or teacher training.

Changes that have come about in ITT over the last few years are largely in response to external, not internal, demands and discussions within institutions tended to focus on how they were going to deal with them in order to stay in business. The AT course tutor acknowledged the lack of explicit and articulated aims but felt that they probably did all share a broadly similar model. Certainly on being asked about this, tutors answered in similar ways. The word 'reflection' was a common one in the college's PGCE one year and AT courses, starting with the Dean's introductory welcome in their first week in college. The course handbooks and the submission document stress the need for thinking teachers and the scope of the AT course in easing the links between theory and practice, 'realised through a growing ability to make sense of experience in schools'.

The submission document also stressed the importance of the student centrality to his/her own learning process. The inference, then, is that the reflection, at least at the beginning of the student experience as 'learner teacher', is grounded very firmly in the student. It will be based on and drawn from the student's own experience, firstly that which they bring with them and secondly their personal interaction with the course. This will provide the way to make sense of what is happening in their schools to make a very personal and idiosyncratic learning experience. In interviews, college tutors further stressed the different experiences which students bring to the course with them, and thus the unsuitability for a structured content-led course that can be applied as a formula to the whole cohort. Added to this is a need for autonomy for themselves. That is not to say that staff were unconcerned about the application of this philosophy and its consequences for entitlement and quality control. Several of the PGCE teaching team held a meeting about this very problem during the second year of my research which was inspired by a paper by the PGCE course director. This discussion emphasized the difficulties, even impossibility of real coordination between staff who teach on a course with discrete elements like the PGCE (and, *ipso facto*, the AT course). With the fragile balance of autonomy and sharing within the college needing continual review it is perhaps a likelihood that sharing perceptions as far as schools is going to be even more difficult.

Implications for Primary Courses

The Articled Teacher course involved small numbers of students, small numbers of schools and therefore small numbers of school staff. In the course I studied attempts were made to incorporate structures which would provide a coherent learning experience for each individual AT while ensuring an entitlement of quality. There was no doubting the efforts of those most closely involved to ensure the course did deliver this; indeed it largely fell upon a very small number of people to do so and one in particular. But with the time and resources available it was never going to be possible to make a real 'team' and the documentation as it stood failed to perform the task of providing for shared understandings. There was no scope to ensure that personnel within schools as well as college were in a cognitive position to take an equal and appropriate part in the team. This would have meant prospective mentors working together with college staff in a way to develop their shared understandings of the structures and functions of teacher training today before they accepted ATs into their classrooms. If this proved so difficult when a course involved such a small number of students and schools, an acknowledgment of the problems faced when we try to give schools a greater responsibility must be made in relation to other courses.

Despite any shortcomings, it would be true to say that the general feeling from almost all the ATs was that they had enjoyed their course, that they were glad that they had chosen this route rather than the more traditional one year course and were sure they were better prepared for teaching than they otherwise would have been. Headteachers and mentors, too, remained enthusiastic about the idea of students training in schools. However, I also studied the one year PGCE students who were following a traditional course. They, too, spoke positively about their course, and in general had fewer criticisms; these tended to focus on particular — and as a part of the course, small — components of their overall experience rather than on the whole. If students have trained in a particular way, they have no other experience on which to make a comparative judgment.

The Articled Teacher scheme ended with the arrival of the new legislation; as one of many routes to Qualified Teacher Status, its practical arrangements may have suited particular students. The new arrangements for primary training only brought a modest increase in the time primary students spend in schools compared to secondary in acknowledgment of the breadth of their curriculum studies. But the same push is there for a sharing of responsibility, an equalling of the partners and opportunities for schools to take the lead. Any change in the balance of responsibility towards schools in primary training must begin to involve those who were not previously involved or involve those who were in different ways. The team will grow. But it is only this integration between partners, that involves shared perceptions that have been articulated and understood, that then leads to a truly shared responsibility and which could result in a preparation for teachers that uses school experience in really profitable ways. A critical and detailed view has to be taken of partnerships. Unless adequate measures are devised to involve schools and HEIs together in ways in which they can really take a meaningful and balanced role, making the most of the growing partnerships, then the changes will be worse than useless. They may in fact lead to a preparation for teaching that will inevitably lack coherence. We risk asking the impossible from those working in schools, providing less than we owe to our teachers in training, and thus ultimately, to our children.

References

BARRETT, E., BARTON, L., FURLONG, J., GALVIN, C., MILES, S. and WHITTY, G. (1992) *Initial Teacher Education in England and Wales: A Topography*, London, Goldsmith's College.

DEPARTMENT OF EDUCATION AND SCIENCE (1989) 'Articled Teacher Pilot Scheme: Invitation to Bid for Funding.' Letter to LEAs and HEIs, 27 June, London, DES.

DEPARTMENT FOR EDUCATION (1992) *Initial Teacher Training (Secondary Phase), Circular 9/92*, London, DFE.

DEPARTMENT FOR EDUCATION (1993) *The Initial Training of Primary School Teachers: New Criteria for Course Approval, Circular 14/93*, London, DFE.

WHITING, C. and HANNAN, A. (1993) 'Never Mind the Quality, Feel the Width.' Paper delivered at the annual BERA conference, Stirling University, September.

Part Three

Professionalism

9 Teachers' Professional Perspectives: Continuity and Change

Marilyn Osborn, Dorothy Abbot, Patricia Broadfoot, Paul Croll and Andrew Pollard

This chapter reports on findings from the first and second phases of the PACE study carried out between 1990 and 1993 concerning the way in which the multiple innovations resulting from the Education Reform Act were impacting upon teachers' professional perspectives and responses to change. The data presented here are drawn from three rounds of interviews with a national sample of teachers in eight regions of England and three rounds of more intensive 'classroom study' interviews with the nine teachers who were currently teaching our PACE 'study children'. A detailed discussion of the research design can be found elsewhere (Pollard *et al.*, 1994).

Teachers are clearly at the centre of all educational provision and the implementation of any new and externally driven policy will inevitably be mediated by the enthusiasm, skills, and practical constraints which characterize every teacher's daily practice. In the case of the introduction of a National Curriculum and national assessment, the policy changes imposed on teachers have been particularly problematic. Much of the thinking behind the reforms has stemmed from a very different political ideology from that which has characterized educational policy making and practice in England in the recent past. Teachers have been asked to change their daily practice in some quite fundamental ways. They have also been asked to change in ways that for many of them are in conflict with deeply held professional convictions concerning how best to provide for the learning of young children.

Teachers' professional ideologies and their beliefs about classroom practice have complex origins, deriving from a blend of personal biography, training, professional experience, classroom constraints, and national cultural and professional traditions (Pollard, 1985; Nias, 1989; Acker, 1990). The research evidence suggests that, for all the above reasons, prior to the implementation of the Education Reform Act, primary teachers in England saw their role as characterized by teacher autonomy, responsiveness to children's needs, and responsibility for a wide-ranging and diffuse set of goals and priorities which included not only academic objectives, but also the personal and social development of the child. This also encompassed responsibilities inside and outside the classroom including extra-curricular and sometimes even community activities, all aspects of school relationships, and accountability to parents, colleagues and the headteacher. Although, in many ways, teachers were constrained by these responsibilities, they nevertheless believed strongly in their autonomy and saw it as central to their 'extended' role that they be able to define and decide for themselves both what they would teach and how they would teach it (Broadfoot and Osborn, 1988; 1993).

In the PACE study, one of our concerns was to investigate how far the sweeping and comprehensive change introduced by the Education Reform Act was affecting these deeply held beliefs about the nature of teaching. We were particularly concerned with how teachers perceived their role to be changing and the extent to which they felt that their professional autonomy and personal fulfilment were threatened by the changes. Related to this was the question of how the changes were affecting teachers' relationships with the children in their class, their perceptions of their classroom practice, and their professional relationships with colleagues.

At a more theoretical level we were concerned with notions of increasing professionalization as opposed to notions of 'intensification' and 'deskilling' (Lawn and Ozga, 1981; Apple, 1986). The argument is succinctly put by Andy Hargreaves (1994) in terms of competing explanations. On the one hand, teachers' roles may be seen to be extended through 'more experiences of whole school development, involvement in collaborative cultures . . . experience of teacher leadership, commitment to continuous improvement, and engagement with processes of extensive school-wide change. In these accounts, teaching is becoming more complex and more skilled.' On the other hand, the intensification thesis is that 'teachers' work is portrayed as becoming routinised and deskilled . . . increasingly controlled by prescribed programs, mandated curricula, and step-by-step methods of instruction.' In addition 'teachers' work has become increasingly intensified, with teachers expected to respond to greater pressures and comply with multiple innovations . . .' (Hargreaves, 1994, p. 118).

In the sections that follow, this chapter investigates the extent to which the teachers in our sample saw themselves as moving from a professional to a technician role or, alternatively, the extent to which they felt able to mediate the changes imposed upon them in order to move towards a new and different type of professionalism.

Changes in Teachers' Perceptions of Work and Role

In the three rounds of interviews between 1990 and 1993 with the eighty-eight classroom teachers in our wider sample, we asked teachers to talk in an open-ended way about their role and how it might have changed as a result of the introduction of the National Curriculum and assessment. Nearly two-thirds of the teachers (65 per cent) felt that their role as a teacher had changed to some extent and, for some, these changes were fairly profound.

Although many teachers felt positive about the overall structure provided by the National Curriculum, for the majority of teachers in 1990 the impact of the changes on their work and role was perceived to be largely negative. They mentioned more administration (47 per cent) and increased planning (39 per cent), a loss of spontaneity and child-responsiveness in their teaching (23 per cent), increased stress and anxiety (25 per cent), a strong sense of the imposition of external priorities (20 per cent), and a feeling of loss of autonomy and of creativity (13 per cent). As one teacher put it:

> I'm just more stressed now. I feel pulled in different directions and I feel the need to fulfil attainment targets and to cover the core subjects as a constant unspoken pressure. The relaxed atmosphere I used to have in my class is gone. I can't spend so much time with individual children and I don't feel able to respond in a spontaneous way to some initiative introduced by the children. I no longer have the luxury of being responsive and creative.

These strongly negative feelings were counter-balanced to a limited extent by the positive feelings of those who saw the changes as having the effect of focusing and confirming their role or of leading them towards closer cooperation with colleagues.

By 1992 and 1993, a number of these changes were perceived by teachers to have intensified, in particular the time spent on paperwork and administration, the level of stress and anxiety experienced, and the sense of externally imposed priorities on the teacher. As one Year 2 teacher in 1992 put it:

> It's just a different pace. There's a pressure and a feeling that you're never doing enough ... You look at the documents and you think, 'How can I possibly fulfil all these demands? How can I fit all this in?' It's just overwhelming sometimes. You feel you're just going through a wheel. You're desperately covering stuff because you must give an assessment for it, and you think, 'This is just not what it's about. Learning is not about this and this is not what it should be like.'

A Year 3 teacher, in 1993, argued:

> There certainly are more constraints, more pressure on you to produce results, having something to show, some evidence that the children have done it.

A number of these teachers expressed a feeling that the things which were of central importance to them in teaching were under attack, but they also asserted that they would defend them no matter what. As one teacher argued in 1990:

> I am not prepared to become somebody walking round with a checksheet, and I will fight it . . . I think my place is with the children, making a relationship with them. It's not fiddling around with bits of paper or spending all my time talking with their parents.

It was striking that, when asked about their own strengths as a teacher, 75 per cent in 1990 emphasized affective skills such as being good at developing relationships with children, colleagues and parents. Only 34 per cent of teachers mentioned classroom management skills as one of their strengths. Yet at the same time, 48 per cent perceived classroom management skills to be of increasing importance under the National Curriculum. It is not surprising, therefore, that nearly one quarter of the sample (22 per cent) felt that their strengths and skills were being eroded by the National Curriculum. Thus one teacher argued that to be a good teacher:

> It's got to be first of all an ability to have a good relationship with children, to be able to encourage, cajole them into working hard, to be lively, full of fun, to provide a stimulating environment where they want to come to school and they want to learn. Some of one's spontaneity gets dampened by the rigorous demands of the National Curriculum. Some of the very special times in a primary classroom are when you just respond spontaneously to children's ideas. There is not much time or scope for that now.

By 1992, an increasing proportion of teachers (50 per cent compared with 22 per cent) felt that their strengths and skills were being eroded by the National Curriculum. This perception of 'deskilling' continued into 1993.

Into this description of professional concern, we should note that, throughout the period of the research, there remained a proportion of teachers (around one-fifth) who saw the National Curriculum as complementing and enhancing their skills and strengths or providing the opportunity to develop them further. As one teacher put it:

> The National Curriculum has been useful in giving us targets and a framework to work within. In a way, it's a bit reassuring. It gives me a focus and another reason for doing things. It helps me feel as though I'm on the right track and releases me to work out new ways of teaching.

These teachers felt positively about processes of reviewing and reflecting on their practice which the National Curriculum had made necessary. They also believed that it had raised awareness among teachers of the importance of providing progression and continuity for children. Similarly, the need to read more widely and to collaborate more closely with other teachers was perceived as an enhancement of their professionalism. It is significant that this proportion of teachers persisted in seeing positive outcomes for their teaching, indicating that there were still strong glimmerings of hope of a new 'emergent' professionalism deriving from teachers' handling of the changes.

To summarize, while there had been a noticeable shift towards perceptions of deskilling amongst teachers by 1992 and 1993, some teachers still felt empowered by the changes, even while suffering from the results of curriculum overload.

Professional Autonomy and Personal Fulfilment

Although at the onset of the implementation of the Education Reform Act it was apparent that the imposition of a National Curriculum would reduce individual teachers' freedom to choose the 'content' of the curriculum, it was not so clear to what extent it might affect their freedom over how they taught. For example, it was argued by David Hargreaves (1988) that having less responsibility for deciding curriculum content would release teachers' energies to engage in developing new pedagogic approaches. Others, however, have argued that external pressures would compel teachers to change their teaching methods (Osborn and Broadfoot, 1990).

Nearly half the teachers interviewed in 1992 felt a loss of autonomy in their pedagogic decision making following the advent of the National Curriculum, and saw it to some extent eroding professional judgment. A large number of teachers talked of a loss of freedom and creativity in their teaching, of feeling increasingly like 'a machine for delivering a prescribed curriculum', as well as the loss of a career structure, and of the feeling of doing a valued and worthwhile job. This feeling continued in 1993, yet at the same time a significant minority of teachers in all three years continued to speak of the positive effect of having a structure and guidelines to work within. This, they felt, released them to be creative in the way they worked with individual children rather than worry about whether they had covered what should be covered. As one Year 2 teacher, in 1992, put it:

> I feel that at least now there is some guideline as to what you should have achieved in the amounts of time that you have had with children ... Up till now I have always felt that in teaching I'm not doing enough. I could always be doing more, which I think every teacher feels. Things were so open that you could never feel you had done a good job.

Such feelings of uncertainty and anxiety among primary teachers prior to the implementation of the National Curriculum were not uncommon. Indeed, several previous researchers have pointed to the insecurity experienced by individual teachers about whether they were covering the right things or whether they ought to have been doing more (Nias, 1989; Broadfoot and Osborn, 1988).

Another teacher in the PACE study talked of the 'vulnerability' of teachers prior to the National Curriculum when:

> You had very little framework, you were very much left to yourself to decide what's to do and I think that is quite hairy really when you look back.

As a result of this previous uncertainty, the majority of teachers (68 per cent) welcomed the structure and guidelines introduced by the National Curriculum, although not its over-prescriptive nature, the rapid pace at which the changes were introduced, nor the sheer volume of work and pressure which resulted. As one teacher of a mixed Year 3/4 class argued, in 1993:

> We're more accountable for what we're doing now than in the past. We don't have the same personal autonomy we once had. At the same time our role has been more clearly defined now. It's probably a clearer route through to professionalism now than in the past. We've got a clearer idea of what we are being asked to do.

When we talked in more depth to our nine classroom study teachers over the three rounds of interviews between 1990 and 1993, it was clear that for some of these teachers, the satisfactions derived from teaching were ebbing away while the frustrations were increasing. For example, in 1992 the Year 2 teacher in one of our classroom study schools, St Anne's, felt very strongly:

> I can see no bright areas of the job whatsoever. Even the simple pleasures of seeing children achieve things. It's more a case of, 'Oh well, I can cross that off my list, mark that box,' and it's not a personal development shared between two people. It's just another task out of the way.

At that time this teacher felt that he would not now choose teaching as a job:

> . . . which is a shame because at times I've enjoyed it. I've realized that I'm good at it, and I've sort of found out what I was meant to be, and it's very disheartening that I'm not allowed to enjoy what I'm doing any more. But, having said that, you know, when I wake up in the morning and think, 'Would I rather go to work in a library, would I rather go to work in an office, would I rather go to work in a school?' school comes down last on the list.

However, by 1993 this teacher, who had moved up with his class as they became Year 3 children, was beginning to feel slightly more relaxed in his teaching and more confident that he could deliver the National Curriculum in a way that fitted with his professional concerns:

Although my approach to teaching has become more formalized, structured and strictured, I find I am beginning to be able to relax more since last year. By becoming more thematic I've been able to cover a lot of attainment targets. In science, for example, we did 'changes'. I managed to cover language, science, geography, maths and cookery, but the National Curriculum doesn't tell you you can do this. You have to think it out. There's no specific advice on what can be done thematically.

As the National Curriculum became more accepted, two of the other classroom teachers interviewed in 1992 also found that the sense of constraint they had experienced had begun to lessen as they became more familiar with the National Curriculum and had the confidence to deviate from it where they felt it appropriate. For example, the Lawnside Year 2 teacher argued:

Now, I don't necessarily think, 'Oh, I shouldn't do that.' I don't feel the restraint in that sense now. I don't feel that it's wrong to go off onto something which maybe has been inspired by the children, whereas before [i.e., in the first few months of the National Curriculum] I used to think, 'I don't have time to do that' . . . I'm not so frightened at going off on a tangent now.

For this teacher, rather than a lessening of enjoyment and fulfilment in work, there had merely been a change in the gains she felt. She now derived satisfaction from working out new creative ideas for meeting the National Curriculum requirements.

Personally, I find it very stimulating because I look at documents and I look at the things that are required and I try to think of ideas and ways of doing things that meet the requirement . . . I find it very challenging to work within a frame but at the same time I want to be free to go outside it to some degree if I think it's worthwhile.

A second teacher, working in the inner city context of Meadway Infant School also argued that:

Before, I felt our goals were becoming woolly and that we had run out of steam with the child-centred approach . . . As long as I can continue my way of working and implement the National Curriculum as I see fit . . . Sometimes it's [the National Curriculum] easy to assimilate and sometimes difficult. It [the National Curriculum], as a whole, is welcome but it's hard work.

These teachers' responses suggest again that some teachers were gaining the confidence to interpret and actively mediate the National Curriculum in ways that suited their own professional ends. They were struggling constructively with their work overload. In rationalizing and prioritizing their goals, they were making decisions which enabled them to cope creatively, *albeit* selectively, with the changes.

Collaboration with Colleagues

When we asked our classroom study teachers how the reforms were influencing their relationships with colleagues, most confirmed that there had been considerable changes in the way they worked both with colleagues and with the headteacher.

Three key themes in teachers' conversation about working with colleagues were those of 'cooperation', 'support', and 'awareness'. All twenty-seven teachers over the three rounds of classroom studies felt that, as a result of the National Curriculum, they were cooperating and working more closely with colleagues and this was usually seen to be a positive outcome, and to give 'a feeling of ownership and sharing. It makes us feel that we are planning towards the common good.' At the same time, they were far more aware of the work colleagues were doing in their classrooms and of the need to avoid repetition and to ensure continuity and progression for children. As the Year 1 teacher at Kenwood put it:

> Now we have a lot more staff meetings when curriculum leaders talk about curriculum areas. We all go on the latest courses . . . We have inservice days regularly. There is an increase in working together. Last year we visited each other in classrooms and we ask each other for help a lot more often now.

In one of the schools, collaboration between teachers had often taken the form of supporting one another to resist aspects of the National Curriculum, which were felt to be inappropriate for inner city children. These teachers, with the tacit support of the head, saw themselves as 'conspirators' working together to implement the National Curriculum selectively in a way that they felt would protect the children and avoid overload. For example, a decision had been made in 1992 to ignore the history and geography programmes of study except where they 'fitted naturally' into topics planned for the core subjects.

There was considerable evidence from the classroom studies and from the larger round of teacher interviews in 1992 and 1993 that teachers were moving towards a more 'collaborative professional' stance, although this mainly involved a substantial increase in planning together and had not yet begun to take the form of shared teaching or more subject specialism. However, there are some limitations on viewing the whole school planning approach as a move towards real collegiality (Wallace, 1991; Warren Little, 1987). Enforced or 'contrived' collegiality can sometimes lead to a lack of ownership in the planned work and hence a loss of interest and spontaneity (Stone, 1993; Hargreaves, 1992). On the whole, however, most of the teachers welcomed the increase in collaboration and partnership with colleagues and felt that it added a new dimension to their professionalism. It would not be putting the case too strongly to argue that there was a definite move towards a more 'collaborative professionalism' (Hoyle, 1992).

Perceptions of Change in Classroom Practice

In our three larger rounds of interviews with eighty-eight teachers across the country, we asked about teachers' classroom practice and how this was being affected by the National Curriculum and assessment.

It was particularly striking that the vast majority of teachers, over 70 per cent, believed they adopted 'mixed' teaching methods. Even in 1990, only 20 per cent subscribed exclusively to forms of 'child-centred' pedagogy, a fact that somewhat belies the sensationalism about progressivism which has sometimes filled the English media in recent years. By 1992 there was a significant fall in the number of teachers declaring themselves to have child-centred approaches and a corresponding increase in those who described themselves as 'traditional' or 'formal'.

When we asked the teachers to clarify these descriptions of their classroom practice, there was a dramatic change apparent between 1990 and 1992. For instance, there was a fall in teachers mentioning forms of integrated day from 29 per cent to 8 per cent, and a rise in teachers mentioning whole class teaching from 4 per cent to 29 per cent. Both these changes are highly significant statistically. A continuity in emphasis on group work and on the curriculum 'basics' was also notable, whilst there was no perceived decrease in the prominence of topic work. The latter finding somewhat contradicts the patterns found through our classroom observation but this may reflect continuing attempts to provide integrated work despite the difficulty of actually doing it.

It was quite clear that these changes were a direct result of the education reforms. Over 85 per cent of the teachers interviewed in 1992 attributed them to the introduction of the National Curriculum whilst 55 per cent identified new assessment requirements. Only 12 per cent spoke of other changes in school and just 3 per cent mentioned personal sources of change. One teacher whose response was fairly typical cited particularly the demands made by the National Curriculum in terms of classroom management:

> I'm finding that the demand of organizing and managing the children has changed a tremendous amount. I'm trying to maximize on time.

This perceived change in teaching approach and philosophy was also reflected in changes in classroom practice. Most teachers (87 per cent) felt that the advent of the National Curriculum had resulted in significant changes to their working day and for 38 per cent in 1990 and no less than 62 per cent in 1992 these changes were seen as major. The most important areas of change involved more time spent on assessment-related record keeping, with over 60 per cent mentioning this in both rounds of interviews, and more time spent on planning and preparation, with this being mentioned by over 40 per cent on both occasions.

Even in 1990 there was certainly evidence for the 'intensification' of teachers' work (in the sense of chronic work overload) (Apple, 1986; Lawn and Ozga, 1981), with many teachers either having to work longer hours or having to work in a more concentrated, less relaxed way in order to get through their workload. There was a general feeling of being swamped by change. 'Too much has happened too quickly,' was the way many teachers put it. While they were developing new ways of working, particularly in the area of record keeping and assessment, more information would arrive which superseded it, meaning that they had wasted their time. For example, keeping up with the documentation which accompanied the National Curriculum was seen by most as 'simply overwhelming'. 'Far too much to assimilate. I have just had to give up on it for the time being,' as one teacher put it.

Many teachers expressed frustration and even anger over the amount of time which was now demanded by government requirements for record keeping and assessment. There were fears that this was beginning to 'take over from teaching', that the heavy burden demanded in time and effort left too little time for planning, for responding to children, for display work, for all the things which were seen by many as 'real teaching'.

In 1992, the pressure on teachers was clearly immense and nearly 25 per cent were beginning to change their teaching methods in order to be able to cope. However, the need to spend such major amounts of time on assessment and on meetings appeared to have declined, presumably because teachers felt that they had come to terms to some extent with the demands of the Standard Assessment Tasks (SATs) and the National Curriculum. One teacher argued:

> I have to put in far more hours than the 1265 hours designated in order to fulfil the needs of the National Curriculum and really the 1265 hours which we're supposed to spend on things in addition to preparation and marking is really extremely questionable. Most teachers are now getting up very early in the morning and finishing very late at night. As a class teacher you need to be in school by a quarter to eight and you need to not leave school before five or six each evening and in addition to that you need to do between two and three hours of work at home and you're still not finished. I certainly spend, I would say, about five or six hours at the weekend, so the 1265 hours really does not address that at all. Because even with doing that amount of work most class teachers feel very much under stress and unable to cope with the workload.

In 1993, this tightening of teacher control was even more in evidence. As the Year 3 teacher at Orchard described it:

I'm far more dictatorial in my approach. There's definitely less sort of 'laissez faire', I would say . . . in the classroom, and I do state far more what the children must do rather than giving them the opportunity to choose and develop activities as they would want to do. I think that means that I'm putting far more of my own emphasis on what they should learn and it's *not* coming from them. Now a lot of the children are not rebelling at all against that but with assessment, particularly, I've felt that they've really got a little bit bogged down with worksheets, photocopied material and that sort of thing and it becomes more difficult to find an alternative approach. I now have very much more teacher speaking, child listening and regurgitating what was said.

We thus have clear signs, from teacher accounts, of tighter classroom structures, tighter teacher control and heavier workloads in response to the National Curriculum and assessment. In the next section we consider how the tightening of 'frame' and the increased pressure experienced by teachers was felt to be influencing teacher relationships with the children in their class.

Relationships between Teachers and Children

In 1990 only 31 per cent of the teachers felt that the National Curriculum had a negative effect on teachers' relationships with children. By 1992 this proportion had increased to 58 per cent, partly as a result of the impact of the introduction of national assessment, but in particular because of a perceived increase in pressure on teachers' time leaving them less relaxed and less able to spend time responding to children. Most teachers had strong feelings about the importance of defending their relationship with the children, feelings which were closely tied to their own sense of identity as primary teachers (Nias, 1989).

Time and again they mentioned the National Curriculum as a definite pressure on the relaxed relationships they had formerly had with children. Contributing to this was the loss of fun and responsiveness to children in their teaching and the feeling of a need to justify everything in terms of the attainment targets. In 1990 one teacher argued:

There isn't anything that you do now that you don't feel, 'Can you actually justify this, what educational guide are the children getting out of it, how can you tie it up with an attainment target or programme of study?' all that sort of thing. Or can you, like you used to be able to, just do it for the pure fun and enjoyment of it?

This feeling of pressure was almost universal amongst the teachers we interviewed. Closely related to this was a sense of loss of the close, affective ties many teachers had developed with the children in their class. As a teacher put it:

> I think there is a tendency to be so pressurized by the demands of the National Curriculum that there isn't so much time to spend discussing emotional and personal issues with the children. It's, 'Right, let's get on. Tell me about it later.' And those issues are just as important as the more academic issues . . . So much of the very nice aspects of being with the children have been lost. And I think the children feel it. I feel they feel very tired and pressurized at the end of the half term.

The feeling of stress and a loss of relaxed, enjoyable time with the children seemed, if anything, to have intensified between 1990 and 1993. As the Year 3 teacher at Audley Primary put it, in 1993:

> I think that you feel always that you've got to urge them on, that there's a big hurry involved because there's so much to get through and so little time, and therefore whereas you would have given them time, more time to carry on with something that they were deeply involved with and enthusiastic about, there's something at the back of your mind all the time saying, 'Oh well, we can only allow so many hours to do this, we've got to move on,' and therefore you can become . . . irritable, if you hurry, because some children are lagging behind and slowing things up. I think this happens subconsciously.

Such feelings were intensified where teachers felt there was a particularly strong conflict between the demands of the National Curriculum and the needs of the children. The Year One teacher at St Anne's working in a socially disadvantaged area in the North of England, felt a conflict between,

> . . . knowing the kind of work you should be doing and which the National Curriculum encompasses, and the restrictions imposed by the kind of children they are. I feel that I'm not able perhaps to take things as far as I would like, it has to be a very simple level, sometimes I'd like to take it one step further and I'm not able to do that.

Throughout the three-year period, there was evidence of a strong determination amongst teachers not to allow the changes to destroy their relationship with the children. As the Year 2 teacher at Valley put it:

> When I feel those frictions I lay off the National Curriculum. When I feel those I say, 'I don't care, we will do something completely different,' and I change my tack, and I go back to being Viv Jones, the 'proper' teacher and I don't care. Margaret [the head] backs me up on this. When I feel those tensions come back into the classroom I stand

back. I make an assessment, make a sensible judgment, and think, 'Enough's enough.'

In spite of the perceived pressures, the responses of these teachers expressed a determination to try to protect their relationship with the children and to mediate the demands of the reforms to acceptable professional ends.

Summary and Conclusions

The evidence presented here suggests that even at an early stage in the implementation of the reforms most teachers felt that they had to change their teaching approach, their classroom practice and their perception of their professional role in ways that they would not have chosen for themselves. This resulted in pressures from lack of time, an intensification of workload, and a loss of job satisfaction. By 1992 and 1993 there were increasing perceptions of a loss of autonomy and fulfilment in teaching. Teachers described themselves as feeling more controlled and less autonomous. Thus, on the face of it, the data appear to support the intensification thesis. However, this impression does not fully take into account teachers' capacity to take charge of events, and to mediate change rather than simply to respond to it. A significant minority of teachers felt that a new professionalism involving creative ways of working with individual children and of assessing them was possible provided they had the confidence to shape the imposed changes to more professionally acceptable ends. This emergent perception of a 'new professionalism' cannot simply be dismissed as 'false consciousness' on the part of teachers (Hargreaves, 1994).

Out of the unpromising beginnings represented by the imposition of a National Curriculum and assessment, some teachers had found creative ways of teaching and many had moved towards new ways of collaborating with colleagues. Often this was evident only at the planning stage of work and there were limits to its effectiveness, but it nevertheless represents an important move towards a new 'collaborative' mode of working.

About 20 per cent of the teachers we interviewed consistently saw some positive outcomes for their professionalism and for their teaching as a result of the reforms. We have called such teachers 'mediators' who were able to take ownership and control of the innovations and to work to develop new forms of practice in pedagogy and assessment while building on what they felt to be good about their existing practice. Some teachers saw particularly positive outcomes in terms of the emphasis placed by the National Curriculum on collaboration between teachers and on the need for teachers to reflect upon and review their practice. A number felt that the changes had helped to focus and confirm their role.

One Year 2 teacher argued that the National Curriculum released teachers from anxiety and vulnerability,

> ... because you've got a framework and you've got a reference, and provided it's used as a tool, which I think perhaps we do here, it can actually release you ... you can relax more because you know that you've got things keyed in at the planning stage ... You can focus much more in depth on areas ... provided that you use it as a tool, and you don't change what you believe is the best way children learn ...

Another argued that as a result of the National Curriculum standards would be pushed up in primary schools, leaving secondary education with less to do:

> Like the science we've been doing over the last couple of years, we've been doing some of the work that would have been done in the first two years of secondary schools, so there ought to be things rebounding off it. Standards should be going up. I think the children are going to be better prepared.

The Year 3 teacher at Kenwood argued that:

> ... in that way the National Curriculum has been quite beneficial because I think it has made teachers come together to try and work on schemes of work, to work together much more. In this school, particularly, that has been quite a benefit.

What were the factors which enabled teachers to take control of the changes in this way and to selectively modify and adapt them? There are many variables at both institutional and individual level which may influence a teacher's stance towards change. Among these are the school ethos and strategy for change, the socio-economic catchment area of the school, and the teacher's ideology and previous beliefs about teaching. For example, Bowe, Ball and Gold (1989) argued that schools that are already well adapted to making changes, and where a collaborative culture has been fostered, are in a better position to make a 'creative' response to change which will involve and support the staff. There was some evidence from our interviews with classroom teachers that teachers who had perceived themselves as strongly child-centred, creative, and spontaneous in their approach were those who often felt they had the most to lose under the National Curriculum, and were, as a consequence, less positive about it.

Conscientiousness, or even over-conscientiousness may be an issue too. Campbell, Evans, Neill and Packwood (1991) cite such internalized commitment to high personal standards as a factor in teacher stress and consequent demoralization, because it made it difficult for teachers to limit their workload. In contrast, some teachers had developed coping strategies which enabled them to constrain impulses to over-conscientiousness in order to protect their personal time, social life and their 'sanity'. For some of the teachers in our study, the ability to adopt such a stance enabled them to make a more positive, creative response to the National Curriculum by exercising choice and rationing and prioritizing the workload. Very often, variables at the institutional level made it possible to take this stance. For example, schools in different types of catchment area experienced very different pressures as a result of the changes, and consequently their teachers often expressed a different set of concerns and anxieties. Thus, in many schools in disadvantaged inner-city areas, anxiety centred on the difficulty of adapting teaching to the perceived needs of the individual children. The National Curriculum was not seen as relating well to the children's needs. It was felt that there was a need for time in order to allow infant school children to adapt to classroom life and to become ready to learn, and that this time was no longer available under the pressures of the National Curriculum. As one inner-city teacher put it:

> There are social and economic difficulties here. You can't start where you would hope to. You have to start building up closeness to the child first. If you don't do that you might as well not bother. I'd hate to get to the point where I think, 'I must do that today and I'm sorry if Emma comes in crying, but she's just got to sit and do it, because the law says I must be doing it.'

In 1992, 62 per cent of teachers in inner-city schools expressed the view that the demands of the National Curriculum took no account of the real classroom situation, compared with 43 per cent of teachers in affluent, middle-class areas and 21 per cent of rural teachers. More inner-city teachers also felt that the National Curriculum was unsuited to special needs children, and more teachers from the inner city (94 per cent) and from settled working-class areas (82 per cent) thought that, in the future, primary education would be less able to adapt to children's needs. Because of their situation, and the very real constraints under which they operated, these teachers often adopted coping strategies similar to those of the 'autonomous' teachers identified by Fullan (1992) who 'cannot be forced to be involved and may very well be doing a good job'. They were often likely to articulate their position in terms of responding to the needs of the children and protecting children's interests.

Teachers in affluent middle-class catchment areas were the most likely to see the changes as enhancing their teaching qualities and skills in terms of enabling them to reflect on their practice (33 per cent of teachers in middle-class areas compared with 11 per cent of inner-city teachers) and collaborate with other teachers (47 per cent and 4 per cent respectively). Those teaching in rural and in middle-class areas were also more likely to perceive the National Curriculum as enabling them to provide greater continuity and progression for children.

Teachers in the inner city had very justifiable concerns about the financial effects of the local management of schools (LMS), about the publication of league tables of standardized assessment results and the effect of such comparisons with schools in more advantaged areas. These, they felt, could in no way take into account the progress individual children had made or the enormous efforts made by teachers. Comparisons in the media, which began to emerge over the period of data gathering, were perceived by many teachers as demoralizing and insulting to both staff and children. Such findings suggest that as the effects of the educational market continue to operate, and teaching in the inner city becomes a harder and less rewarding job, the eventual outcome might be a flight of teachers from the inner-city schools to 'easier', more affluent areas — as often occurs in France as a primary teacher's career develops. This could mean a considerable loss to inner-city children of committed, confident and experienced teachers.

All these factors apart, the teachers who felt able to make a creative response to the National Curriculum were those who had the confidence to make choices and to be selective in how they implemented the programmes of study. They were often supported in these choices by their headteachers and by a strong culture of collaboration within the school (Nias, Southworth and Yeomans, 1989). They felt able to benefit from the structure and guidelines of the National Curriculum without letting it drive them or destroy what they knew to be good about their practice. More detailed case studies of such teachers' beliefs and classroom practice are presented elsewhere (Osborn, forthcoming).

While only a minority of the teachers in our sample could be described as 'mediators', there were many more, in fact a majority, who welcomed the guidelines and structure provided by the National Curriculum. Indeed, it is likely that if such teachers had not been swamped by the sheer pace of change, and if they had been given an opportunity to take ownership of the innovations, 'mediation' and creative response to the changes might have been the predominant response.

While the Dearing Report (1993) is likely to result in some reduction of workload, there remains the challenge posed to teachers' sense of professionalism from a continuing barrage of criticism in the media and from policy makers. Our evidence suggests that, in spite of the pressures and the generally inept central management of the introduction of the Education Reform Act, some teachers still saw a movement forward to a new clarity about their role. The research presented here points to a need to build upon this new sense of focus, to establish a constructive dialogue between the makers and the implementers of educational policy and to involve teachers more closely in the process of policy change.

References

ACKER, S. (1990) 'Teachers' culture in an English primary school: Continuity and change', *British Journal of Sociology of Education*, **11** (3).

APPLE, M. (1986) *Teachers and Texts: A Political Economy of Class and Gender Relations in Education*, London, Routledge.

BOWE, R. and BALL, S. with GOLD, A. (1992) *Reforming Education and Changing Schools*, London, Routledge.

BROADFOOT, P. and OSBORN, M. (1988) 'What professional responsibility means to teachers: National contexts and classroom contexts', *British Journal of Sociology of Education*, **9** (3), pp. 265–87.

BROADFOOT, P. and OSBORN, M. (1993) *Perceptions of Teaching: Primary School Teachers in England and France*, London, Cassell.

CAMPBELL, R.J., EVANS, L., NEILL, S.R. ST J. and PACKWOOD, A. (1991) *The Use and Management of Infant Teachers' Time: Some Policy Issues*, Warwick, University of Warwick Policy Analysis Unit.

DEARING, R. (1993) *The National Curriculum and its Assessment: Final Report*, London, School Curriculum and Assessment Authority.

FULLAN, M. (1991) *The New Meaning of Educational Change*, London, Cassell.

HARGREAVES, A. (1992) 'Contrived collegiality: The micropolitics of teacher collaboration', in BENNETT, N., BARTON, L., FURLONG, J., GALVIN, C., MILES, S. and WHITTY, G. *Individual and Organisational Perspectives*, Milton Keynes, Open University Press.

HARGREAVES, A. (1994) *Changing Teachers, Changing Times: Teachers' Work and Culture in the Postmodern Age*, London, Cassell.

HARGREAVES, D. (1988) 'Educational Research and the Implications of the 1988 ERA,' Paper given at BERA Annual Conference, University of East Anglia.

HOYLE, E. (1992) 'An Education Profession for Tomorrow'. Paper given to annual conference of British Educational Management and Administration Society, University of Bristol.

LAWN, M. and OZGA, J. (1981) 'The educational worker: A reassessment of teachers', in OZGA, J. (ed.) *Schoolwork: Approaches to the Labour Process of Teaching*, Milton Keynes, Open University Press.

NIAS, J. (1989) *Primary Teachers Talking*, London, Routledge.

NIAS, J., SOUTHWORTH, G. and YEOMANS, R. (1989) *Staff Relationships in the Primary School: A Study of Organisational Cultures*, London, Cassell.

OSBORN, M. and BROADFOOT, P. (1990) 'French lessons: Some international comparisons of teachers' classroom practice', *Times Educational Supplement*, 9 November.

OSBORN, M. and BROADFOOT, P. (1992) 'A lesson in progress? French and English classrooms compared', *Oxford Review of Education*, **18** (1), March.

OSBORN, M. (1996) 'Teachers mediating change: Two case studies at Key Stage 1', in CROLL, P. (ed.) *Teachers, Pupils and Primary Schooling*, London, Cassell.

POLLARD, A. (1985) *The Social World of the Primary School*, London, Cassell.

POLLARD, A., BROADFOOT, P., CROLL, P., OSBORN, M. and ABBOTT, D. (1994) *Changing English Primary Schools: The Impact of the Education Reform Act at Key Stage One*, London, Cassell.

STONE, C. (1993) 'Topic work in the context of the National Curriculum', *Journal of Teacher Development*, **2** (1), pp. 27–38.

WALLACE, M. (1991) 'Flexible planning: A key to the management of multiple innovation', *Educational Management and Administration*, **19** (3), pp. 180–92.

WARREN LITTLE, J. (1987) 'Teachers as colleagues', in RICHARDSON-KOCHLER V. (ed.) *Education Handbook: A Research Perspective*, London, Longman.

10 Creating Atmosphere and Tone in Primary Classrooms

Bob Jeffrey and Peter Woods

Introduction

School ethos has for long been recognized as a highly significant factor in pupil achievement, both in secondary (Rutter, Maughan, Mortimore, Ouston and Smith, 1979) and in primary schools (Mortimore, Sammon, Lewis and Ecob, 1988). The same is true of 'classroom climate', which bred a whole research industry in America following the pioneering work of Lewin, Lippitt and White (1939). Much of this work has been guided by quantitative or experimental research methods, which can establish the framework of significance and its generality without, however, getting to the heart of what school 'ethos' or classroom climate constitutes. For this, we need qualitative methods. In a previous attempt to characterize a particular secondary school ethos through such methods, Woods (1990, p. 77) conceived of ethos as 'a moving set of relationships within which different groups and individuals are constantly in negotiation. It is expressed largely in symbolic form, notably in language, appearance and behaviour.' In this chapter, we seek further characterization of the quality of ethos or climate in relation to primary classrooms.

Our work formed part of long-term research into 'creative teaching in primary schools'. Initial identification of this phenomenon (Woods, 1990) was followed by study of exceptional educational events (Woods, 1993), and adaptations of creative teachers to the National Curriculum (Woods, 1995). We have also been concerned with portraying the nature of creative teaching. Prominent features include innovative behaviour, teacher ownership and control of the pedagogical process, and relevance to pupil cultures and generally accepted social values. None of the early focus was on climate. We gradually became aware, however, that that was one of the most prominent features of creative teachers' work. The exceptional events certainly generated exceptional climates. But there was also a feeling of exceptionality about these teachers' classrooms from day to day outside these events. Much of this was to do with how they created 'atmosphere', and their use of 'tones'. We came to see these as important constituents of classroom climate, particularly in the way in which they generated feelings amongst pupils and teachers alike conducive to learning. In their effective construction lies the key to the 'subtle art of teaching'. Sue, a deputy head Year 5 teacher, comments on how essential she feels this area is, and how underplayed it is in the National Curriculum:

> Basically, this is my big bone of contention with the NC. If you're working in industry you can work by assessing measurable quantities and qualities. We work in a business which is about producing people who can cope and it's all about immeasurable quantities, immeasurable qualities. You can't overlay your plastic transparency of the NC, tick it all off and say, 'there you are sixteen, made a little person there, well done'. You can't do that. We work in a totally subjective atmosphere with subjective qualities and quantities every day. You can't suddenly put objective measurements on top. Yes, you can on very very simple things, like can this child count up to ten, can this child count to 20? In many ways I've found it quite offensive to the art of actually teaching because it gives it a simplistic quality that it doesn't have.

The Research Project

The creative teaching project from which this chapter is drawn took place over two to three years with mainly one researcher working with five schools, drawing on over twelve teachers' work but working in depth with five teachers. The classrooms of these five teachers were visited at least once weekly from one to three terms. The work of teachers and pupils together with their interactions were recorded by the use of observational field notes, photographs and tape recordings. This data was then used to stimulate separate taped conversations with the teachers and pupils concerning their practice. This is how, together with field notes and conversations with other adults who worked in the same classrooms, we triangulated the research.

The relations between researcher, teachers and pupils became quite close and many conversations were held that had little direct connection with creative teaching but nevertheless were part of the business of constructing 'rounded' (Atkinson, 1990) characters. The researcher was expected and agreed to assist with some of the classroom activities in a limited manner for this is the culture of primary classrooms.

The conversations with the teachers were varied in that they took place in snatched moments — on staircases, during breaks — and in more extended circumstances — appointments after school, in cafes, and in homes. They were often discussions rather than interviews, hence we use the term conversations.

The conversations with the pupils took place both individually and in groups, whilst they were engaged in activities and in more formal settings designed to encourage the expression of opinions and discussion. Photographs were particularly useful in that they not only provided *aide-memoirs* for specific situations but they allowed the pupils to reflect and analyse situations in more depth. It also became clear that asking pupils to imagine what other pupils in the photograph were thinking and feeling was more productive than asking them to describe their own reactions. In the latter situation, children appeared concerned about their image within the group and with the researcher. In the former situation, the children did, we believe, use their own experiences and their imagination to describe others, less constrained by worries about image and they were able to express themselves more elaborately because they were focusing on an 'other'.

Lastly, the teachers were invited to act as respondent validators in that they were all given any papers resulting from the research and asked to comment in any way they wished.

Classroom Atmosphere

We have noted the following characteristics — anticipation and expectation, relevance, achievement and success, and satisfaction.

Anticipation and Expectation

These teachers are skilled in the construction of situations and their sense of timing:

> There's a wooden frame on the carpet with two end supports, a bar across the top with some pulleys hanging from it. The children sit in a circle around it as they arrive and whilst some curious children examine it, most await Mary's introduction and take part in the early morning routines. She doesn't mention it while she deals with the morning jobs and pleasantries.

Visual aids were a common stimulus, as when Judy showed her children some cooking utensils one morning, Rolf showed some materials to make ancient clocks, and Freda began one morning with a tank full of water by her side. These activities often had a 'hands-on' quality to it but above all, they heralded 'something new', which was a constant feature. Ira (Year 5), one of Sue's pupils, commented

> She likes doing stuff to do with machines, maps and Tudor gardens. She does a lot of imaginative work, a lot of finding out about different times and a lot of experimenting, like science, and she tries out new stuff from books.

Exciting out-of-school events, such as trips to museums, art galleries, sporting venues, ancient sites and community projects like film units and arts centres, were eagerly anticipated. New people were often in evidence as teachers used volunteers and invited specialists to assist in particular projects; e.g., Tudor dance instructors, puppeteers, sports specialists, sculptors. These brought a charismatic quality to the projects in which they took part, as discussed in Woods (1995).

There was a theatrical quality about the way in which these teachers acted, noted by Maria, a support teacher, of Mary:

> It's a talent I suppose, its a kind of suspense she creates, not all the time, but the children are aware of her at all times in the class . . . it's a lively kind of theatre in a way.

Relevance

We were able to expand on the importance of 'relevance', identified in earlier work (Woods, 1990). A key aspect of these classrooms was that all identified with and experienced the atmosphere. Pupils felt it, and were moved by it. They felt their experiences were valued, and that they were able to contribute to the 'world of knowledge' being created and explored. Teachers made sure, therefore, that pupils felt a strong sense of involvement. They did this in various ways. Firstly, they used children's personal experiences and interests as part of the curriculum. For example, Tricia encouraged them to draw on family histories to construct evacuation stories, and Susan helped them establish connections through letters and photographs with children from a school in Wales. The influence of their teacher in establishing personal relevance is well illustrated by a group choreographing part of their musical on their own:

> Val talks to the whole group together and then we just tell her our ideas, and other people comment on them and suggest this and that and then we put it all together. She lets us talk about it more than other teachers. She let's us have our own conversations and arguments and then gets us back to the point. She lets us speak, she lets us vote although we're not eighteen . . . She lets us breathe more. Most of all, she listens, unlike other teachers who jump to conclusions.

Secondly, in relating the curriculum to the pupil, teachers take account of cultural, 'race', gender and social class distinctions, aiming for an harmonious ethos that is fair to all pupils. As Burwood (1992) argues with respect to reducing working-class children's under-achievement, teachers constantly seek to 'reduce the gap between everyday experience and classroom experience' (p. 320). Thus, Mary chose to focus her geography topic on a West Indian island because many of her children have West Indian connections and one of her children visits there regularly. Sue emphasized the role Queen Elizabeth I played in supporting women writers. Sean's Year 2 class focused on similarities and differences between Bangladesh and English family life in his school which had a large Bengali population.

A third aspect of relevance is the way learning is related to children's feelings. As Drummond (1991) notes, learning is an emotional enterprise and not solely a cognitive one. Thus, Junior (Year 2), whilst looking at some photographs of his performance in a dance drama which was the culmination of a term's project on 'worlds', told us that 'I thought I was a fish, swimming like a fish. I thought I was water . . . It was like I was in a picture.' Asked what he enjoyed about doing the dance, he said, 'I like stretching, closing, twisting and skipping and running . . . I liked following the music like I was in the mood.' Junior's use of technical dance language is illustrative of how many of the children in this project picked up the language and used it to help articulate their actions.

A fourth feature of relevance is a constant sense of purpose. Sue explains one way in which this works:

> I want them perhaps do something with imagination during the day, that's quite important, but most of all, the overriding factor is, sometime during the day you want them to have an end product in their head. One finished thing. If I've got a target or any, any target or the day, it's that during the day one thing needs to be finished and in their heads. So they go home and someone says, 'Right, what did you do today?' as they inevitably do, and they can say 'I did so and so, I did that today'.

Many activities have an end in view that the children recognize. In Sue's class the children were asked to construct a vehicle that can roll, design the best leaflet to go home to parents informing them of an outing, write a newspaper report for parents of their sports day, construct flower designs for the harvest festival, simulate the experiences of explorers who first recorded particular flowers discovered in South America by drawing some of them meticulously, and construct a chess board for classroom free time. Tricia's class constructed 'proper' books in which to put their evacuation stories, made puppets for a live performance of a play with a proper theatre, and built sculptures to enhance the school exterior. Thus clear purposes cemented the sense of relevance.

Achievement and Success

A mood of achievement and success is a distinctive feature of the classroom atmosphere. There is a sense of high teacher expectations, and confidence in children's abilities to meet them. Thus, constant encouragement by publicly praising pieces of work is done with the whole class two or three times a day. More informally, the teachers punctuate the various activities by stopping the class to comment on an individual's or a group's work. These public expressions of achievement were often developed by the teacher into a supportive dialogue between members of the class as to the possibility of further enhancing the quality and rigour of the work. Thus, Mary expected her group of children to report back on their science investigation into the use of pulleys to overcome friction, and the other children were invited to ask questions and the answers were discussed and evaluated. This approach is not just related to the content of an activity but to developing dialogue as a part of the atmosphere of the classroom. In these interactions the teachers sustained a sense of need for quality. Thus, when one of Rolf's groups had not made much effort to organize a presentation of their clock constructions, they were sent away and given five minutes to re-present their activity. They did so and Rolf described it as a more polished and organized presentation.

This pupil engagement can lead to a collaborative atmosphere of positive encouragement and critique, a kind of 'empathetic challenging' (Bonnett, 1991). Val's class at work on book reviews provides an example. After listening to some of the reviews and teacher comments on them in terms of content and depth, the children were then put into groups to listen to each other's reviews and assist each other in developing them. Here, Lee and Ian comment on Jamie's review which he has just read to them:

Lee: It's like a story isn't it.
Ian: You're telling a story aren't you. At the end you've got 'I like the story, it was interesting.'
Jamie: That's part of the review.
Ian: Yes, but you can't write a story. You've got to think about 'I like the book because [certain] parts happened in it.'
Lee: Yes you can't write 'I like this book because *all* this is happening.'
Ian: You've got to explain at the beginning what the book is all about. You can't just start with a part of it.
Lee: Yes, and you've got to write down the different characters.

Their teacher, Val, commented:

They're taking a role in teaching themselves. They've learnt something and they can pass it on. There's a huge value for them to know that they have that skill . . . I think it's motivating, it does motivate them 'cos they will look at that [other perspectives and skills] and they will go away and try that or they will try another angle.

She was aware of the risks in this. Children can be 'insensitive', and can 'slip out of the mutually supportive framework very easily'. But she based her approach on the conviction that 'deep down there is a caring attitude towards each other and that they have an understanding of learning difficulties and support each other through them'. Her role was important in 'pushing the positive'.

In 'pushing the positive' teachers make a distinction between praise and encouragement. The former may be beneficial in terms of self-esteem but the latter is more directed towards development. Madeline (Year 5) exemplifies this difference in describing her relationship with Sue:

> Well, I think that if you do something wrong she never really lies. Some teachers lie. If they don't think its very nice they say, 'Oh that's brilliant'. And they just say that will have to do, but Sue, if you do something wrong just says, 'OK, that's not very good, go and do it again.' She doesn't say it horribly, 'Oh that's really stupid, go and do it again' . . . when I finish a piece of work you sort of feel like you've achieved something. You sort of know that you've done it and won't have to do it again. If you didn't like it you know that you're finished and you just feel good about it.

Satisfaction

Achievement leads to feelings of satisfaction and the sense of 'a job well done', as when Madeline finished her map: 'I felt like it's a whole block of work and . . . I just thought "wow that's really good" and I did feel quite good about it.' Similarly, a great deal of satisfaction is derived from the public display of children's work. Madeline (Year 5) identified what it meant to her:

> Well I think, if you look at it up on the wall you say 'That's mine and that's somebody else's' and then you compare them and I think its nice to look at them because you know what you've done. And if you're just finishing something like that you look at on the wall you can compare them to see if you've progressed.

This confirms the well-known effect of the situation — classroom organization, furnishings, props, displays — on how it is experienced (for example, Delamont, 1987; King, 1978). Displays in these classrooms were a prominent component of their atmosphere.

Judy suggests that this sense of satisfaction can be seen on children's faces as a result of being stretched and working hard. Here she refers to a group with whom she is keen to develop their factual and descriptive writing:

> We have got quite a good tuition group and they're really being quizzed with their work, about how they're complicating their stories, what sort of resolution they're working towards and where they're going with their work. They're having to work out what their intentions are and how they can bring all their diverse ideas into it and how they are weaving them all together and they really are beginning to structure their thinking about it. I'm really pleased. They are complaining a little

bit about the amount of work they are having to do, but I actually feel this is a sign of success. There's a sort of self-satisfied thing in there. They say to their mums, 'Oh all we ever do is work, work, work, work.' But it's in a rather self-satisfied way. You sort of feel that they are actually quite pleased about it.

The Tone of Classroom Life

By 'tone' we refer to the sound quality and levels, rhythm, pace and tempo of classroom life. In these respects, an artistic lesson has affinities with a piece of music, with its variations designed for effect, its range of instruments to produce them, and with the teacher as orchestrator and conductor. Different tones produced different moods for different purposes, for example seriousness when dealing with an issue of behaviour, or calm or excitement for a particular activity. These states of mind and feeling are as important for the teacher as for the pupil,

> Sue spoke of how she moved from tiredness to active involvement and when asked what drove her she answered 'enthusiasm'. Not the enthusiasm of the individual teacher, but of the situation, the context of the children and teacher together which increased the adrenaline. She was swept along by the good times. (Field Note, 16 June 1992)

Common resources used by teachers are humour and metaphor. There is much warmth conveyed in smiles and twinkles of the eye. Even admonishments are done in this manner for they recognize children more as people than as 'clients' (Berlak and Berlak, 1981). Hera's (a Year 5 girl), view of Sue exemplifies this approach:

> I did a piece of writing and in the middle I stopped and I found out I'd skipped a line. She kind of put her hand on her hips and kind of pretends to be a bit angry, but really she's just joking while she does make us do it again but, like, she's not furious.

Metaphors are used constantly, differing ways of describing activities are created, puns are enjoyed.

> Sue is looking for instructions that are 'real teasers', 'tricky dicky' clues. Clues that need 'brain power', not hand power. She asks them to create a 'state secret'.

Here, we use our own metaphor in trying to convey the main moods identified, likening the lesson to a piece of music. There are many kinds of moods in creative classrooms. Three prominent ones we consider here are 'andante', 'legato', and 'spiritoso'. These differ in both physical and subjective space. In the 'andante' mood the teachers usually have the children close to them. In the 'legato' mood the children spread out into the corridors and use the floors and carpets. The 'spiritoso' mood is often used in a space halfway between these two where, for instance, the whole group may be seen at times trailing through the school on an adventure. But, even more importantly, perhaps, the varying of the mood is also another way of varying the psychological space. As Harvey (1989) notes, space

> . . . has direction, area, shape, pattern and volume as key attributes as well as distance. We typically treat it as an objective attribute of things which can be measured and thus pinned down. We do recognise of course that our subjective experience can take us into realms of perception, imagination, fiction, and fantasy, which produce mental spaces and maps as so many mirages of the supposedly 'real' thing. (p. 202)

In this way, changes in mood add breadth to a daily learning experience that is generally confined to the more limited space defined by the four walls of a classroom.

Andante (to be performed in moderately slow time)

This mood is generated by the teacher to establish seriousness and to create tension. Rather similar to the 'ripple effect' (Kounin, 1970), where humour spreads through a group, so quietness creeps over a group, where a teacher is trying to bring a class to order. Members of the group sensitive to the 'creeping quietness' encourage others to conform and the varied use of stares, mock gestures of disapproval tinged with humour sometimes, establishes a settled atmosphere. Admonishments to individuals are delivered in quiet whispers so as generally not to embarrass or create martyrs. This does not mean that a soft approach is being used, for whispered, quiet admonishments can be delivered with some considerable conviction and intensity. Individuals are brought into the teacher's 'space'. It rather ensures that a quieter level of interchange is the norm and louder utterances are saved for times of enthusiasm, affirmation and congratulation. Teachers did not keep themselves apart, creating a division between teacher and pupils. They addressed individuals at similar height levels on a one-to-one basis, often with a warm touch of the hand on the arm or shoulder.

Sue's children often seemed spellbound. She emphasized particular vocabulary, used a slower manner of speaking and deliberate pauses to generate an atmosphere of intensity, excitement, and importance, Her description of Elizabethan Times had all the ingredients of mood built up by an *andante* presentation. The group of children were due to visit the National Gallery one afternoon to look at portraits. In the meantime they had been preparing their own portraits of Queen Elizabeth I and making their own scrolls. In this extract, Sue describes the modern speedy process of making a book, and then goes on to tell the children about printing in Elizabethan Times. The children's general hum gradually died down as Sue leant forward to tell her tale:

In Elizabethan days if you wanted a book it had to be copied out by hand and it might take as long as five years to publish it [*She begins in a factual tone emphasizing the 'five years' but it has a 'Once upon a time' mood to it*.]. A man very early on before Elizabethan Times had discovered how to print books, William Caxton, but even so, to buy a William Caxton book was extremely expensive and even when it was printed in his machine it took nearly a year to make. So you can see you didn't just nip out to the Canonbury's Art Shop [*she adds humour by referring to the shop next to the school*] and buy a paperback for £1.99, you couldn't do that. It is only very, very recently that ordinary people like you and me could go out and say we want a book. Books used to be for the very very rich. [*Her voice lowers slightly and she slows her delivery emphasizing 'very very' and 'fabulously wealthy'*.] They were a sign that you were fabulously wealthy and when you look at the portraits this afternoon, you look for what you see behind those portraits, because what you see behind those faces of the people in the pictures, those are the stories that tell you about the people in those pictures, not the false faces that the artist has given them, not the flattery that the artist has been paid to do, but you look behind those pictures and you see the real Elizabethan life. You will see the books which say, 'I am filthy rich. I can afford books.'

Look at the land. That tells you that these people ruled the land. Look at the clothes. Look at the maps and it tells you that these people travelled [*The story takes on a poetic style in the way she uses the word 'look' three times*.]. Until very recently, the last 150 years, people expected to be born, live and die in one place and if these people were travelling it was because they were fabulously wealthy and powerful. You look at what's behind those pictures, behind those people and behind those very very serene faces, a lot of which have got nothing to do with the real people behind them [*'Real' is the next word to be emphasized and she brings the metaphor of the detective to help put the children in control of the afternoon activity. There is a long pause after 'lies' and nobody interrupts. She uses the lists to help create the mood*.]. Look for the clues this afternoon. Be the detective when you look at those pictures, because that's where real Elizabethan England lies. Look behind those pictures and you'll see dogs, animals, horses, not mongrel dogs, but pedigree hunting dogs, fabulous Arabian horses, because behind those people are their very precious possessions. You know that in Ancient Egypt the Pharaohs were buried with their precious possessions, yeah! In Elizabethan England, in portrait painting, possessions were put behind people to show just like the Egyptians how powerful they were. Egyptians took their belongings to their grave [*She brings in the Egyptians to prove her point drawing, on the children's knowledge of a previous topic.*]. People from the Elizabethan age, the Victorians, the Stuarts, took their possessions to the grave with them, in the pictures they left.

We know exactly who they were, we know exactly where they stood, we know exactly what power they had, because it's there in the pictures, yeah! [*She finishes by including the pupils in the repetitive 'we know.'*]

Both researcher and children were entranced by the richness of the language, the poetic construction and the clear images. Sue is sure that the creation of mood is an important part of her craft:

Capturing the audience is a difficult thing in teaching, isn't it? It's this elusive thing students call discipline . . . it's the captivation, it's creating a pause, and then bang in on the pause. It's the pause where JPR Williams would have nipped in, picked up the ball and been off, it's that sort of change of direction, skidding off one surface and on to another. It's that which you're creating, it's capturing the audience . . . in the palm of your hand. You're doing basically what an entertainer or performer does. If you actually analyse what a stand up comic does, it's very akin to what a teacher does.

Here, Sue refers to the art of 'timing', such an important ingredient of the comedian's skill, which Eisner (1979) feels is intrinsic to the artistic teacher's role. There is also a sense of emotional as well as cognitive engagement of the audience, so that all are captured in a spirit of *communitas* (Woods, 1993). Sue finally comments on her role as facilitator, building on children's own experiences in giving them an emotional charge towards new knowledge.

Legato (smoothly and connectedly, no gaps or breaks)

This tone was adopted as the general working atmosphere of the classroom. It had a steady rhythm which the teacher occasionally slowed down to emphasize something of importance. Pupils also had more personal space and time than in the *andante*, being given more control of their activities, and working in small groups or as individuals, rather than as the whole class under the teacher's direction. Thus, when Sue's children were creating their portraits of Queen Elizabeth I, there was a quiet buzz as they went about their work, some on their own, some together. They showed initiative in finding tools and space, and in starting work. As the activity progressed, there was a steady movement as pupils stepped over each other to borrow items, but mostly they stayed in their selected space purposefully engaged in the detail of their own activity. Sometimes they sought help from or assisted each other. One child, usually chatty, whistled quietly to herself as she did some extended detailed work. A group of six talked quietly, mostly in relation to task. This all contributed to the sense of a 'working noise' (Woods, 1983, p. 136). The teacher was constantly on the move, orchestrating from within the class, moving from site to site, keeping the rhythm and smooth pace going. She constructed a sentence with Philip, advised a group on a colour, knelt down to assist Tom, validated another child's writing as 'authentic Elizabethan', now engaging with a group at desk level, now sitting in a spare chair talking to an individual about their work, anxieties, or behaviour and now bringing the class closer, metaphorically speaking, by commending somebody's efforts out loud.

It is in this *legato* mode that the tone is set for enquiry and dialogue. Tricia, in describing the construction of a script for a puppet show the children were producing, noted that where they had to work as a group, 'they enjoyed building up their dialogue with each other, and came out with some really good, interesting, funny dialogue, and learnt it all.' In another example, Sue, established a *legato* tone in which a constant dialogue was heard emanating from all the groups as her class of 7-year-olds constructed their publicity about a trip to Brighton. She suggested that they took on the role of travel agents. They had to decide, in groups, how much money to take with them. Then they planned a letter to their parents about the outing. Some wrote the letter, others suggested what they should take with them and others designed the front cover. The groups tackled the task in their own way. Sue brought some examples to the attention of the whole class and new ideas or methods were generated amongst the whole class. This is typical of *legato* mood, in the profusion of ideas, involving children in some practical or investigative activity, with close attention to language and vocabulary.

Spiritoso Mood ('with spirit')

A *spiritoso* mood involving animation, vigour and liveliness generates excitement, joy, interest and enthusiasm. There is much humour, and many smiling faces. It is commonly used to 'arouse appetite' (Hargreaves, 1982), for example, stimulating the whole class in a unifying venture such as an assembly, or in preparation for activities, or for effect in telling stories. There is often a quicker pace, more noise, and more variation in pitch.

The celebration phase of critical events (Woods, 1993) is often characterized by such a mood. Such was the case with the preparation by some Year 6 children of a musical based on a story of Henry VIII and his six wives as the culmination of a term's topic on the Tudors. The pupils decided who was to play each part, and contributed some choreography and musical compositions. They were excited at the thought of performing, even more so because they were all dressed in very elaborate Elizabethan costumes.

The classroom was a hive of activity as last minute amendments were made to the costumes by the teacher, Val, and a parent governor. There was lots of calling out 'Look at me!' and other humorous comments, accompanied by much giggling. As they were on their way to perform it to their parents they were asked about their feelings. They all seemed to have a high charge of adrenaline. Michael was 'looking forward to the cheering and the laughter and my mates trying their very hardest and their very best.' Nicola was excited and said she felt 'Good, lovely' and laughed loudly. She was 'looking forward to getting the whole play right and nothing wrong.' She was 'nervous ... But after I've done it, I'll probably want to do it again.' Georgina spoke with a large grin over her face. She felt she was 'looking forward to doing it, I don't know why, but I am, although I don't want to do it. I'm frightened of getting one bit wrong, but I still want to do it.' Wayne said he would overcome his nervousness by 'just carrying on and not thinking about it'. He became so overcome with emotion during his solo — he told us so later — that he began to cry. However, he did carry on, with everyone in the hall willing him to finish his song.

As they lined up to go in, some called out excited comments about other characters' costumes and roles. Gradually, Val lowered her voice and paused more often, generating a more *andante* mood. Eventually, the children came to order and they gracefully descended the stairs to begin their performance. They were quiet and, as exemplified in their comments, full of contrasting emotions of nervousness and excitement.

The teacher also becomes carried along with the excitement her planned activities will generate. Susan reported how she had been reading about 'Til Owlyglass' who 'gets up to all sorts of mischief and the children adore it'. She had told them, 'I can't wait to read this to you. I took it home at the weekend and I read it and couldn't put it down.' Susan's enthusiasm is taken up by the children and the story becomes valued because of the feelings of excitement Susan generates in the children for her story. The content and presentation of the story is not the only stimulus to interest.

Conclusion

Hargreaves (1994) has argued that without 'desire, teaching becomes arid and empty. It loses it's meaning' (p. 22). Unfortunately, desire, or teachers' and pupils' emotional involvement in teaching and learning, has not figured prominently in government policy of late. Rather, during the 1980s and 1990s, it has been marked by an increasing emphasis upon rationality in teaching, the close delineation of ends to be achieved, summative assessment with which to measure success, and bureaucratic structures and processes with which to monitor the system. Teaching is in danger of losing its 'emotional heart', even more so since, in the preoccupation with cognition, it has never been properly identified. The same might be said for learning. However, some teachers at least, are still managing to cultivate what they consider to be the 'subtle art of teaching'. Through the artful construction of atmosphere, teachers imbue pupils with the desire to learn, with the feeling of deep personal involvement and purpose, and with a strong sense of intrinsic rewards. They create and sustain moods appropriate to the task in hand through the skilful deployment of a variety of tones which make subtle use of time and space. Jackson (1992) argues that we must look at the minutiae of school life through an interpretive frame, cultivating a 'heightened sensitivity to the nuances of schooling' (p. 90). Atmosphere, tone, mood are hardly minutiae, but they do contain significant nuances. It is in this area that the teachers give an 'aesthetic form to their existence through their own productive work' (Foucault, 1979). We have tried to indicate the potential fruitfulness of this area and of the qualitative approach to its study, seeking to understand some of the more intangible, but highly significant constituents of the art of teaching.

References

ATKINSON, P. (1990) *The Ethnographic Imagination*, London, Routledge.
BERLAK, A. and BERLAK, H. (1981) *Dilemmas of Schooling*, London, Methuen.
BONNETT, M. (1991) 'Developing children's thinking . . . and the National Curriculum', *Cambridge Journal of Education*, **21** (3), pp. 277–92.
BURWOOD, L.R.V. (1992) 'Can the National Curriculum help reduce working class under-achievement?' *Educational Studies*, **18** (3), pp. 311–21.
DELAMONT, S. (1987) (ed.) *The Primary School Teacher*, Lewes, Falmer Press.
DRUMMOND, M.J. (1991) 'The child and the primary curriculum — From policy to practice', *The Curriculum Journal*, **2** (2), pp. 115–24.
EISNER, E. (1979) *The Educational Imagination*, London, Collier Macmillan.
FOUCAULT, M. (1979) *The History of Sexuality*, Harmondsworth, Penguin.
HARGREAVES, A. (1994) *Changing Teachers, Changing Times — Teacher's Work and Culture in the Postmodern Age*, London, Cassell.
HARGREAVES, D.H. (1982) 'The teaching of art and the art of teaching: Towards an alternative view of aesthetic learning', in HAMMERSLEY, M. and HARGREAVES, A. (eds) *Curriculum Practice: Some Sociological Case Studies*, London, Falmer Press.
HARGREAVES, D.H. (1994) 'The new professionalism: The synthesis of professional and institutional development', *Teaching and Teacher Education*, **10** (4), pp. 423–38.
HARVEY, D. (1989) *The Condition of Postmodernity*, Oxford, Blackwell.
JACKSON, P.W. (1992) *Untaught Lessons*, New York, Teachers' College Press.
KING, R.A. (1978) *All Things Bright and Beautiful*, Chichester, Wiley.
KOUNIN, J.S. (1970) *Discipline and Group Management in School Classrooms*, New York, Holt, Rinehart and Winston.
LEWIN, K.R., LIPPITT, R. and WHITE, R.K. (1939) 'Patterns of aggressive behaviour in three "social climates"', *Journal of Social Psychology*, **10**, pp. 279–99.
MORTIMORE, P., SAMMONS, P., LEWIS, L. and ECOB, R. (1988) *School Matters: The Junior Years*, London, Open Books.
RUTTER, M., MAUGHAN, B., MORTIMORE, P., OUSTON, J. and SMITH, A. (1979) *Fifteen Thousand Hours: Secondary Schools and their Effects on Children*, Cambridge: MA, Harvard University Press.

Bob Jeffrey and Peter Woods

Woods, P. (1983) *Sociology and the School*, London, Routledge and Kegan Paul.
Woods, P. (1990) *Teacher Skills and Strategies*, London, Falmer Press.
Woods, P. (1993) *Critical Events in Teaching and Learning*, London, Falmer Press.
Woods, P. (1995) *Creative Teachers in Primary Schools*, Milton Keynes, Open University Press.

11 Gender and School Leadership: Using Case Studies to Challenge the Frameworks[1]

Lisa Smulyan

So I'm learning how to be an administrator. I didn't want to be an administrator, either, you know. I sort of got pushed, and it seemed the wrong thing not to do. You know what I mean? It seemed cowardly — and I didn't think they'd pick me. I was as surprised as anybody, and then I kind of thought, 'Well heavens, if they think I can, then I guess I can.' (Interview, October 1991)

In 1989, in her integrating study of women in educational administration, Charol Shakeshaft wrote: 'Histories, case studies, and ethnographies almost always center on the male principal or superintendent. Consequently, we know little of the individual lives of the women who occupy these positions' (p. 56). The quote above describes how one elementary principal entered her job. It represents both her personal story and the experiences of the many women who have entered and worked in the principalship. Individual cases allow us to see the complex interactions between women principals' personal and professional lives and the social and cultural frameworks within which they work.

In this chapter I present a brief overview of some of the prior literature on effective school leadership as well as recent work that examines the role of gender in school administration. The exclusion of gender (and race and class) from work in school leadership makes its generalizations problematic, while the research on women in school administration tends to be limiting in its focus on gender as the determining factor in a woman administrator's experience. Both bodies of literature remain abstracted from the concrete, daily work of school leaders and the immediate choices, decisions, and strategies they use within a dynamic school context. I therefore turn to a case study of a woman principal to illustrate how the characteristics of effective leadership and gender interweave with other personal and professional issues and actions in the ongoing work of a school administrator.

Theoretical Background

Many calls for school reform and school restructuring in the late 1980s and 1990s focus on site-based management, developmental/child-centered approaches to teaching, alternative forms of assessment, and teacher empowerment and involvement in decision making. All of these strategies depend on 'effective principals' whose traits, roles, and skills have been described and analyzed by many researchers (Blase and Kirby, 1992; Barth 1990; Blumberg, 1987, 1989; Deal, 1987; Blumberg and Greenfield, 1986). The literature on effective schools suggests that the strong school leader takes initiative; has confidence; tolerates ambiguity; has a clear vision for the school and communicates that vision to teachers, students, and community; sets goals and evaluates them; uses a democratic-participatory style; focuses effectively on people and their needs; and establishes an open, warm and supportive school environment for teachers, students, and parents (Blase and Kirby, 1992; Buell, 1991; Barth, 1990; Griffin, 1990; Porter, Lemon and Landry, 1989; Goodlad, 1984; Sweeney, 1982). Interestingly, the leadership styles described often parallel styles attributed to women administrators by those who examine the role of gender in educational leadership.

None of the general literature on the tasks, roles, and skills of an effective principal addresses the influence of gender (or race or class) on an administrator's actions or interactions. The implication is that all principals experience common demands and need similar strategies to be successful; the primary variables mentioned are school and district cultures and requirements (e.g., Barth, 1990; Blase and Kirby, 1992) and, less frequently, the social, psychological and intellectual history the individual brings to the job (Blumberg, 1987). Blumberg (1987, 1989) refers to the latter as the individual's 'baggage,' and comments that despite 'idiosyncrasies' in how each person interprets events and acts in situations, principals' actions and interpretations share a common character: 'that which is personal is generalizable.' Although there are certainly generalizable characteristics of principals and their jobs, calling the effects of gender, race, and class either baggage or idiosyncrasies minimizes the impact of these social constructions and power relationships on both the role of the principalship and the people engaged in it, suggesting that the influences of gender, race, and class are individual interpretations rather than powerful social and political aspects of experience. Yeakey, Johnston and Adkison (1986) and Blackmore (1993) explain the neglect of gender in this literature as the acceptance of the 'rational man' model of organizations which grew out of the emphasis in the early 1900s on school administrators as professional experts who should run their schools as effective businesses. 'Educational theory and administrative practice have been dominated by men, who have acted as "gatekeepers" in setting the standards, producing the social knowledge and decreeing what is significant, relevent and important in the light of their own experience' (Blackmore, 1993, p. 27). Therefore the body of theory and research on educational administration tends to reaffirm the status quo and the existing power structures without questioning them.

The literature on women in educational management focused initially on issues of access and discrimination, then on career development, and more recently on male and female differences in management style. Research on women's access into school administration probes the reasons behind the decreasing numbers of women principals in the past fifty years, especially surprising in light of the large majority of women in the teaching profession. Explanations for women's underrepresentation include discrimination in hiring and promotion; socialization patterns that do not provide women with the skills and behaviors needed for administrative success; women's lack of training, experience, mentorship and support; and women's choice to avoid principalships because of the change in relationship, commitment, and possible role conflicts the position might bring (Edson, 1988; Fauth, 1984; Biklen, 1980; Clement, 1980; Gross and Trask, 1976).

Other studies have examined the similarities and differences in men's and women's career paths into educational administration (Grant, 1989; Shakeshaft, 1989; Edson, 1988; Fauth, 1984; Prolman, 1983; Clement, 1980). This work suggests that the traditional notion of career needs re-examination when applied to many women in education (Smulyan, 1990; Grant, 1989; Sikes, 1985). Women choose teaching, remain in teaching, change as teachers, and enter educational administration in ways that reflect both personal and socio-historical pressures on their lives, and ways which differ from the men whose lives have, for the most part, been used as the norm against which women are examined. For example, research suggests women generally enter teaching with no plans of moving into administration (Polczynski, 1990; Grant, 1989; Sikes, 1985). If they do leave the classroom, it tends to be after many years of teaching — and possibly raising a family — to work in special curriculum areas (e.g., reading, curriculum development) rather than direct school administration (Mitchell and Winn, 1989; Shakeshaft, 1989; Prolman, 1983). Their graduate work is more often in curriculum development, supervision, special education, or counseling than administration (Fauth, 1984; Weber, Feldman and Pling, 1981).

The different career paths of male and female administrators contribute to differences in both the particular roles and tasks they emphasize and the style in which they carry out those tasks (Eagly, Karua and Johnson, 1992; Shakeshaft, 1989; Schmuck, Charters and Carlson, 1981; Gross and Trask, 1976). As school principals, women tend to pay more attention to curriculum, interact more frequently and regularly with students and teachers, involve teachers in decision making, and focus on developing the school as a people-centered community than do male administrators (Shakeshaft, 1989; Marshall, 1985; Tibbetts, 1980). Studies that focus on differences in management style tend to dichotomize male and female approaches and skills, emphasizing women's traditional skills of collaboration and care. The focus also, at times, seems to obscure the larger social fabric within which people work, providing the impression of a homogeneous cadre of caring, collaborative democratic women leaders.

More recently, studies have begun to focus on the organizational structures of schools and their reflection of larger social structures that perpetuate gender, racial and class inequities. Shakeshaft (1987), Ballou (1989), Marshall (1985) and Adler, Laney and Packer (1993) all argue that the male dominated structures, processes and value systems in society and in schools limit the number of women chosen as administrators and then constrain their actions once hired. 'What is provided is a different view of organizational reality. By grounding organizational social theory in the larger social structures, in the organizational realities from which it emanates, the weight of the evidence reveals that the position of racial minorities and women in organizations is inseparable from the relative position of women and racial minorities in the larger social system' (Yeakey *et al.*, 1986, p. 118). While this approach continues to emphasize a gender difference in style, it locates that difference in larger institutional and social structures, questions its source, and examines its effect on outcomes.

In field as diverse as psychology (Schaef, 1985) and political science (Ferguson, 1984) researchers argue women bring to their work social, interpersonal and institutional experiences that differ significantly from men in society and that operate as subsystems within the larger patriarchal structure. Schaef (1985) argues that the White Male System 'surrounds us and permeates our lives. Its myths, beliefs, rituals, procedures and outcomes affect everything we think, feel, and do' (p. 2). Women live both within their own Female System and yet learn to function within the White Male System in a variety of ways, sometimes by being like men or by acting out the role of the traditional woman. Ferguson (1984) has argued that 'women's experience is institutionally and linguistically structured in a way that is different from that of men' (p. 23). The male bureaucracy, which permeates all public and most private institutions, creates self-perpetuating mechanisms that make it difficult for individuals, especially those in token roles such as women and minorities, to see, let alone resist, the structures. Both Schaef and Ferguson suggest that women can begin to create alternatives once they recognize the larger structures within which they operate, but also describe the limitations on resisting within the existing bureaucracies and structures which characterize institutions such as schools.

Marshall (1985) presents a set of approaches to women educators' dilemma of working within a male dominated structure, approaches which focus on women maintaining their traditionally expected roles while adopting enough of the male ways of functioning to be acceptable. For example, she explains that women can choose 'denial and retreat,' modifying their aspirations, retaining culturally defined roles, and remaining either teachers or child-centered principals who avoid district involvement. Or they can adopt a stance of impressions management: 'Gradually they learn that passing is the only way they can gain tentative acceptance in administrators' and the women's groups. They adopt a grateful, apologetic, supportive, good-natured front. This is a front that must be consciously devised and consistently maintained' (Marshall, 1985, p. 44).

Thus women learn how to balance being gender appropriate and carrying out the expected administrative tasks in acceptable (i.e., male) ways. Marshall presents no option for women to have a conscious set of goals (e.g., *choosing* to be a child-centered principal), a vision of how they would like to lead and of the kind of school or district in which they would be most comfortable, and a plan for working toward those goals and visions. She implies that the existing school structure is here to stay and women must learn how to operate success-fully within it if they choose to be a part of it. We lose here any sense of the person as an intelligent actor who can, perhaps, see the existing power struc-ture and make choices that allow her to redefine power and how she uses it.

Adler *et al.* (1993) explain that feminist educators have several options: they can stay in the classroom, avoiding promotion and minimizing the com-promises they have to make. They can ascend the career ladder and follow male styles of management, adopting a 'liberal feminist' stance that suggests that women can be as successful as men at their own game, or that androgy-nous approaches to leadership are most effective (Swiderski, 1988). Alterna-tively, they can ascend the career ladder and adopt a more female management style, recognizing the possible backlash and difficulties involved. Or, they can leave the profession and continue to work for social change in other ways. Although Adler *et al.*'s approaches provide a more active, positive approach for women principals, they still focus on gender as the primary (indeed only) influence on the educator's actions and experiences. This perspective, while important, limits our view of the women principals' life and work.

Women and men experience the patriarchal social system and the bureau-cratic structures of schools differently. They operate within different constraints and may respond differently within similar situations as a result of actual and perceived differences in status, experience and roles. Women may consciously choose to use gender as a framework as they act and respond as leaders or they may unconsciously make choices that draw on their experience as women in the larger society and the school context. Perhaps leadership approaches described as 'female' can be seen as conscious or unconscious acts of resist-ance within the larger school and social structures, actions which have the potential to challenge the dominant culture of the school institution and of the larger patriarchal society. While Ferguson (1984) avers that resistance leading to institutional change is close to impossible within existing bureaucratic struc-tures, both Ferguson and Schaef (1985) suggest that developing a feminist discourse which reflects women's experience may lead to the development of a female system which can challenge and redefine the dominant discourse and institutional structures. If women approach leadership as feminists and want to develop different approaches, goals, and processes, they may be frustrated and limited in what they are able to do in the school context. But for many women, their more 'female' management styles may be less conscious. Despite the fact that they may be acting in ways which reflect the constraints of the system and their roles in it, they maybe unaware of doing so and, conse-quently, less likely to challenge the system.

Neither the literature on effective school leaders nor the work on women in educational administration provide a complete picture of the life and work of a woman administrator. Gender is only one variable in determining an individual's leadership style and effectiveness. While gender shapes the female administrator's world view, school and life experience, and modes of interacting with others, it is one of several interacting factors that influences an administrator's behavior and effectiveness (Charters and Jovick, 1981; Schmuck, 1981). In both the individual's life and in the community in which she works, issues of race, ethnicity and class come into play, as do the particular organizational structures in the school district and community and other issues, events and experiences in the life of the individual. The case history approach provides an opportunity to illustrate, challenge, and expand our views of the styles and experiences of women administrators, even as it provides insight into the complexity of elements interacting in an individual's life and work in a school. If, in fact, women's leadership styles match those of effective school leaders, we need to see how those behaviors look when used in the real, complex world of a school by individuals who bring their own personal and professional experiences to the process. Such an examination leads us to question, and perhaps to begin to refine, the categories of effective leaders and women administrators.

Methods

While qualitative approaches have begun to help us understand the complexity of teachers' lives and work (Cohen, 1991; Weiler, 1988; Connell, 1985), there are few similar examples of the use of these methods to examine the experiences of school administrators (Wolcott, 1973, is the one prominent exception). The case study project from which this chapter is drawn can be categorized generally as ethnography in its use of participant observation, unstructured and structured interviews, and document collection and analysis with the goal of generating a rich description of people's lives and the settings within which they work (Hammersley and Atkinson, 1995; Woods, 1986). I have also drawn on the more specific approaches described as life history and case study research and, more marginally, on some of the recent work done in narrative analysis.

Several recent studies have emphasized the key relationship between teachers' individual, personal identities and their work identities as teachers in a particular school context (MacClure, 1988; Ball and Goodson, 1985; Connell, 1985; Nias, 1985). Life histories suggest that one's sense of self develops before one's teaching career begins, throughout one's personal life, and within one's teaching career. A teacher brings this sense of self to the school and classroom context and is, in turn, influenced by the constraints and possibilities determined by a school's management, values, and organization (Ball and Goodson, 1985; Connell, 1985; Nias, 1985). If there are conflicts between one's sense of self and the identity demanded by the teaching situation or school context, the individual may need to change — herself, her context, or her career. How the individual teacher or administrator responds to educational reforms, job changes, and personal challenges is influenced by prior experiences and present values and beliefs, all a part of her identity.

The focus on the interaction between the educator as individual and the school as a social context has led to the reappearance of the life history approach for examining teachers and schooling. This approach, popular in the 1930s, has been revived as a way of providing insight into how an individual's experience influences, and is influenced by, the broader socio-historical context within which he or she acts (Foster, 1994; Beynon, 1985). In education, in particular, where national directives, local priorities, and school needs are all filtered through the individual teacher or administrator, the life history approach provides important information about how an individual's past and present experience influences his or her actions and responses. As Beynon (1985) says, 'Unless we first understand teachers we can hardly claim to understand teaching' (p. 158). Life history relies on the unstructured interview as a means of data collection, although personal and institutional documents, observation, journals, and other materials can be used to verify and challenge interview data (Burgess, 1984, 1982; Simons, 1981; Bogdan and Taylor, 1970).

In this project, life histories are one key element of each of the three case studies, one of which is presented in this chapter. Robert Stake (1994) describes a case as a bounded, integrated system which has patterned behavior and exists in a significant context. Descriptions of life history and case history approaches appear similar in the literature; like life histories, case studies provide a depth and detail of experience which contribute to our understanding of social institutions, the people within those institutions, and the actions and interactions which occur on a daily basis. They help us locate the individual within her own life experience as well as within the changing historical context which contributes to and reflects that experience (Stake, 1994; Smulyan, 1992; Burawoy, 1991; Goodson, 1991; Ball and Goodson, 1989; Plummer, 1983). More can be learned, case researchers argue, from the detailed description of the particulars of one case than from the comparison of a few attributes across several cases (Stake, 1994; Burawoy, 1991). 'The importance of a single case lies in what it tells us about society as a whole rather than about the population of similar cases' (Burawoy, 1991, p. 281).

Although this study draws on the first person narratives of the principals involved and reflects some of the philosophy behind narrative analysis, it does not use the linguistic approaches that characterize much of this kind of research. Like narrative enquiry, these case studies rely on the voices and reflections of the principals as they tell their stories as a way of discovering the meaning they make out of their experience (Riessman, 1993; Cortazzi, 1993). Sandra Acker (1990), in an ethnography of a primary headteacher in England, explains that current studies of school management focus on lists of tasks, skills that can be taught, and the fragmentation and unpredictability of the head's day. These studies fail to describe the simultaneous, dramatic quality of events, the detailed content of the activities and the emotions that accompany them, and the sense of the continuation of issues and events over time. Narratives, on the other hand, provide insight into the complexities of the principal's actions and the life of the school. This study weaves the principals' narratives and reflections with the researcher's observations and the reflections of other key constituents — teachers, parents, and other administrators — to create an integrated, complicated picture of the work that goes on in each school.

The larger project from which this chapter is drawn uses life history and case history methods to examine the experiences of three elementary school principals. In each case, I was a participant observer at least once a week in the school for a full school year. During that year I also conducted four to six unstructured life history and career history interviews with each principal as well as more structured interviews with teachers, parents, and other school administrators in that district. By adopting diverse methods of finding, recording, and interpreting data (triangulation) I can develop a more complex picture of the work of each principal in her school.

In order to construct a detailed description of each principal's life history and school experience and effectiveness, I have analyzed the data both during and after data collection using processes described by Becker (1958), Glaser and Strauss (1967), and Schatzman and Strauss (1973). In the first step of this process, preliminary analysis of data indicates salient questions and patterns of experience and action. In the second step, these questions and patterns are used to focus further data collection. Other patterns emerge during this process, and new data are used to clarify, redefine, and assess the accuracy and validity of identified patterns. This process is facilitated by the use of HyperRESEARCH, a new computer program useful in the analysis of qualitative data. In the third step, themes and patterns are incorporated into a case study that is grounded in the data and which can be analyzed using theories of gender and school administration and prior work in school restructuring and change. These cases are shared with the administrators and their responses incorporated into the final case description, thus allowing the subjects a voice in the interpretation of the description and analysis presented.

In gathering data for the case study presented in this chapter, I spent one day a week in 1991–92 as a participant observer 'shadowing' an elementary school principal. I also attended evening meetings of the Home and School organization, Back to School night, district administrative council meetings, faculty meetings and some committee meetings. All observations were documented and annotated. In addition, I conducted six two-to-three hour interviews with the principal which covered life experience and current issues in her work. I interviewed teachers, administrators in the district, and parents about their perceptions of the school in general and of the school principal. All interviews were transcribed. The data collected has been analyzed for patterns in the life history and career history of this school principal, and those patterns have been placed within the framework of questions about gender and school administration, effective approaches to school improvement, and the role of case study methods in contributing to principal growth and school change.

The Case

Jeanne Price has been principal of the Greenfield-Weston Elementary School for five years. The district serves a middle–upper-middle-class, predominantly white community (Greenfield) and a smaller working-class community (Weston). An 'American black' (her term) in her early fifties, Jeanne taught in this same district for twenty years without ever considering a move into school administration. During the past five years she and others say she has learned a great deal and begun to establish a style of leadership and a school atmosphere that clearly reflects her own values and vision for the school. She has, in effect, moved through the stages identified by Parkay, Currie and Rhodes (1992) of socialization experienced by first time principals, focusing first on issues of survival and control, moving through a period of stability and maintenance, and then developing an interest in leadership and professional confirmation in which she focuses on developing a vision for the school and a school atmosphere that allows teachers to work with her toward that vision. 'The pieces are all falling together, that this is an excellent staff, excellent school, and the vision is coming. And the mechanics are in place to start moving to the vision. Five years is a short time, but probably the only amount of time you could do it in' (Interview, June 1992). And yet she realizes that it is not an easy task: 'You've got the vision, so you're scared. And you also have the pride. Like I said, I can't walk away from here until I've done a good job' (Interview, September 1991).

This year, in particular, evidence suggests that she is trying to become a better manager, even as she holds on to the interpersonal approaches and creative emphases that are clearly her hallmark. Questions that arise around this shift include: Do the organizational structures of schools and districts demand a particular management style? Can school principals be effective/efficient managers and maintain the more cooperative, person-centered approach that they believe in and feel most comfortable with? Jeanne points out that she wants to be able to do what the other administrators (all white males) in the district can do, but she certainly does not want to be the kind of leader she sees in them. When asked if she wanted to become more like one of the other principals she said, 'No — oh my god! No! Oh! No! Maybe inadvertently in places I will become, have some things like him, but I don't want to be like any of them . . . But there are things about them I think I have to be' (Interview, October 1991). It becomes a balance between giving the district and community what they want even as she holds onto her own ideals:

> I had an idea about schools and how they should work, but that idea can't be carried out in the structure I work for. So I've had to back off of my ideas, and that sometimes makes me very unhappy. On the other hand, when I'm faced with wanting to escape it or to say, 'I'm not compromising my stuff,' I look at the positive that's happened or the positive input I've been able to get . . . And then I figure, 'All right. I'll be this kind of principal (the kind the school district wants) and then I'll just run around and do the other stuff.' . . . I don't want to lose those pieces of me. There are sometimes I think — there are moments when I know I was giving up my soul and some of my ways, but I've been able to recover and find another little niche to worm out in and just go along. (Interview, October 1991)

Lacking role models, paths, patterns, and sometimes support for her own way of operating, she works to forge a new style that integrates effectiveness (in terms of getting what the school needs from the district and within its own operation) and a unique sense of creativity, energy, and care that reflects Noddings' (1988) and others' views of what schools might be.

In this chapter, I choose and follow one story, Jeanne's work with an individual African-American student, that illustrates her approach to leadership. The story reflects her own perspectives, those of teachers, parents and administrators, and the influences of her family, schooling and earlier teaching experiences on actions and decisions. A picture emerges of a woman elementary school principal whose style reflects, to a large extent, that described in the literature on women managers, administrators, and effective school principals, but whose uniqueness clearly results from her own upbringing, personal experience, beliefs about teaching, and unusual (in terms of gender and race) role in the district and community. The school in which she works is effective in terms of student achievement and school climate, but her somewhat indirect style of leadership makes some of those around her wonder what part she plays in that effectiveness. As one parent said, 'If you just took this community, you wouldn't get any straight answer about what this school should look like. So it's partly Jeanne dancing on water to make the school look enough like whatever anyone else wants it to look like, and that's a real time thing, in terms of energy, that's a tough job' (Interview, June 1992).

The Story

Alan came to Jeanne's attention in October during one of her regular monthly meetings with a first/second grade teacher. When she finished with some other issues she wanted to raise with Emily, she said to her, 'So, tell me about your life.' Emily launched into a story of an 8-year-old child in her class who had been held back in kindergarten, did not know his letters, was 'way behind,' and was tested at one point but received no special attention. She spoke very quickly and intensely, angry for the child who had fallen between the cracks and for herself because this child took up a disproportionate amount of her time in the classroom. Jeanne interrupted her along the way, at one point saying, 'What do you like about this kid? What would you like to have happen?' A few minutes later she said, 'I don't even know if you like Alan.'

When Emily finished her story, Jeanne took the floor. She suggested that Emily visit Alan's home, in part because she may have some inaccurate assumptions. She described another African-American child whom she drove home every day and said, 'I see a clean orderly home devoid of literature. There's no chaos. I see his mother who just beams when I say he's doing well.' She told Emily that she is glad it was she (Emily) who discovered him and that she was embarrassed because she (Jeanne) was principal and didn't know about this child even though he is an 'American black child and I lie awake at night thinking I'm going to save them.' Jeanne offered Emily some help in the class and some suggestions for working with Alan for the moment. Toward the end of this mini-lecture, Jeanne said to Emily, 'I hope he [Alan] is in your goals. American black males are dying in the street' (Field notes, 10 July 1991).

Jeanne followed up on this conversation in the following weeks. The reading teacher began to work with Alan, and Jeanne herself tutored him regularly. The school psychologist carried out another core evaluation of Alan, and he and the teachers recommended that the child be transferred to another elementary school in the district where he would be in a self-contained special needs class. Jeanne overrode this decision, saying that they would keep him in her school and meet his needs there. In March, she explained that she met with him nearly every day:

> Yeah, I was going to get him a tutor. That was my piece for keeping him here. I didn't know where . . . I don't want to just let him go to a casual tutor. And it's getting me into whole language too. I read a wonderful article that sounded so convincing. I still think you have to know what you're doing to teach whole language. This article talked about you learn from the company you keep. I loved that phrase. But Alan doesn't put the endings on his words. You've got to teach him to do that. But he's a sweet child, he's got a lot going for him. And I know Emily will be successful. And we'll have him next year. And if you learn by the company you keep, he sure as hell (won't learn) in that special ed class all day. (Interview, March 1992)

Emily, in an interview, explained that she was angry at Jeanne's decision, saying that Jeanne was not aware of this child's low functioning. 'But she didn't see his test score and didn't take into account his age. She just looked at his disadvantaged background and the fact that he's black and therefore made special considerations for him' (Interview, April 1992). She also pointed out that there is a larger black population in the other elementary school, which might have provided more of a community for Alan than exists at the

Greenfield-Weston School. She was able to see Jeanne's side, however, and said that since Alan seemed to be succeeding, 'Maybe she was really right . . . Somebody once said, fair is not always equal. So maybe she's right. Maybe by going out and giving these kids something extra to help them, but it seems unfair that so much energy goes to this small group' (Interview, April 1992).

During the summer, Jeanne arranged for a parent who has close ties to the school to continue tutoring Alan while she was away. This parent and Jeanne have since helped Alan's mother enroll in a General Education Diploma (GED) program to get her high school equivalency degree.

Reflections on the Story

Jeanne has lived and taught in the Greenfield-Weston district for twenty-five years. She has made a commitment to that school district and has found a comfortable home in this predominantly white community. As a principal, however, she challenges the system, the community and her teachers when it comes to working with black children. Are her actions those of a female administrator? An American black woman? An effective leader for school change?

Jeanne was raised in and around Cincinnati. Her father went to bible school when she was nine and preached on Sundays but always had other jobs during the week. Her mother cleaned houses and raised foster children along with her own. Her parents believed in education; Jeanne attended a rural Catholic school until eighth grade, when her family moved into the city. Following one year in the regular public school, she tested into and attended a public preparatory high school. She went to the University of Cincinnati Teachers College on a scholarship from the school's parent–teacher organization, falling into teaching as she later tripped into the principalship: 'Ever since I was little I wanted to be a nurse but someone gave me a scholarship, so I just walked off. . . . Everybody I knew and loved were teachers. People I cared about. I fell in love with teachers. They saved my life. . . . But I didn't plan to be a teacher, and never did I look for any other thing to do' (Interview, October 1991). She also moved away from home during college, after years of growing alienation and what she describes as emotional abuse from her family, especially her mother. Her first teaching job was in the inner city of Cincinnati, where within two years she was given the Cincinnati Teacher of the Year award. She tosses the award aside, saying,

> I knew how to make kids mind, you know. And I knew how to organize and I could see what people wanted. I mean, I was a manipulator to survive in my own family. And it didn't take me long (as a teacher) to figure out, 'What, you want some of that? I can do that.' That's just how you survive. . . . I was a good teacher, but I don't know how they found me. . . . But when I came here (to Greenfield) it was on my resume, because it happened. God, Greenfield took it

up and carried it around like it was a gift from the king on a purple platter. (Interview, October 1991)

She moved from Cincinnati to Greenfield with her husband, then had a child and stayed home with him for a few years. She returned to teaching in Greenfield when she and her husband divorced.

Her commitment to working with the black children in the Greenfield-Weston schools has intensified during the past five years, as she is able to use her position as principal to make a difference. It is a personal commitment that comes from her own background — both her experience as an African-American woman but also her experience as an abused child:

> Whenever I go back to an American black community like home, to my family, or to another school, somewhere where I see the community, my psyche cannot stand it. It is the abuse I suffered there that prevents me from going back there. So, I will never be able to manage that. Never. But I can do something here. I can do something, not only for the American black kids that come here, which I'm just beginning to, after being here three years . . . But I can also do something for the rest of the population. (Interview, September 1991)

Deciding to stay and work in Greenfield was not always easy to reconcile, and yet she has convinced herself that she has an important job to do here and that she can make an important contribution. Her own ease with her racial identity now allows her to make it an issue, just as the principalship gives her a new platform from which to act.

> I know enough about being black that I can be black, you know. I can talk the jive I need, if I need to. I can survive, nobody's going to hurt me walking into town or anywhere else. And I've figured out what I can do here. I had to figure out why, there was a crisis at some point about staying here and I chose to stay teaching here. Because there are enough black kids here . . . and there were enough white kids who needed to know about me. . . . And I know how I can be helpful here. . . . These kids are going to make decisions about a lot of people. For a lot of people. You know, that's input. It's powerful for every new kid that comes here (to see a black woman principal). . . . I can connect with the black kids right away, you know. But it's got to be different. I know I make a difference for them. (Interview, November 1991)

Jeanne is, in a sense, reclaiming her connection to the African-American children in this community and choosing to make race an issue in her principalship. bell hooks (1989) talks about this kind of reclamation and choice as both difficult and necessary for creating change. As hooks says, Jeanne may be able to act on these issues at this point in her life because she can step back and examine her past and begin to name her goals:

> One of the clear and present dangers that exists when we move outside our class of origin, our collective ethnic experience and enter hierarchical institutions which daily reinforce domination by race, sex and class, is that we gradually assume a mindset similar to those who dominate and oppress, that we lose critical consciousness because it is not reinforced or affirmed by the environment. We must be ever vigilant. It is important that we know who we are speaking to, who we most want to hear us, who we must long to move, motivate, and touch with our words. . . . Maintaining connections with family and community across class boundaries demands more than just summary recall of where one's roots are, where one comes from. It requires knowing, naming, and being ever mindful of those aspects of one's past that have enabled and do enable one's self-development in the present, that sustain and support, that enrich. One must also honestly confront barriers that do exist, aspects of the past that do diminish. (hooks, 1989, pp. 78–9)

Jeanne's work with Alan, and her focus on African-American children and on a multicultural/multiracial curriculum, reflect a stage in her life when she has both the personal insight and strength and the professional position which allow her to act in ways that, in her mind, make a difference to the individuals, the community of Greenfield-Weston, and the larger social structure.

Edson (1988), in her study of 142 administrative aspirants, found that both affirmative action and community pressure contribute to the hiring of minorities. Some of the minority administrators Edson surveyed believed that even if hired in part because of gender or racial quotas, they would prove their competence once in the job; others felt that they were segregated to assistant or lower level administrative positions as a result of race and gender. Most agreed, however, that competence was responsible for their achievement, not their ethnicity or race (Edson, 1988; Doughty, 1980). Jeanne was somewhat aware of the symbolic and political role of race, gender, and class in her selection as principal; she knew the superintendent wanted her to have the job, 'Because he admired me. Because he's smart, you know, he's no dummy. That's a lot of tickets I bring in. I'm a black female principal. And I live in this town. And the people love me. But underneath it he's a poor, blue collar person too. And it makes him feel good that I've made it because of him' (Interview, October 1991). Thus, Jeanne entered the principalship aware of the issues of race and class, although it is now, in her fifth year, that she has chosen to make them a more public issue. Her approach to the principalship is clearly influenced by her own personal and professional background and her consciousness of her racial identity and role as a black woman principal in a predominantly white community.

Jeanne's work with and decisions about Alan also reflect — and challenge — the usual expectations of women administrators. Jeanne's movement into the principalship reflects a typical female path of advancement. She taught in the district for twenty years, had no plans to become a principal, and was more than a little surprised when the district selected her. As the brief description of her personal and professional past, above, suggests, this career path results in part from prior experience, but also is determined by her gender (Polczynski, 1990; Mitchell and Winn, 1989; Paddock, 1981). Most male administrators plan to pursue administration as they enter the teaching profession and many teach for only a short time before moving into administrative positions. Networks provide them with support systems that many women lack, and management styles develop out of prior socialization, their comfortable assumption of positions of authority, and the ways in which others expect them to behave. Male administrators often tend to be less interested in classroom issues, individual children, or community building and more interested in district expectations and less personal aspects of administration (Ballou, 1989, Shakeshaft, 1989). As is the case for many women principals, Jeanne's lengthy tenure as a teacher contributes to her concern for individual children, in this case Alan, and perhaps to her sense that his needs could and should be met by the classroom teacher (Shakeshaft, 1989; Charters and Jovick, 1981; Prolman, 1983).

Jeanne's attention to this individual child and her decision to work directly with him is a style more typical of women principals than men (Gross and Trask, 1976). A principal focusing on building management might have agreed to send Alan to another school in the district where he would have been able to take advantage of an existing, effective program. He or she would also have been more likely to use and uphold the administrative process by which that decision was made. Jeanne, again reflecting women's approaches in general, focuses less on immediate effectiveness or traditional rules in this decision and more on the experience of the individual child and her desire to develop and maintain a diverse and supportive community in the school.

In order to keep Alan at the school, however, Jeanne has to pull rank, overriding the decision made by Alan's teacher and the school counselors. Some of the literature suggests that women administrators tend to collaborate with teachers and involve them in a process of democratic decision making (Eagly *et al.*, 1992; Charters and Jovick, 1981). While Jeanne certainly involved Emily in the process of determining Alan's program, she herself decided that he would remain in the school and that she would tutor him. Her unilateral decision-making process is reflected elsewhere in the school, although it is certainly tempered by her work to develop a strong school-based management program that involves teachers in all aspects of decision making in the school. One area in which she consistently tends to act more independently is in the work she does with individual minority children and in promoting multicultural awareness throughout the school. For example, students and teachers have a monthly meeting or assembly, during which they develop the school's theme, recognize outstanding students, and watch students perform. Each month the school works on a poem, and several months in a row, Jeanne asked all the students to memorize Langston Hughs' poems. This, in conjunction with her attention to African-American students in the schools, has made some of the teachers uncomfortable.

> I've never seen her mothering the poor white kids, the way she would a poor black one. I don't know that that's bad at all. But going to the home, bringing them here, it's wonderful that a principal would do that. But I haven't seen her do it for other kids. . . . It doesn't seem right. Maybe it is uncomfortable — it's embarrassing, and I'm not sure why. To hear her gleam about teaching Alan — any kid would want tutoring. . . . And I think the more global picture is that she's right, we've got to do something. We've got to do something. But I'm not sure she should do it in the school where she's the principal. I think it sets up all kinds of social conflicts for the child. (Interview, March 1992)

Other teachers are comfortable with Jeanne's looking out for individual minority students and multicultural issues in general, seeing it both as natural and as a benefit to the school: 'As much as she's proud of her heritage, she's very much interested in everyone else's culture. So, she's really well-rounded like that. And I don't, I think it's more interest than a bias, really' (Interview, June 1992).

Jeanne herself became aware of some of the teachers' discomfort with her championing of African American kids, and although she was not about to give up her more direct approach to this set of issues, chose to address it in ways which again reflect a female approach to management, one which emphasizes communication, interpersonal interactions, and participation (Shakeshaft, 1989; Charters and Jovick, 1981). At a faculty meeting she raised with teachers her concern that they might not bring black children to her attention because she might think they were prejudiced or because she might act on her own without listening to their views. It was not at this point a topic for discussion, but more an opening of the issue, with Jeanne owning her own prior actions and saying that perhaps it was a problem in her own perception of the issues. Her willingness to open up the topic for discussion reflects a concern for her continued interpersonal relationships with these teachers, because through those relationships she runs the school. Even in an area where she tends to be less collaborative in her style, she is at least aware of the responses of others and thinking about how to include them in a conversation about the decisions she makes. It is not clear that this overture led to further conversation or addressed teachers' discomfort, however. It could be seen as a conversation opener or as a conscious or unconscious move by Jeanne to let people know that she knew of their discomfort but wanted to keep it under control.

Alan's story also has, for Jeanne, implications for school reform. In particular, ideas for two changes have grown out of this experience, ideas that will take time to develop and implement, but which reflect the vision Jeanne has of the school as a place that can serve all students in exciting and challenging ways. First, Jeanne wants to find ways to make the school a more supportive community for its African-American (and other minority) children and a more diverse community for all of the children at Greenfield-Weston. In the fall of 1992 she gathered together a group of parents and professionals to talk about the possibility of developing a tuition-free program through which minority students outside of the district could attend the school. The group opposed this idea, but has continued to work with Jeanne to develop multi-cultural curriculum and approaches at the school that would better serve the needs of the majority and minority students who are there.

Second, Jeanne has been developing ideas of how to better meet the needs of students identified as in need of special education. She has begun with a small summer tutoring program for Alan and a few other students, hoping to expand it into a full-year school for these children, in particular, but also for any students who need and want it. She is also interested in examining both the special education program and the classroom process to see how to better meet the children's needs. From thinking about Alan, her thoughts move to other children and to new programs:

> So I'm talking about Alan, I'm talking about special ed and the goal.
> He just personifies what the other kids have. And the richness of their
> environment prevents us from having them often; they're being taken
> care of or learning to compensate in some other way. But we need to
> be ready to do it here, within the school year, the context of the
> school day, and be more flexible. . . . The other piece, now this is the
> vision part, is that I'm really looking forward to having a Tradewinds
> School (local school for able children with reading disabilities) here.
> And I want to, and I probably told you this, ask Bob Welsh when he
> comes, 'Before you retire, Bob, I want a ropes course here.' So he'll
> be working from a physical standpoint. . . . And that's leading into the
> extra stuff for kids who need the confidence to learn. (Interview, June
> 1992)

Her ideas here are very much at the level of speculation. In practice, several parents have expressed concern about the school's lack of response to their children's special needs both within and outside of the classroom. But as a school leader, Jeanne is beginning to develop a vision, and a possible set of programs to meet it. It is a vision based on meeting the needs of students and teachers (but students first) and developing a school community that is diverse, supportive, and focused on growth. And it is a vision that grows out of her experiences as a child, a teacher, an African-American and a woman. It remains to be seen whether she can translate this vision into practice.

How did I get to be this principal? It's bewildering, you know. I don't know how the hell I got to be a principal. When I talk to people about how I came along — I look back and I think it was very ordinary and it was an escape from other things. But in fact, it was doing all the things that got me to be here. And it never occurred to me that it was a rich path. And yet it was very rich. And I've been looking over a rainbow trying to figure out, you know, how to have a rich life beyond and it's right here. So now I want people to know, 'Kids, that what you're doing right now is, is rich and right.' (Interview, October 1993)

Conclusions

In response to the calls in the 1970s and 1980s for school reform that emphasized the content of change, many recent studies have examined the process of change (Lieberman and Miller, 1990). These studies document the critical importance of collaboration, teacher participation, and a focus on practical issues in effective school improvement. Practices associated with successful innovations include the opportunity for teachers to interact around professional issues, the provision of technical assistance, the adaptation of ideas and programs toward a fit with school and classroom regularities, and opportunities for reflection (Griffin and Barnes, 1984). These studies emphasize the need to develop a professional, supportive work environment for teachers that parallels a positive climate of learning for students. School change only occurs if the individuals most closely involved and affected are engaged in meaningful and positive ways (Smulyan, 1990).

In order to understand how to make collaboration work, how to engage teachers in the process of change, how to establish a positive school environment, we need to know more about school leaders and their ways of working toward effective schools. The current literature on effective school principals focuses on the traits, roles, and skills which characterize good leaders. These attempts to encapsulate or propose static models for the dynamic process of leadership that we see in Jeanne's case run into problems; this research still lacks a sense of what leadership looks and feels like in action. The literature also loses some of its credibility by its neglect of issues of race, class and gender, because teachers, students, and administrators all function within personal, school and larger social contexts where these aspects of self and role influence actions, reactions, beliefs and values.

Recent work examining the relationships between gender and school administration provides some insight into the complexity of leadership. We see a school principal's actions and responses as a part of her experience within a social and bureaucratic system which may make her more conscious of power relations, more aware of the roles and experiences of those around her, and more interested in developing alternative management approaches which allow her to neither dominate nor be dominated. This literature also has its limitations; women experience the existing power structures and their own gender differently. Little of this literature, for example, points out that the patriarchal system is also white and middle class. In Jeanne's case, race is a crucial determinant of many of her actions and responses, often modifying or dominating responses which may otherwise be seen as gender related. Women of different generations, religions, and social classes, women who have had varied life experiences and who work in different school environments will face unique challenges and will respond to them in unique ways. The work done on gender and school administration makes us more aware of the complexities in describing effective leaders, but it, too, may limit our view.

Any list of leadership characteristics, gender-based or otherwise, reveals only a small part of what it means to be an effective principal. To say that Jeanne is female, African-American, focused on individual children, and concerned about relationships with teachers and with developing a democratic management style only begins to provide a sense of what it would be like to teach and work with her. For example, we see a unique intersection of influences of race and gender in her approach to working with Alan; her commitment to working with and for African-American children at this point in her career modifies her usual more collaborative approach to working with teachers. As she develops her vision of what the school could and, she believes, should be, she tries to develop a style that allows her to work with others to achieve that vision. It seems possible that a more participatory or democratic style of leadership would be ineffective in meeting some of Jeanne's goals for both African-American and white children in the school. She therefore needs to develop leadership skills that allow her to involve others in decision making even as she remains more directive in some areas of concern. Thus, literature suggesting that effective principals are democratic or that women administrators tend to focus on interpersonal issues and use more collaborative rather than directive approaches, oversimplify a complicated process. It remains interesting that prescriptions for effective school leaders tend to match descriptions of women's leadership styles, but we need to see more of how those behaviors look when applied within the real, complex world of a school by individuals who bring their own personal and professional experiences to the process.

Case studies such as this one begin to illustrate the complex interaction of the many variables that influence a school administrator's goals and actions. Future research in educational administration needs to continue to examine the lives and work of the individuals involved in schools to understand how lists of traits, roles, and skills of effective administrators translate into responses to children, teachers, parents, and other administrators; into ideas and actions; and into school practice in a particular context that may lead to change.

Lisa Smulyan

Note

1 Research for this project was supported by the Spencer Foundation and by Swarthmore College.

References

ACKER, S. (1990) 'Managing the drama: The headteacher's work in an urban primary school,' *Sociological Review*, **38**, pp. 247–71.

ADLER, S., LANEY, J. and PACKER, M. (1993) *Managing Women*, Milton Keynes, Open University Press.

BALL, S.J. and GOODSON, I.F. (1985) 'Understanding teachers: Concepts and contexts,' in BALL, S. and GOODSON, I. (eds) *Teachers' Lives and Careers*, London, Falmer Press, pp. 1–26.

BALLOU, M. (1989) 'Male administrative orientation: Patriarchy in school administration,' *Contemporary Education*, **4** (60), pp. 216–17.

BARTH, R. (1990) *Improving Schools from Within*, San Francisco, Jossey Bass.

BECKER, H. (1958) 'Problems of inference and proof in participant observation,' *American Sociological Review*, **23**, pp. 652–60.

BEYNON, J. (1985) 'Institutional change and career histories in a comprehensive school,' in BALL, S. and GOODSON, I. (eds) *Teachers' Lives and Careers*, London, Falmer Press, pp. 158–79.

BIKLEN, S. (1980) 'Introduction: Barriers to equity — women, educational leadership, and social change,' in BIKLEN, S. and BRANNIGAN, M. (eds) *Women and Educational Leadership*, Lexington, MA, DC Heath and Co., pp. 158–79.

BLACKMORE, J. (1993) 'In the shadow of men: The historical construction of educational administration as a "masculinist" enterprise,' in BLACKMORE, J. and KENWAY, J. (eds) *Gender Matters in Educational Adminstration and Policy*, London, Falmer Press, pp. 27–48.

BLASE, J. and KIRBY, P. (1992) *Bringing Out the Best in Teachers*, California, Corwin Press.

BLUMBERG, A. (1987) 'The work of principals: A touch of craft', in GREENFIELD, W. (ed.) *Instructional Leadership*, MA, Allyn and Bacon, pp. 38–55.

BLUMBERG, A. (1989) *School Administration as a Craft*, Boston, MA, Allyn & Bacon.

BLUMBERG, A. and GREENFIELD, W. (1986) *The Effective Principal: Perspectives on School Leadership*, Boston, MA, Allyn & Bacon.

BOGDAN, R. and TAYLOR, S.J. (1970) *Introduction to Qualitative Research Methods*, New York, John Wiley and Sons.

BUELL, N. (1992) 'Building a shared vision: The principal's leadership challenge,' *NASSP Bulletin*, **76**, pp. 88–92.

BURAWOY, M. (1991) 'The extended case method,' in GAMSON, J., BURAWOY, M., BURTON, A., FERGUSON, A., FOX, K., HURST, L., JULIUS, N., KURZMAN, C., SALZINGER, L. and SCHIFFMAN, J. (eds) *Ethnography Unbound*, Berkeley, University of California Press, pp. 271–87.

BURGESS, R.G. (1982) *Field Research: A Sourcebook and Field Manual*, London, George Allen and Unwin.

BURGESS, R.G. (1984) *In the Field: An Introduction to Field Research*, London, George Allen and Unwin.

CHARTERS, W.W. and JOVICK, T.D. (1981) 'The gender of principals and principal–teacher relations in elementary schools', in SCHMUCK, P., CHARTERS, W.W. and CARLSON, R. (eds) *Educational Policy and Management*, NY, Academic Press, pp. 307–31.

CHUSMIR, L.H. (1989) 'Male–female differences in the association of managerial style and personal values,' *The Journal of Social Psychology*, **129** (1), pp. 65–78.

CLEMENT, J. (1980) 'Sex bias in school administration', in BIKLEN, S. and BRANNIGAN, M. *Women and Educational Leadership*, Lexington, MA, DC Heath and Co., pp. 131–38.

CLEMENT, J. (1981) 'Sex bias in school administration,' in BIKLEN S. and BRANNIGAN, M. (eds) *Women and Educational Leadership*, Lexington, MA, DC Heath and Co., pp. 131–8.

COHEN, R.M. (1991) *A Lifetime of Teaching: Portraits of Five Veteran High School Teachers*, NY, Teachers College Press.

CONNELL, R. (1985) *Teachers Work*, London, Allen and Unwin.

CORTAZZI, M. (1993) *Narrative Analysis*, London, Falmer Press.

DEAL, T. (1987) 'Effective school principals: Counselors, engineers, pawn brokers, poets . . . or instructional leaders?' in GREENFIELD, W. (ed.) *Instructional Leadership*, Boston, MA, Allyn & Bacon, pp. 230–48.

DENZIN, N.K. (1989) *Interpretive Biography*, California, Sage Publications.

DOUGHTY, R. (1980) 'The black female administrator: Woman in a double bind,' in BIKLEN, S. and BRANNIGAN, M. (eds) *Women and Educational Leadership*, Boston, DC Heath and Co., pp. 165–74.

EAGLY, A.H., KARUA, S.J. and JOHNSON, B.T. (1992) 'Gender and leadership style among school principals: A meta-analysis,' *Educational Administration Quarterly*, **28** (1), pp. 76–102.

EDSON, S. (1988) *Pushing the Limits: The Female Administrative Aspirant*, Albany, SUNY Press.

FAUTH, G. (1984) 'Women in educational administration: A research profile,' *The Educational Forum*, **49** (1), 65–79.

FERGUSON, K. (1984) *The Feminist Case Against Bureaucracy*, Philadelphia, Temple University Press.

FOSTER, M. (1994) 'Resisting racism: Personal testimonies of African-American teachers', in WEIS, L. and FINE, M. (eds) *Beyond Silenced Voices: Class, Race and Gender in United States Schools*, Albany, NY, State University of New York Press, pp. 273–88.

GLASER, B. and STRAUSS, A.L. (1967) *The Discovery of Grounded Theory*, London, Weidenfeld and Nicolson.

GOODLAD, J. (1984) *A Place Called School*, NY, McGraw Hill.

GOODSON, I. (1991) 'Teachers' lives and educational research,' in GOODSON, I. and WALKER, R. (eds) *Biography, Identity, and Schooling*, London, Falmer Press, pp. 137–49.

GRANT, R. (1989) 'Alternative model of "career",' in ACKER, S. (ed.) *Teachers, Gender and Careers*, London, Falmer Press, pp. 35–50.

GRIFFIN, G. (1990) 'Leadership for curriculum improvement: The school administrator's role,' in LIEBERMAN, A. (ed.) *Schools as Collaborative Cultures: Creating the Future Now*, London, Falmer Press, pp. 195–212.

GRIFFIN, G. and BARNES, S. (1984) 'School change: A craft-derived and research-based strategy,' *Teachers College Record*, **86** (1), pp. 103–23.

GROSS, N. and TRASK, A.E. (1976) *The Sex Factor and the Management of Schools*, NY, John Wiley and Sons.

Lisa Smulyan

HAMMERSLEY, M. and ATKINSON, P. (1995) *Ethnography: Principles in Practice*, New York, Routledge.

hooks, B. (1989) *Talking Back*, Boston, South End Press.

LIEBERMAN, A. and MILLER, L. (1990) 'Restructuring schools: What matters and what works,' *Phi Delta Kappan*, June, pp. 759–64.

MacCLURE, M. (1988) 'Teachers' jobs and lives: An interim report,' Centre for Applied Research in Education, University of East Anglia.

MARSHALL, C. (1985) 'The stigmatized woman: The professional woman in a male sextyped career,' *Journal of Educational Administration*, **23** (2), pp. 131–52.

MITCHELL, J.P. and WINN, D.D. (1989) 'Women and school administration,' *Journal of Instructional Psychology*, **16**, pp. 54–71.

NIAS, J. (1985) 'A more distant drummer: Teacher development as the development of self,' in BARTON, L. and WALKER, S. (eds) *Education and Social Change*, London, Croom Helm, pp. 3–28.

NODDINGS, N. (1988) 'An ethic of caring and its implications for instructional arrangements,' *American Journal of Education*, **96** (2), pp. 215–29.

PADDOCK, S. (1981) 'Male and female career paths in school administration,' in SCHMUCK, P., CHARTERS, W. and CARLSON, R. (eds) *Educational Policy and Management*, New York, Academic Press, pp. 187–98.

PARKAY, F.W., CURRIE, G.D. and RHODES, J.W. (1992) 'Professional socialization: A longitudinal study of first-time high school principals,' *Educational Administration Quarterly*, **28** (1), pp. 43–75.

PLUMMER, K. (1983) *Documents of Life*, London, George Allen & Unwin.

POLCZYNSKI, M. (1990) 'Getting there,' *Momentum*, **21**, pp. 28–30.

PORTER, A.W., LEMON, D.K. and LANDRY, R.G. (1989) School climate and administrative power strategies of elementary school principals,' *Psychological Reports*, **65**, pp. 1267–71.

POWELL, G.N. (1988) *Women and Men in Management*, Newbury Park, Sage Publications.

PROLMAN, S. (1983) 'Gender, career paths, and administrative behavior.' Paper presented at the Annual Meeting of AERA, Montreal.

REGAN, H. (1990) 'Not for women only: School administration as a feminist activity,' *Teachers College Record*, **91** (4), pp. 565–77.

RIESSMAN, C.K. (1993) *Narrative Analysis*, Newbury Park, CA, Sage Publications.

ROGERS, J.L. (1988) 'New paradigm leadership: Integrating the female ethos,' *Initiatives*, **51** (4), pp. 1–8.

SCHAEF, A.W. (1985) *Women's Reality: An Emerging Female System in a White Male Society*, San Francisco, Harper and Row.

SCHATZMAN, L. and STRAUSS, A.L. (1973) *Field Research: Strategies for a Natural Sociology*, Englewood Cliffs, NJ, Prentice Hall.

SCHMUCK, P. (1981) 'The sex dimension of school organization: Overview and synthesis,' in SCHMUCK, P., CHARTERS, W.W. and CARLSON, R. (eds) *Educational Policy and Management*, NY, Academic Press, pp. 221–34.

SCHMUCK, P., CHARTERS, W.W. and CARLSON, R. (eds) (1981) *Educational Policy and Management*, NY, Academic Press.

SHAKESHAFT, C. (1987) 'Theory in a changing reality', *Journal of Educational Equity and Leadership*, **7** (1), pp. 4–20.

SHAKESHAFT, C. (1989) *Women in Educational Administration*, NY, Sage.

SIKES, P. (1985) 'The life cycle of the teacher,' in BALL, S. and GOODSON, I. (eds) *Teachers' Lives and Careers*, London, Falmer Press, pp. 27–60.

SIMONS, H. (1981) 'Conversation piece: The practice of interviewing in case study research,' in ADELMAN, C. (ed.) *Uttering Muttering*, London, Grant McIntyre Ltd., pp. 27–50.

SMULYAN, L. (1990) 'Moving the mountain: The individual and school change.' Paper presented at the Implementing Educational Change Conference, Centre for Educational Development, Appraisal and Research, University of Warwick.

SMULYAN, L. (1992) 'The artist as INSET coordinator: A problem in design,' *Journal of Teacher Development*, **1** (2), pp. 95–110.

STAKE, R. (1994) 'Case studies,' in DENZIN, N. and LINCOLN, Y. (eds) *Handbook of Qualitative Research*, California, Sage.

STATHAM, A. (1987) 'The gender model revisited: Differences in the management styles of men and women,' *Sex Roles*, **16** (7/8), pp. 409–29.

SWEENEY, J. (1982) 'Research synthesis on effective school leadership,' *Educational Leadership*, **39** (5), pp. 346–52.

SWIDERSKI, W. (1988) 'Problems faced by women in gaining access to administrative positions in education', *Education Canada*, **28**, pp. 24–31.

TIBBETTS, S. (1980) 'The woman principal: Superior to the male,' *Journal of the NAWDAC*, **43** (4), pp. 15–18.

WEBER, M., FELDMAN, J. and PLING, E. (1981) 'Why women are underrepresented in educational administration,' *Educational Leadership*, **38** (4), pp. 320–2.

WEILER, K. (1988) *Women Teaching for Change: Gender, Class and Power*, MA, Bergin and Harvey.

WOLCOTT, H. (1973) *The Man in the Principal's Office*, IL, Waveland Press.

YEAKEY, C., JOHNSTON, G. and ADKISON, J. (1986) 'In pursuit of equity: A review of research on minorities and women in educational administration,' *Educational Administration Quarterly*, **22** (3), pp. 110–49.

Notes on Contributors

Dorothy Abbot taught in primary schools for many years before joining the PACE project at the University of Bristol in 1989 as a research officer. She worked on the project until her retirement at the end of 1994.

Edie Black is a Research Associate in the School of Education, University of Bristol. Currently her main research interest is in primary schools, particularly the changing role of teachers and headteachers.

Paul Black is Emeritus Professor at King's College, London, where he held the Chair of Science Education from 1976 until retirement in 1995. He has contributed to a range of Nuffield curriculum projects and to several research projects on the learning of science. He has also worked in assessment, his principal contributions being as joint director of the Assessment of Performance Unit's monitoring of science and as chair of the government's Task Group on Assessment and Testing in 1987–88.

Ezra Blondel worked on the Progression Project at King's College, University of London, from 1991 to 1993. She is a primary teacher with teaching and inservice experience in aspects of primary mathematics in England, South East Asia and the Caribbean. She has worked as an advisory teacher in the London Borough of Camden and is presently doing research in the role of inservice training in the professional development of teachers in primary and special schools.

Patricia Broadfoot is Professor and Head of School, University of Bristol, School of Education, and Director of the Centre for Curriculum and Assessment Studies. She has published widely in the field of assessment policy and practice and on curriculum issues both in the UK and internationally. She has directed a number of major national research projects and is currently a co-director of the PACE project.

Margaret Brown is Professor of Mathematics Education and Head of the School of Education at King's College, London. After teaching in primary and secondary schools, she has been director of sixteen research projects in the area of the learning and assessment of mathematics. She is currently co-directing two projects on the effective teaching of numeracy in the primary school, one on primary pupils' perception of mathematics and science tasks, and one on national assessment at age 11.

Rita Chawla-Duggan is a former Research Fellow in CEDAR at the University of Warwick, where her research interests were in the study of the primary school curriculum and research methodology.

Paul Croll is Bulmershe Professor of Education at the University of Reading and was previously Professor and Associate Dean of Education at the University of the West of England. He was one of the co-directors of the PACE project and is now conducting research on policy and provision in the field of special educational needs.

Sandra Duggan is an experienced researcher in education and psychology. She recently worked for three years with the Exploration of Science Team at Durham University and is currently continuing research into childrens' understanding of scientific evidence. She has published several articles and is joint author with Richard Gott of a book on investigative work in science education.

Richard Gott is Professor of Education at the University of Durham. His interests over the past few years have centred on pupils' investigative work in science. He has carried out a number of research projects in this area and published a book and series of articles.

Uwe Hameyer is a former Research Director at the Institute for Science Education (IPN) at the University of Kiel. Since 1990 he has been a full professor at Kiel University where since 1994 he has directed the Institute of Education. He has published widely in the areas of education, innovation research and planning, one of his recent books is *Pädagogische Ideenkiste Primarbereich* (1994).

Andrew Hannan is Reader in Education and Director of Research in the Rolle School of Education of the Faculty of Arts and Education at the University of Plymouth. He is currently involved in research about rural racism, the effects of the introduction of television to St Helena, the impact on primary schools of new requirements for special education and the effects of new technology on teaching and learning in higher education, as well as researching teacher education.

Bob Jeffrey is a Project Officer at the Open University in the Centre for Sociology and Social Studies department of the Faculty of Education. He has recently completed the Creative Teaching project, from which his chapter was drawn and the full report will be published by Open University Press in February 1996 with Peter Woods as co-author. Currently, he is conducting a project partly funded by the Open University and the ESRC on the effects of Ofsted inspections on primary teachers' work.

Penny Munn lectures in Developmental Psychology at the University of Central Lancashire, Preston. Her research interest in the development of literacy and numeracy began with post-doctoral work on one of Rudolph Schaffer's projects for Strathclyde Region Education Department and continued with the project described in her chapter. Current research is examining the implications of these findings for development at slightly later stages.

Marlene Morrison holds a joint post with CEDAR and the Sociology Department at the University of Warwick. She has recently completed an ESRC-funded project on teaching and learning about food and nutrition in schools and is currently engaged in research into aspects of legal education. Previous research has included projects on inservice training, school development plans, supply teaching, and libraries in primary schools. Articles and reports reflect her research interests. A joint author of *Implementing In-service Education and Training* (Falmer Press, 1993). She co-edits (with Sheila Galloway) *The Supply Story: Professional Substitutes in Education* (Falmer Press, 1994).

Marilyn Osborn is Research Fellow in the University of Bristol School of Education, and Deputy Director of the Centre for Curriculum and Assessment Studies. She has researched and published in the field of teachers' work and teachers' professional perspectives, both in a UK and an international context. She is co-director of two funded projects on teachers, pupils and primary education.

Christopher Pole is a Lecturer in Sociology with CEDAR at the University of Warwick. He teaches courses in Research Methods and Sociology of Education. His research is concerned primarily with higher education, in particular, the socialization and training of research students. He has recently completed a feasibility study in the Internationalization of Research Training for the European Union. His publications include: *Assessing and Recording Achievement: Implementing a New Approach in Schools*, (Open University Press, 1993), *Strategies for Managing and Supervising the Social Science PhD*, (with Bob Burgess and John Hockey) in *Postgraduate Education and Training in the Social Sciences* (Jessica Kingsley, 1994).

Andrew Pollard is Professor of Education at the University of Bristol. His current research interests include pupil learning and careers in primary schools and the impact of national policy on school and classroom practices.

Shirley Simon is a Research Fellow at King's College, London. She has undertaken research and development into the use of Open-Ended work in Science (OPENS), focusing on strategies for teaching investigations in secondary science. As a researcher on the Progression in Learning in Mathematics and Science project (PIMS), she studied how children progressed in their understanding of forces, and produced teaching materials for primary science. She is currently co-director of an ESRC project on primary Mathematics and Science Tasks (MAST), which is concerned with children's perceptions and performance of tasks.

Lisa Smulyan is Associate Professor in the Program in Education at Swarthmore College, Pennsylvania where she teaches courses in educational foundations, adolescence, women and education, and school and society in addition to supervising student teachers. Her publications include several articles and two books, one co-authored with Sharon N. Oja, entitled *Collaborative Action Research: A Developmental Process* (Falmer Press, 1989) and the other co-authored with Andrew Garrod, Sally Powers and Robert Kilkenny entitled *Adolescent Portraits: Identity Relationships and Challenges* (Allyn and Bacon, 1995). Her research focuses on school-based research with teachers and administrators and the use of life/career history as a basis for understanding school practice and providing effective staff development.

Caroline Whiting is a research officer at London University's Institute of Education, working on the Modes of Teacher Education research project with Professor Geoff Whitty. This post follows the completion of her PhD at the University of Plymouth which focused on Articled Teachers. An experienced teacher at both primary and secondary level, she is also currently teaching 'A' level psychology and sociology at a community college in Devon, and contributes occasionally to degree and postgraduate courses at the University of Plymouth.

Peter Woods is Professor of Education at the School of Education, The Open University, Milton Keynes. He spent eleven years teaching before joining the Open University in 1972, where for a number of years he was Director of the Centre for Sociology and Social Research. His main research interest is school ethnography. His is the author of numerous articles and books, including *The Divided School, Sociology and the School, Inside Schools, The Happiest Days?*, and *Teacher Skills and Strategies*. He has recently been researching creative teaching in primary schools.

Index